THE GROUND I WALKED ON

GEORGE N. SHUSTER

The Ground I Walked On

REFLECTIONS

OF A COLLEGE PRESIDENT

New York

FARRAR, STRAUS AND CUDAHY

CONTENTS

PROLOGUE

More than forty years have passed since I marched from
Langres as a young lad dressed in khaki, with an absurd flat
helmet on my head and a gas-mask over my shoulder. (It was
Langres which had startled Julius Caesar by reason of the hill
rising straight up out of the landscape like a man in a mosque
at muezzin-time.) We were to proceed through Baccarat to a line
of trenches dug from hill to hill. During the first sunny afternoon of the march to the front, rival artillery batteries fired at
whimsically irregular intervals. I recall, in the last shell-pocked
town we walked through, a shapeless woman who stood with
her arms on her hips in front of an *épicerie*. Spring was everywhere in Lorraine then. I spent my first night lying in a louse-
infected dugout next to an old French soldier who reread the
plays of Aeschylus from a dog-eared book before he went to
sleep. Cuckoo birds welcomed in a dawn all fog and forest.

What comes most vividly to mind as I look back is that, once
the *épicerie* had been left behind, the world in which we were
to live during the months that followed was one without women.
They were everywhere except where we were. They were in
mourning, or providing sordid hours of pleasure for men on
leave, or being so many more arms in factory or field, or they
were teachers in classrooms, nuns praying, nurses in hospitals.
But our incredible, grim, dirty, bloody world—of which we
asked over and over again why we were in it without ever having an answer—was nevertheless an oddly fascinating place.
There one was liberated from all care except the ultimate fierce
anxiety about life and death. Nothing had to be hidden from
the others, apart from the fear you sought to conceal from yourself. I hated the war world with a furious detestation words

1

è - pice - rie = grocery articles

could not express. But shamefacedly I sometimes loved it, because the courage which had to be more commonplace than daily bread was not begotten for oneself only but for the others as well. There were times when men got blood on their hands from being kind to others, inexpressibly, pathetically kind.

I mention all this at the beginning of a book about a later period because there, in that world, I learned what in any deeper sense I know about education. First in the order of things there came character, integrity, loyalty to one's hidden best self for the sake of the others. Whatever you wished to call it, this thing was the opposite of sham. And so it has been with us in college. An educated man does not read philosophy in order to hang onto the erroneous notions he had when he began to read. He realizes full well that the laboratory cannot be hoodwinked. Above all, he understands in the end that he must live bravely and genially with his ignorance because being ignorant is a very large part of being human. Yet also, while remaining unable to answer questions which desperately need an answer, he realizes that peering into the mystery engirdling him is a heartening, cleansing, ennobling experience. Second, there was what the French soldier with his dog-eared Aeschylus had, without at all wishing to, shown me. This was that fragments of beauty cannot lose their freshness or meaning because the world in which one happens to be living is false and tawdry. These fragments are like pieces of quartz in the sand, like flashes of color in sea waves. For one who understands and respects them, my French companion seemed to say, the lines of the great Greek are as impervious to war as the sunset is to a man's desire for day. During seven years I had studied Greek, and in my turn had dapperly translated passages from the *Agamemnon*. But in Lorraine I found out what they mean.

Like everybody else who has made a profession of education, I have talked a great deal about it. There are always statistics and the question of where the money is coming from to give such figures "human interest." We discuss what should be included in the course of study, just as doctors talk about what ought to go into the diets of patients. There are many other similar things we argue about. I do not wish to disparage such concerns, but in the final analysis the sole thing that matters is that a boy or girl go away from college with an unfettered mind, knowing that the only treasure which will not trickle away is the small change of beauty and truth he keeps in his soul. That kind of intellect will give him all he needs to elbow his way along. The rest will keep him company. Of course it is agonizingly true that not every Senior who marches past on Commencement Day is that sort of person. I often feel that some are like men lost in battle—or indeed occasionally akin to those who ran or deserted. But, thank God, there are many who go as we would have them go. Then also it has been for me a very enlightening and, in more ways than could be spelled out, a rewarding experience to have had a rather special chance to think about the kind of world men and women could build together if they really wanted to.

When I first came to it, the world of Hunter College seemed just eddies of women, swirling and milling about. Each one was different in individuality, no doubt, and yet each was curiously like another. It is in a way strange that I, all of whose higher educational experience had been gained in the company of men, should find myself on an island which seemed at first more bizarre than any Gulliver had hit upon, where days would pass without bringing more than a glimpse of a masculine face. Later on the scene would change somewhat as the college became in part coeducational, but the basic impact remained.

I hasten to add that of course I did not, as the years went by, manage to acquire an understanding of women. I am not being humorous about it. I simply do not know what it means to be feminine. Perhaps I could write sketches of women young and old whom I have come to visualize rather clearly. If I did you would probably recognize the one or the other, but the most important thing about each one, the mystery, would be missing. Some few things I have, however, found out. One is that you ought not to educate a woman as if she were a man, or to educate her as if she were not. This may be a paradox, if you like, but it has taken me a long time to realize that it is also simple fact. For some reason or other English culture, after the Renaissance had faded into more than relative dimness, put the feminine mind into the bargain basement. I have sometimes fancied that this happened because the English had made plain-featured Elizabeth into the likeness of Burleigh and murdered the beautiful Queen of Scotland. At any rate the result was that the seventeenth century in England went on bowing around such worthy humdrum ladies as Anne Killigrew and Catherine Phillips while in Spain there was Teresa. The situation in not a few other cultures was quite different also. Whatever may have been the cause, it has taken us a fearfully long time to see that, however great may be the intellectual sacrifice woman must bring by reason of her primordial function as the bearer of life, there is no reason at all why her share in the community of scholars and artists should be of a lower order than is that of men.

It seems to me that it has been one of the special glories of Hunter College in my time to have had an opportunity to make this manifest. I can allude to it all the more warmly and candidly since, in the nature of things, I have had nothing whatever to do with it except knowing it was there. At any rate, the quality of teaching and scholarship which the women of the Hunter College Faculty have to their credit is so genuine of texture and so far-reaching in its diversity that if the institution ceased for some reason or other to exist tomorrow, their contribution could not be erased from the pages on which American academic achievement is inscribed. All this means that women do some things quite as well as men. It has been a signal honor for me to be associated with this effort, upon occasion to have recognized its worth, and in some bumbling manner to have been of assistance. Perhaps a way has been shown to escape from the fog created by our ancestors.

Yet if on the one hand the moral of this experience would appear to be that we must avoid educating a young woman as if she were not a man, it does seem to me that the other part of the paradox is valid also. We cannot think of woman sensibly or without some banal reservations unless we bear in mind her role in Nature. The Pauline Epistles probably overdid things a bit, but the core of what they said still has validity. It is absurd to say that intellectually women are inferior to men, but that they depend on men here and in other aspects of life is true. I am therefore persuaded that the education of women is most successful when, by reason of the presence on the campus of distinguished male scholars, they come to realize early that their own work, at whatever scholarly level, is likely to be most successful and rewarding when it is done in the company of respected men. This I believe I should be able to illustrate if called upon to do so. Perhaps the reason why the pinnacles of achievement have been reached by men rather than women is also thus accounted for. It is of course true that women have excelled in some forms of literature and research. Emily Dickinson remains the best of the American Victorian Age poets, and I should not be at all surprised if Willa Cather were to outlive Ernest Hemingway.

Were we to face earnestly the possibility of a community in which men and women would find their several parts in the quest for knowledge and in the transmission to the generations which are to come, I believe we should not be confronting the unknown but rather be reliving some of the best hours in our collective human past. The obstacles to be surmounted are real and formidable. There is probably nothing which dominant forms of salesmanship have so successfully marketed to the wide public as they have their version of woman. As they see her, she is without a mind. It is unnecessary to say more. The insipidity of the image is as deplorable as are the results. If there be anything of which Hunter College can be proud it is that during the years I have known it a protest against that kind of doctrine about women has been implicit in its achievement.

These, I may add, are the hidden themes of this book, though to be sure it is discursive, if you insist, given to conjuring up the past. This past will, I perhaps fondly hope, not be uninteresting to you. But there is quite a little in it about the future as well. At any rate, it has given me a chance to think about life in a great city and a great College.

I.

THE GROUND I WALKED ON

Nothing could happen in New York City government in the summer of 1939 (and I was obviously something that was happening) unless Fiorello La Guardia had affixed to it a blessing. The first thing that came to pass, after I agreed to act as president of the second oldest municipal college, was that Ordway Tead, Harper editor and chairman of the Board of Higher Education, took me out to a sprawling house in Queens where the fomidable Fiorello was holding summer court. When we arrived, the place was buzzing with hangers-on and insects of the season, while the Mayor sat with his shirt sleeves rolled up, eating frankfurters and potato salad.

What we said to each other was hardly worth travelling all the way to hear, but I went away conscious that a trickle of foreboding was more than lazily moving down my spine. If city government was to have its finger in the academic pie, what pressures would one have to expect? The question was not an idle one. As a person somewhat vehemently and perhaps quixotically pledged to the idea that man is supposed to be a perpendicular creature, I realized that being asked to buckle under when a principle was involved would soon find me without a job.

The dispensing of patronage had previously affected almost every aspect of municipal college activity, from appointments to the staff to the awarding of contracts for things as diverse as buildings and washing soda. But a profound change had now set in. New York under La Guardia was on the mourner's bench and reforming its ways. The sole pertinent question was whether one would be cleansed and purged to within an inch of one's life. This Mayor had been swept into office by a wave of protest against all that was lush and wasteful in the time of easy money which had come to an end with the quake of 1929. In one big city after another, the entrenched machines were temporarily smashed; and New York was singular only in that reform would be in command for a long time. Jimmie Walker, well-groomed and debonair, nimble of wit and light of heart, was the symbol of what most of us yearned to be as private citizens but were committed to holding anathema in public life.

On the one hand the La Guardia government was as frugal as a housewife on a meager budget. It was depression time, and would soon be war time. One had to be prepared to find that what was available to spend today would no longer be there tomorrow. Yet on the other hand we were passionately concerned with the general welfare. The Mayor took an interest in every pot and pan in the citizen's kitchen. Sometimes he was more than a little flamboyant in expressing his good will, by literally rushing off to see that fires were put out or by giving advice as to what to cook and how. Yet all this was merely foam on the ale, sometimes a good deal of foam, but the draft itself was strong and crisp. It was not anything less than absolute sincerity that brought William Hodson, La Guardia's new Commissioner of Public Welfare, close to august Biblical mandates in the instructions he issued in 1934. His concern, he said, was with the "thousands of people who through no fault of their own are unable to provide for themselves and those near and dear to them." He said to his staff accordingly, "My first request and order is that you deal with them as you would have them deal with you, remembering that except for lucky chance you, too, might be in their ranks."

La Guardia kept this mood dominant by his mastery of political in-fighting. He was crude or urbane, vicious or conciliatory, as the situation demanded; and he was fully prepared to be called a dreadful oaf and ogre so long as the people did not vote for Tammany. And yet, in spite of doctrines and practices easily dubbed radical, the man himself was spiritually and intellectually very conservative. He thought of public and private morals as the common people think of them, in traditional terms, without frills or concessions. This may no doubt have been due in part to his simple Arizona background, to his training in the law, and to his exemplary family life. Some of it stemmed from the influence of Charles Burlinghame. But anyhow this was his faith and he lived by it, sometimes of course to the consternation of his friends but seldom to the delight of his enemies.

My task it inevitably was to live as amicably and effectively as possible within the framework thus established. The City's higher education system was also being reformed, as conditions beyond any question required. La Guardia had appointed a group of earnest, distinguished citizens to the Board of Higher Education and given them each a bright new broom. The premises were swept from top to bottom and disinfected. A lookout was posted in every window to ward off possible marauding political mosquitoes, by creating a "democratic Faculty organization" which so distributed authority that almost everything had to be done by caucus. The arrangement was as productive of oratory as measles are of spots; and, while it was still novel, one could be certain that a decision ordinarily to be arrived at in five minutes would still be under discussion at the end of five hours. But the spectre of patronage had assuredly been laid. It was as dead as half a doorknob.

La Guardia very seldom interfered, which was perhaps remarkable in view of his quite nostalgic interest in higher education. Very probably he would have liked to end his career as president of a college or university, though one cannot imagine that he would have escaped academic boredom for long. He was one of the first to realize the magnitude and significance of New York City's commitment to the training of young people. There were times when none of the several colleges was quite large enough for him. Once he tried to induce President Conant to leave Harvard and become Chancellor of an educational domain to be created by piecing together all the parts. And sometimes, when in a competitive mood, he suggested that City, Brooklyn and Queens Colleges pool their manpower resources and muster in a sturdy football team. That for the time being left Hunter out of the calculation, for it was then strictly feminine. But we did attempt to please him by trying rather desperately to merge our violinists and horn-players in a single orchestra. It proved to be a rather spectacular failure.

On the rare occasions when he did venture to intervene, he made history of a not always commendable kind. The City College's nomination of Bertrand Russell to teach mathematics was approved in a most perfunctory fashion by the Board, on the same night that I was named to the presidency of Hunter. Almost immediately afterward it was challenged, following a public protest from the Cathedral of St. John the Divine, and the Board found itself sorely divided on the issue. A week or so later, La Guardia peremptorily took out of the budget the amount of money required to pay Sir Bertrand's salary. The action was highhanded, indeed; and his own "reform" appointees to the Board had recourse in vain to legal action in the hope that they would be able to rescind the Mayor's solution of the problem. It was not that they wanted Russell, but they had given him a contract and felt obliged to honor it. For this the Mayor never forgave some of them, and upon occasion peppered them with language not normally used in polite society. Of course his indefensible veto was not due to his having succumbed to "pressure." His own simple moral code made him feel that Sir Bertrand, allegedly committed to free love and atheism, would have no beneficent influence on the youth of the city. As always, he thought he knew what was good for everybody, and the rest of the world could go hang.

My own relations with him remained delightfully pleasant, though upon occasion a brimming measure of diplomacy was required to keep them so. He came to the College for the inaugural ceremonies, and sat listening to Van Wyck Brooks who was extremely nervous and Jacques Maritain who was not. He then made quite the sprightliest speech of the afternoon. It was thus that I first came to experience La Guardia's almost unbelievable ability to go anywhere without an oration in his pocket, listen attentively to what others said, and then mould his own remarks round texts supplied by them. Since one part of him was a quite puckish showman and another a shy, almost secret, but very real, well-nigh austere spirit concerned with ethical and spiritual values, these improvisations would be couched in the jargon of the boxing ring or in the language of the Bible, as the case might be. The fighter in him might likewise rise like a spurt of fiery lava from Mount Etna. He could build fifteen minutes of withering comment round a sentence selected willfully from the address of someone he disliked, however inappropriate the occasion. Once that happened while I was presiding over a civic function. With the speaker who preceded him he had had a glorious row, and there was nothing to do except listen while he poured paragraphs of ridicule on something innocuous the poor man had said. Yet even this callous brutality was remarkable, viewed merely as a rhetorical feat. Bourke Cochran, renowned in the annals of Churchillian oratory, could weave a half-hour of purple prose round the theme of an occasion to which he had given no thought prior to coming out on the platform. Once as a college boy I was serving as an usher while the guests walked in to a convocation Cochran was to address. When he was passing by, he stopped and asked me, "Young man, what is this meeting about?" Quite startled, I supplied the answer. He nodded, went in, and covered himself with glory. But he did not have the drive and meat of La Guardia at his best.

For several reasons the Mayor took a special interest in Hunter, its educational philosophy and achievements. No doubt one of the reasons was the feminine clientele, for his was a quite archaic, almost sentimental chivalry. One therefore never quite knew when his eye would be fixed on the premises, benevolently or otherwise. Shortly after taking office I discovered that the Hunter Elementary School, maintained theoretically as part of the teacher training program, was the mecca of many of the most influential parents in town. All conceivable forms of influence were used to secure the admission of children to it, and teachers were expected to coddle chosen darlings forever after. Recommendations came from virtually every source, including to my astonishment the Vice President of the United States and the Papal Secretary of State. The spirit of reform now urged us onward. The Board formally and solemnly resolved that thereafter admission was to be based strictly on the order of application. No exceptions to the rule were to be countenanced. The new system had its disadvantages—a young couple, for example, appeared in my office immediately after their marriage to register their prospective first child—and had to be altered later on. But on the whole it operated rather well, though at the time it did not add to my popularity in some segments of the community.

At any rate, not long after the reform had been enacted, my private telephone rang. The Mayor was calling. After a few introductory remarks, his voice reflected the autumn chill outside. "Doctor," he said, "Jimmie Walker has come back to the city. He tells me his kids can't get into your Elementary School. I want them admitted!" It sounded like an ultimatum delivered without gloves. "Your Honor," I replied with a nonchalance I did not feel, "you are probably aware that the Board has ruled that children are to be admitted only in the order of application. But if you wish, I can suggest a supplementary resolution to read as follows, 'Resolved, that the Board rescind its previous action, in order to permit Mayor La Guardia to place Jimmie Walker's children in the Elementary School.'" There was a pause, which probably seemed longer than it actually was. No doubt he was picturing to himself just how such a resolution would look in the papers, even if the Board were to adopt it, which was highly unlikely. "Forget it!" he said and hung up. Of course no personal gain or advantage was involved for him. He happened upon occasion to feel a fantastic measure of good will towards men he had defeated politically, just as some boxing champions have been known to shed tears for opponents they had knocked out. This odd quirk of temperament gave rise to some of the sternest criticism made of him in his later years.

The principal controversy in which I was engaged with him had to do with our High School. This was then and still is an academic high school of excellent quality, serving girl students chosen for their ability. "The Little Flower," as he was jocosely called and as he sometimes loved to refer to himself in private, had imbibed two ideas about education of this character. The first was that the Board of Higher Education had no business trying to operate anything except colleges. The second was that a school which professedly had for its purpose the training of the gifted was anathema to all true democrats. Paradoxically he took the initiative in having Townsend Harris High School at the City College abolished—it was an excellent school for the training of gifted boys—while doing everything he could to induce the Board of Education to maintain the Bronx High School of Science and the High School of Music and Arts, which also catered to selected students. He could approve the recognition of special aptitudes for the professions, but the idea that something comparable ought to be done in so far as the liberal arts were concerned was not included in his educational philosophy. Therefore he kept up a species of drum fire against Hunter High, in which effort he was aided and abetted upon occasion by interested citizens. It was a ticklish situation, for there was no doubt that he could quite easily have closed the place down. Finally I said to him in desperation, "Before you decide to do something drastic about our High School, do at least come and take a look at it." He tapped his finger on the desk for a moment and replied, "I won't come. I might like it!" At any rate that ended the discussion, and our High School has gone its more or less merry way ever since.

When you called on him, which of necessity was rather frequently because nothing ever burgeoned budgetwise unless he had given it the stamp of approval, etiquette demanded that you walk right into his office, then a big room to the south of the first floor of City Hall, and sit in as conspicuous a place as you could find, waiting your turn. One day there was seated next to his desk a woman in whose judgment he had a great deal of confidence. Before him was a request from the Board of Education. "Look at this crazy idea!" he sputtered. "They want five school psychiatrists. We didn't have any of them when I went to school, and look at me!" The woman beside him icily replied, "Yes, look at you!" Without another word, he signed the request, and no doubt the psychiatrists led a busy life thereafter. Upon another and later occasion, he was discussing Civilian Defense. The talk got round to the linguistic marvel which ordered that during blackouts "illumination shall be extinguished on these premises." La Guardia agreed with labor leader Sidney Hillman that the text should read "Get dark, stay dark!" But characteristically Hillman suggested that the word "Please" should precede the command. "O. K.," said the Mayor, "provided you end with—or else!" That was the essence of his spirit.

There were of course times when I had as much success with him as I might have had going out with an axe to chop off a piece of a slab of carborundum. When the old building burned down on the Park Avenue site, La Guardia agreed that a handsome structure of sixteen stories was to replace it, with the help of Federal funds. But though he was with one side of his personality proud of the achievement, the other frugal side kept on feeling remorse over the fact that a college building had been erected on expensive Park Avenue property. Just above us on the Avenue there was the Guggenheim Mansion, surely the most beautiful house ever erected in the city. It had been designed as a memorial to a son killed in the First World War. Entering you were in a breath-takingly lovely Spanish patio, imported intact from abroad, to which young people came from all parts of the East to absorb its matchless radiance and, if they were interested in art, to sketch. The house had been willed to the Metropolitan Museum, with the proviso that if it were razed and the art works transferred to the Museum the property could be sold. I badly wanted to have it retained because it seemed to me to contribute to aesthetic education as nothing else quite could. I proposed that it be transferred to Hunter and used as a center for art studies. This idea was warmly supported by the director of the Metropolitan, and by others, but the Mayor was as frightened by the suggestion as if I had proposed arson or rifling the City treasury. There was nothing whatever to be done. One of the most entrancing buildings New York will ever see was torn down, the patio went into the Museum's cellars, and we now have on the site as ugly an apartment house as could have been designed. But New York has always been too busy and restless to bother about beautiful things. It prefers to cram them into a few show cases, where they can be duly inspected on selected afternoons.

Everyone who really knew Fiorello La Guardia need not be told that although he was a reformer whom nothing was too slight to interest—most of his idiosyncracies stemmed from the too discursive pattern of his concern for human welfare—his mind could take in larger vistas with extraordinary lucidity. As V-E Day was approaching, I was besought by the Office of War Information to assume responsibilities in Germany and Austria which that agency then thought would fall to its lot. Patriotic duty was not to be taken lightly; though my craving for the task was minimal, I found the answer difficult to give. Therefore I decided to ask the Mayor for quite personal advice. At the time he was no doubt greatly disappointed at not having had a more dramatic part to play in the war effort, but of that he breathed not a word. The counsel I received was negative. He forecast the impending demise of OWI (it actually died a little sooner than he had predicted), said that the sole agency of any importance over there would be the Allied Control Council, if indeed even it could function, and then added almost prophetically, "Roosevelt will get to exactly the same place Wilson did—by trying to avoid all of Wilson's mistakes!" The comment reflected the genius of a politician who could project the human nature he knew well to the international scene.

During his final days at City Hall he was very tired and, it must be confessed, irritable. The old touch of magic was no longer there, no doubt because the lingering disease which would take his life was busily at work. They buried him from the Cathedral of Saint John the Divine. There was a vast crowd and a solemn service. But I thought it out of character. How much more fitting it would have been if his coffin had been borne on strong shoulders through the garment district to some church in a crowded neighborhood, so that the people he loved could have jammed the streets and mourned as his body passed! For though there was something of Cola di Rienzi in his blood, there was also a concern for humanity no social worker has ever equalled. He had put the stamp of civic virtue on the great city he served—etched it in so deeply that a long time will have to pass before it can be eradicated. He had all the faults of a Dickens novel—some people do not like Dickens, so much the worse for them—but also its entrancing contagious vitality.

It is good to recall him as he was at his exuberant best, thrilled by the joy of haranguing, or conducting an orchestra (this had to be thoroughly disciplined, or it would have lost its way in the wake of his eccentric beat), flaying enemies who often had been and again would be his friends with language ranging all the way from Isaiah to the gutter. It is impossible for me to forget a night when we sat side by side on the platform of Madison Square Garden, where Rabbi Stephen Wise was presiding over a great meeting of protest against Hitler's treatment of the Jew. The program was scheduled to begin with the blowing of the shofar horn and to close with a rousing speech by the Mayor. But as so often happens on such occasions, the lesser fry who were to speak first were as full of words as the world is of sin; and as the hours dragged on, more and more people left. All the while La Guardia kept whispering to me that this was his favorite meeting place, and that he could be heard from the railing without a microphone. Finally, at a little after midnight, I got up to drop my capsule of words into the now almost deserted gloom. Then he rushed forward and flung all his eloquence into the vast space.

In a sense it is true that something comparable happened with his life. He created no Party organization or machine. That he called himself a Republican was due only to the fact that he could not be a Democrat while Tammany Hall stood. He was no doubt the quintessence of the Independent; and though this is a noble breed, it has no effective progeny. Yet how can he be forgotten? He could be noble when he wished to be, and often vulgar when he did not actually desire to seem that. A compound of Garrison and taxi-driver, of cop and preacher, of dictator and humble servant, he was the man to whom a great city responded for years on end, because nobody else was more like all sides of its character than he was. For my part I was sometimes afraid of him, and upon occasion annoyed by his antics. But looking back I cannot imagine any man in City Hall association with whom could have been so signal an honor.

La Guardia's departure from City Hall did not open floodgates of corruption. In so far as we in higher education were concerned, the number of telephone calls and letters from officials urging this or that for consideration greatly increased. But there was no steam-roller behind them. One Mayor was an im-

posing figure who had an unusually beautiful and intelligent
wife. The other was a man who undoubtedly was interested in
education but seldom tinted his concern with the hue of his personality. William O'Dwyer's career as mayor of New York did
not end on a note of triumph, but I have always been convinced
that he deserved a far better fate. Even his glaring faults were
endearing. One was his quite remarkable amiability, compounded
of Celtic charm, presence and a measure of the rarest kind of
social tact. But alas, it resulted in a far too great readiness to
untie his tie and put his feet on the table when cronies asked
him to do so. Still another ingrained characteristic of his was
delight in talk about the colorful days he had spent abroad in
connection with the war effort. When he succumbed to this
amiable pasttime, the business of filling La Guardia's shoes faded
from view like a banshee on the Shannon.

I saw him often enough on social occasions to realize that he
had excellent nimble brains which could have bolstered an appeal
to the citizenry. If he had known how to carry it off, this would
certainly have given him a far more illustrious part to play in
our national political life. I shall confess that I used to itch for
a chance to take him in hand—to see that his speeches were as
good as he deserved that they should be, that the men he gathered round him had a probity and intelligence which would have
reflected credit on his administration, and that he was placed
on a rigid diet of civic business. But even if some one had hinted
at this secret desire of mine, I am sure he would have heartily
laughed it off. For Bill O'Dwyer "the Doctor," as he always referred to me with a mixture of reverence and contumely, lived
in an ivory tower from which no staircase led to the ground.
How could he have known how ruggedly versed in the ways of
the world I unfortunately was! But it is a great pity that nobody
took him in tow as Charles Burlinghame did La Guardia when
he had come to the great crossroads in his career.

Here I shall do no more than allude to the grim but nevertheless poignant, almost wistful story that might be written about
his one calamitous attempt to dictate to the Board of Higher
Education. Who talked him into that inept business, I do not
know. My own private brush with him was over a matter which

should perhaps be chronicled for the minor benefit of future historians of New York. It had been decided that the seat of the United Nations was to be in the city or some place near it, and for a time sites as diverse as Connecticut's Mianus Gorge area or the water-front near Little Silver, New Jersey, were suggested with considerable gusto and fanfare. Then the idea caught fire that the really important thing to do was to find a place in which the Security Council could be housed adequately. Would not this body, after all, settle every really significant international dispute, thus leaving only minor chores to other more or less peripheral agencies? But where could it be set up in business? Like many another citizen I had given some thought to the matter and come up with what I believed was an excellent way of tiding things over until a permanent site for the United Nations organization had been found. The idea was to place at the disposition of the Security Council the large Assembly Hall of Hunter's Park Avenue building. At the time, a considerable amount of office space was vacant in structures near by; and the plan assumed that the various bureaus of the Council could be housed in the neighborhood while its meetings were held in the Hall. I shall say no more in praise of it than that Abraham Feller, entrusted with the cause of UN sites, surmised that it was a good idea, though this surmisal came too late.

Meanwhile, however, the Borough President of the Bronx, flanked by the omnipresent Grover Whelan, had come up with the notion that the Hunter College campus in his domain was the answer to the Security Council's prayer. This Bronx campus had been expropriated by the Navy during the war for the purpose of training the WAVES. The College had thus been deprived of half its plant, all its athletic fields, and much of its specialized equipment, but not a complaint had been voiced by us. If training the WAVES on our broad acres would help win the grim struggle, we were all prepared to say Amen. Of course the situation thus created was sometimes difficult, for people generally thought we were still in formal control of the campus. For example, one day I received a letter from a woman in St. Paul, Minnesota, which read as follows: "Dear Mr. President, I am sending my only daughter Susan to your college to be a

WAVE. Please send her back to me as sweet and wholesome as she was when she left."

Facing the prospect of doing without this campus for another indefinite period, or perhaps forever, was a bleak assignment and I demurred. But to our credit be it said that the opposition was based far, far less on our needs than on the rather obvious fact that requiring the various delegations to travel every day to the edge of New York City and back again seemed calamitously wasteful of their time and energy. It was impossible to find living quarters or office space in that area. All this later on became quite clear, for after having turned the Hunter Gymnasium inside out and spent a modest fortune transforming class-rooms into offices, with bi-lingual signs on every door, the Security Council departed for Lake Success. But not until Mr. Gromyko had walked out, the Cold War had reached almost the nadir of frigidity, and the Borough President had acquiesced in the facts of geography. For my part, the departure was a relief in more ways than one. Our responsibility for virtually everything the United Nations did or did not do was assumed by the public. On one occasion, after a bar had been opened on the premises for the edification of the delegates, I received a sheaf of protests from the Women's Christian Temperance Union. But then came a letter from a Cleveland bartender, enclosing an addressed postcard. "Mr. President," the letter read, "what is the most popular cocktail you serve?"

The meeting called at Mayor O'Dwyer's office to discuss the matter was most cordial. It was of course quite clear that our cause was as lost as Burnside's at Fredericksburg. The chairman of the Board of Higher Education had pledged his cooperation; and I also knew full well that, education or no education, the great Borough of the Bronx was not going to be deprived of the glory of playing host to the Security Council. A considerable number of personages were on hand, and we reminisced during half an hour about the war, Italy and a number of other subjects with the requisite nostalgia. Then we got down to business and I tersely recited the reasons why the Security Council ought not to look upon our campus as its predestined home. Nobody advanced any reasons why it should. We parted most amicably

—it was a pleasant, sunny afternoon—and history took its course. I attended the ceremonies which marked the opening of the Security Council's deliberations and had my picture taken with Borough President James Lyons and Grover Whelan. Those photographs are doubtless safely deposited in appropriate morgues, but thank God thousands of live youngsters now stroll more or less busily about the uptown campus. I know as well as I know anything that if I had not kicked up a fuss, Hunter would never have got back there. That is as good a reason as any for having been a college president.

My liking for Bill O'Dwyer still abides with me, as does regret that he was not fated to be what he might have been. But in more ways than could be enumerated, it was fortunate that my sojourn in office should have come to an end under the friendly reign of Robert Wagner. The government of the City was now transformed into almost the opposite of what it had been under La Guardia. First-rate men were installed in subsidiary offices and were given a large measure of responsibility, though the Mayor remained personally accessible—really more than for his personal well-being he should have been. This new order of things brought John Theobald to the office of Deputy Mayor from Queens College. It was therefore inevitable that the municipal colleges should move into an unprecedented tide of prosperity. The pernicious financial anemia from which we had suffered for so long responded admirably to treatment, and in a short time parity had been established, in terms of salaries and allowances, with the best-groomed colleges and universities. We also began to receive a larger measure of State aid, and here again it was Dr. Theobald's spade which dug the first channels of communication. But, alas, while money is a highly beneficial substance, it will not remove all the ills of life. At an old college like Hunter, the passing of time brought it about that many a senior member of the Faculty departed, and we were knee-deep in the thickets from which fledgling instructors must now be extricated.

It is far too early to write an epitaph for Robert Wagner as Mayor, but I may record that it was of genuine interest to me that with him the "German element"—to which I also belong—

reentered New York political life. Oddly enough, with singularly few exceptions, notably Wagner's distinguished father, German-Americans have shied away from the popularity contests which are no doubt the prime ingredients of the "democratic process." How different a story there is to tell if one thinks of generals, admirals and military men in all ranks! Or also of educators, writers, business men. Since Bob Wagner has never belied his origins, we had been associated prior to the War in the leadership of an anti-Nazi organization known as Loyal Americans of German Descent. It was thus that I first came to know his remarkable urbanity, which is not to be compassed within the meaning of the German word *gemuetlichkeit*, though this has also not been absent. No doubt this Mayor has lacked the hard, relentless drive of La Guardia, but he has been able to prove that a gentleman's government can in some measure survive in New York.

Yet even from a relatively crass political point of view, the most awesome force to be contended with in New York, and it may be anywhere in the United States, is public opinion. The average citizen of this great city assumes, and beyond any doubt will continue to do so, that every municipal college, Hunter included, is gloriously spotted with whatever hue of skullduggery is the favorite at City Hall. That venerable edifice, concerning which Henry James remarked in his time that it was peopled with "large florid ghosts," looms in the citizen's thoughts as a curious blend of Mecca and Monte Carlo. It is near enough to Wall Street, he believes, to have acquired the gambling habit and yet so snugly set up against Trinity Church that it has taken on a deceptive patina of respectability. Were he required to believe that Hunter or any of its sister institutions was immunized against the miasmas seeping in from its political surroundings, he would be sorely tempted to strip it of importance. On the other hand if there were to be a scandal of however unimportant a kind, he might well ride to hounds and chase the poor offending president to kingdom come. This is an environment in which a college like Hunter must live, with whatever blend of irony and serenity it can conjure up.

I believe that the authentic residents of the city, used to its history and customs, realistically take it for granted that efficient democratic government will involve costs which do not appear in the budget. I recall that Dixon Ryan Fox, first-rate historian who was also president of Union College, was wont to say that the cities of the United States were better governed than many in other countries because those in charge could count on a certain amount of patronage with which to reward those who could keep the complex machinery oiled. At one time I thought this a very cynical view to take of the situation, but I now feel he may have been right. Perhaps if the handouts were ampler, there would not be so many concessions to union leaders who more or less do the same thing in another way. Possibly there might even be more jobs for youngsters who are now juvenile delinquents. I do not know and I assuredly do not want to sound like an advocate of corruption. But unless one is bent on governing the city as Fiorello La Guardia did, by feeling the pulses of all God's children, it seems indispensable to find a viable substitute arrangement.

Now I should doubtless reflect a bit on major centers of public opinion in New York. The most important of these is certainly that to which New Yorkers refer as the "Power House" on Madison Avenue. This is the residence of the Cardinal Archbishop of New York, flanked by the office of his Chancellor. From both there is supposed to issue a never-ending stream of clerical and lay Friar Josephs who shape legislation to their heart's desires, bestow benefices on a variety of proteges, and knife enemies of the Lord with subtlety and finesse. Therefore I should no doubt report that during more than two decades Francis Cardinal Spellman never tried to bring any influence whatever to bear on any aspect of the changing fortunes of Hunter College. After having been named to the presidency, I went to call on him, admittedly for the purpose of sniffing out what the climate might be. Archbishop Spellman, for that was his rank and station at the time, indicated very frankly that it would not be his policy to interfere in any way in public education, including the college over which I would have the honor to preside. This promise he scrupulously respected. No Friar

Joseph made his shadowy presence felt. Instead there were occasions on which the Cardinal supported this or that campus activity with modest generosity, with no thought of a favor to be granted in return. It is true that a personal feud with one of his Chancellors, begun in my editorial days on *The Commonweal*, continued unmerrily on. For this His Eminence was in no way responsible; and though it undoubtedly caused me inconvenience and annoyance, it did not affect the educational chores to which I was committed.

When I first talked with the newly consecrated Archbishop he suggested that I would be well advised to forget my days as an editor and refrain from voicing opinions on controversial issues. No doubt he had in mind views of Naziism, General Franco and Father Charles Coughlin which I had up to that time assuredly not concealed. This friendly counsel which, if followed, would have added considerably to my personal tranquility went, I fear, through both ears without delay. (I may add that at the convocation which marked my retirement, I alluded to this conversation. The Cardinal interrupted to say, "I wish I had taken my own advice!") Perhaps I may have thought arbitrarily that a prelate fresh from Rome and New England could not be very familiar with the New York situation. At any rate, after a dozen bruising years of editorial activity, I had come to realize full well how difficult it is for many men of good will outside the Catholic Church to view it without a measure of aversion or even of dread. This was a mood into which they had more or less been born; and it seemed to me highly improbable that a change would take place unless Catholics stopped sounding like a blend of D.A.R., Bruce Barton and a random devotee of Torquemada. Therefore I went resolutely down the path I had set for myself, with the result that my isolation was upon occasion as grimly complete as that of a lone sailor clapped in the brig. Later on, when Father Lawrence McGinley pinned Fordham University's Insignis Medal on me, he said whimsically but with a good measure of truth that there had been times when there seemed to be two kinds of Catholics in America— George Shuster and all others. Today this has of course rather startlingly changed. The scene is now abuzz with young Catholic writers, philosophers and even theologians whose utterances I would have found, even in my most outspoken days, rather venturesome and challenging.

No doubt these things should be said primarily because the very few occasions on which Cardinal Spellman entered the arena of public debate with a certain amount of verbal passion have in my judgment obscured the genuinely impressive though quiet contribution he has made to the preservation of a liberal climate of opinion in his part of New York. Life in other boroughs of the city has sometimes been scarred by bitter, often quite unintelligible, conflicts in which religious differences played a notably deplorable role. But in Manhattan, despite social problems of the utmost gravity which primarily grow out of racial divergences and forms of segregation stemming from them, we have had a prevailing equanimity of temper. I would be less than honest were I not to say that for the preservation of this Cardinal Spellman is entitled to his due measure of credit. It gives me great satisfaction so to attest, for granted both the situation and the character of Hunter's president, a man in his august office could have made things unpleasant indeed.

Once more I shall admit that the average New Yorker, were he perchance to read this chronicle, would hardly be persuaded by it that a man in an educational position so exposed to the varied winds that blow would not have to rig his sails accordingly. Of course the city is amply supplied with pressure groups, some of which would like to have a special corner of the College for themselves, or be given half a chance to help run the show. These are in the main of two kinds. Feeling like a victim of discrimination is one of the maladies to which Americans are most addicted, often, alas, with good reason. In dealing with the disease it was of great advantage to me to know that nobody was really being mistreated in so far as we were concerned, while realizing also that a variety of organizations developed by minority groups for the protection of their rights simply have to find something to make a fuss about if they are to stay in business. I am afraid that I gradually developed an attitude of dispassionate languor toward whatever outcries of this character were voiced. Sometimes the complaint was that we were not appointing to the Faculty an adequate number of representatives of one or the other group. But we went right on selecting the best people we could find, regardless of their affiliations. The second form of pressure is attempted by those who wish to eliminate from campus opinion ideological views of which they do not approve. These are they who, for example, consistently get their feathers ruffled over something a brash young editor has written in the college newspaper. Or they wish to censor the list of speakers invited to the campus. Perhaps none of their protests has amazed me as much as has the inability of relatively mature citizens to realize that many opinions which a young man or woman cherishes at twenty will be lived down more or less painlessly at forty.

On the other hand, Hunter does have a quite astonishing amount of credit in the bank of public opinion. Embedded in all the layers of the City's generations there are memories of cherished mothers, formidable aunts, sisters, sweethearts, wives, teachers doted on or feared, who were trained at Hunter while it was a normal college or later on a college of liberal arts for women. Perhaps there were times when ladies who had come up the social ladder found it desirable to forget so proletarian an Alma Mater. And it may also be that upon occasion it happened to be a rather drab and shabby place. But rooted in the benevolence, aspiration and criticism of the common man in the community it has long since been. This is the proudest thing it can say of itself; and I shall fondly hope that no monolith of public higher education in New York will ever deprive it of that heartwarming individuality—or rather, it is not too much to say, that personality.

You may pardon a random sampling of what this means. Some years ago, Fordham University celebrated its hundredth anniversary and asked President Harry Truman to deliver the address. The guests doomed to academic enrobement had been asked, for security reasons, to present tickets at a certain gate. Finding that I had forgotten to bring the precious piece of paper, I told the policeman stationed there who I was and begged his pardon for my forgetfulness. "Go right on in, Doctor," he said. "My aunt graduated from your great institution. Go right in!"

Nelson Rockefeller stood immediately behind me, confessed like-wise to having been absent of mind, and gave his name. "I don't care if you are Napoleon Bonaparte," snapped the custodian of the law, "you can't get in here without a ticket!" I stepped back and said, with a mild deviation from the truth, "It's quite all right, officer. He teaches at Hunter." "In that case, Doctor," was the reply, "of course I'll let him in."

This identification with the needs of a great community is a constantly shifting, greatly expanding reality. For many people recent years have been times of tragic exile from their native lands, and some of the fortunate among them found a haven in New York. This may not have given them riches, but did provide employment, freedom, satisfaction. On the day before Christmas a few years ago, I hailed a taxi in front of the Carnegie Endowment Building and asked to be driven to the college. When I had got in the driver began to explain jubilantly that his daughter had graduated from Hunter the previous June, that she and her alma mater were quite the most precious of females, and that it had assuredly been the hand of Providence which had brought her and him safely out of Estonia to the land of liberty. In his eyes its shores had taken on the coloring of Marvell's Bermuda. So eloquent did he grow as we proceeded through traffic and the lightly swirling snow that at a stop light the driver of a limousine behind us got out and said to my cabby, "Please don't wave your hand around like that! I can't tell which way you want to turn." "Oh, excuse me," my happy companion replied. "A merry Christmas to you, and three cheers for Hunter College."

Upon occasion, to be sure, the omnipresence of the Hunter student and graduate can prove to be a problem. I have met them everywhere in the East and the West, in Paris and the Tyrol. One morning in Rio de Janiero, I stood on the balcony of the Royal Hotel as the body of President Vargas was being borne through the streets hemmed in by machine-gun squads to the airport. Suddenly a voice beside me asked, "Aren't you President Shuster?" It was a charming graduate, of course. I have often found it expedient to walk about keeping half an eye on the passing throng lest I failed to greet a woman with the stamp of

Hunter more or less upon her. And so misfortune inevitably occurred. One afternoon on Fifth Avenue I felt certain that a trim young lady in a flowered pink hat was one of my very own. I raised my hat and smiled. But she threw a furious glance in my direction and said, "If you don't stop grinning at me, I'll call the police."

But when everything has been said, Hunter owes the relative equableness of its history above all to Manhattan. This, it may be said, perhaps has no point of view other than that there are points of view. Its neighborhoods cling to its torso of big buildings less like ribs with flesh on them than like the ships which hug the banks of the Hudson. In all of them the loyalties and samenesses of population groups are cabined up snugly, and occasionally they manifest their identities with long, shrill toots of the whistle. Anybody who loves the borough knows that the discovery of these several presences is the heart of the matter. It is something the stranger will never find out or savor. Why should one add anything about the Bronx, for this is more of the same? It is the fanned out dormitory of Manhattan. No one save a few officials knows where it begins or ends. A congeries of neighborhoods which exist because Manhattan does, it reflects the well-being, the poverty, the problems and the social engineering requirements of the great pinnacled streets to the south. Many of the city's institutions have their brick-and-mortar habitats there—universities and colleges, hospitals and homes for the aged, botanical gardens and golf courses. But everyone knows that the voices which speak through them and for them come from elsewhere. One could hardly symbolize this more effectively than has been done by Fordham University in planning a place for itself in Lincoln Center. The hallowed old campus which for decades brought the Third Avenue Elevated to a dignified conclusion will keep right on housing boys. But the platform from which the University's voice will speak to the city, and no doubt in time to the nation, can only be built where in this mad but glorious metropolis platforms belong.

This is the scene on which, for more than twenty years, I tried to earn my daily wage.

II.

THE COLLEGE PRESIDENCY

A college or university presidency is normally a calling incomprehensible to those engaged in it, and misunderstood by those who are not. I fear that anyone who reads what follows may at the end feel more mystified than ever. But one thing is quite simple and clear. Unless one has bad luck or the college is beyond redemption, being First Man on a campus is a fairly enviable fate, as fortunes go in this world. Campuses are things Americans love almost more than they do churches or movie stars. They pour tubs full of money into them. Nobody knows what college education costs in the aggregate, but it certainly is a sum which would look impressive in the balance sheet of General Motors. Other signs of public affection are not lacking. Even the demand for admission on the part of those whom it would usually be a kindness to turn away is so great that there would be a major boom on all the Broadways of the nation if the disappointed chose to go to the theater. Perhaps they should. It is also so obvious that our urban-technological society needs large numbers of at least partly educated citizens that even what looks like, and sometimes is, academic luxury does not make anybody feel that Alma Mater has been on a binge.

There exists a basic American image of the college campus which young people and their parents perennially try to conjure up as a reality, yet the various institutions are so different that the dream picture is always only partly in focus. What is the picture? It is of a place round which moral fences have been built fairly high and strong; where ivy, wistaria or something similar dangles from every paling; where there will be a chance to meet "nice" boys or girls, as the case may be; where opportunity will be given to meditate upon the sages, the poets and the artists of mankind; and from which the youngsters will nevertheless emerge equipped with skills to make enough money to join the Country Club. But in cold, hard fact one college is situated in a not too interesting small town and housed in buildings which require unflagging effort to keep their shabbiness genteel. Faculty members here usually know one another wisely and too well; and the students, not moulded into anonymity by numbers, learn to outwit teachers and townfolk with canny solidarity. Another may be a large urban seat of higher learning in which out of thousands of faces a few hundred become identifiable during four years. There the only place at which the whole Faculty meets regularly is the bursar's window on pay-check day. Many other kinds exist—some segregated in terms of sexes, others coeducational; some priding themselves on fidelity to "liberal arts" conventions, others pledged to creating through experiment something like twelve-tone education; some with religious commitments, others frankly secular; some, finally, manifestly down at the heels, others hardly able to get away from blissful contemplation of their solvency. Henry James once described a character's face as "an accidental cohesion of relaxed angles." No better phrase could be invented to define higher education in the United States.

If a man lets himself be cajoled into becoming the president of a college, he must have good fortune or wit enough to select a campus on which he can function without twisting his psyche wholly out of shape. Some people can, it is true, live themselves into almost any rôle. But as I have looked about me during these past years and contemplated my own relative fair fortune, it has seemed that most of the sad failures have been due to good men being in the wrong places. Nobody would ever assume that just because someone can manage a large hotel efficiently he could just as admirably keep a steel-mill going. But because the "basic image" is so fixed, or for other reasons I cannot fathom, the picture of a college president which not a few well-meaning Boards conjure up tends to have the same cast of feature. Or good institutions may come to feel that lightning strikes several times in the same place. Thus there are colleges which once having had at the helm a successful, scholarly professor of Latin believe that the thing to do is to find still another such professor. And when the poor man discovers that he is expected above all to cajole graduates and raise money, he is as unhappy as can be imagined and gets out of the assignment more or less alive.

It would be impossible to establish many rules of thumb, but a few do seem demonstrable. If the task is presiding over a large institution, the president must be a man who can talk effectively to large groups, meet a great many people and like them, possess a stomach for public dinners, and act through the deputizing of authority. This is no job for somebody who likes a "family atmosphere," desires to run the whole show himself, or bumbles about when there are more than a couple of hundred people in the hall. It is even more important that the president be in tune with the traditions of a given campus (if it has any, and it usually has) without being hidebound about his allegiance to them. This is not at all easy. It need hardly be pointed out that being the president of a Lutheran college necessitates sympathy with the Lutheran attitude toward life and education. Equally important, however, is the realization that no two Lutheran colleges are alike. I have often been impressed by the fact (for example) that Jesuit institutions of higher learning, though supervised by a Society committed to strict religious discipline, are usually the most delightfully disheveled places imaginable. But, you may take it for granted, there is no such thing as a Jesuitical disorderliness!

Yet even when the planets are in the proper configuration and the right man is in the right place, the task is by no means simple or always agreeable. But it is challenging, in very many ways rewarding, and certainly as necessary as any in American life. What does a president do? The answer is of course, that his job is a veritable deck of cards. Despite the widespread fostering of public higher education, ours is by and large a free enterprise system, which means that the budget is never what it ought to be. Therefore the president is first of all expected to find money somewhere. This is one task he cannot hire anybody else to perform. It is an ornery business which nearly everybody finds extremely unpleasant at the outset. Here nothing helps as does a measure of success. The first check is like a first baby or a first published book. Indeed, I have come to feel that money-raising is like smoking: one's first experiments are sickening, but after a while the thing acquires a fascination quite its own. You have formed the habit. The difficulty is that no matter how much money a president extracts from people, it is never enough either in his own estimation or—what is vastly more oppressive—in that of his colleagues.

The indispensable rule is to glamorize the product. Those engaged in public educational administration now find this somewhat easier to manage than do their colleagues in private universities and colleges (formerly the opposite was the rule) because the great demand makes its own dramatic case. People want campuses for their children just as they want lights on their streets; and legislatures tend to feel that the state and national interest is well served by education. Yet even so the public battle is never won. That is why it fascinates some men, who carry on with brilliant tenacity and seem to enjoy the public relations effort which is required. Even they, however, come upon days when there is no give in city and state budgets—when the blunt truth of the matter is that the citizenry are conscious of taxation and little else. As a matter of fact there are areas in which the prospects for privately financed education may be better. This also finds a notable asset in the national psychology. Over a period of time, some citizens find themselves making money in embarrassing amounts. They cannot, as the sage maxim indicates, take it with them. Indeed, the normal course of daily living may sternly dictate a choice between the tax collector and a worthy cause.

But what will induce a person who can give to think benevolently of *your* college? Looking for the answer to this question makes addiction to benzedrine unnecessary for the average president. Naturally the most favored among American institutions —Harvard, Yale, Princeton and a few others—need only keep alive the flame of adoration which gleams brightly in the bosoms of their graduates and friends. The rest of us, however, have got to get into battle dress and capture our places in the sun. Therefore we pose our colleges in the most favorable light available. Every charm must prove endearing. And sometimes, we do rather dreadful things, from buying a football team to banning Mrs. Roosevelt, from sponsoring an experimental curriculum merely to attract attention to giving away honorary degrees with tongues in our cheeks. Even so some of us do not succeed and crack under the strain. Others do and new buildings blossom on their campuses like dandelions. One must have some luck in this undertaking as in all others. In the final analysis I believe I know that meretricious practices very, very seldom usher in good fortune.

But no amount of coin collecting will enable a president to sense that his is a successful college, unless he is sure that it knows what training the mind means and can point with confidence to a Faculty which is earnestly devoted to teaching and scholarship. Boards of Trustees are sometimes inclined to think that a president need not have a stake in these concerns—that their specific situation calls for "a good business man" or a famous somebody-or-other who can jack up the endowment total or get the building program under way. Now and then they are right—but not often. It is far, far easier to teach a man with genuine scholarly interests how to raise money than it is to supply a top-notch sales manager with the key to Faculty respect and confidence. Unless these eminently necessary assets are in an institution's bank account, poverty of every kind will in the long run be inescapable. Some Faculties have a greater sense of corporate responsibility to their institutions than do others. Yet even the best must find a tonic quality in the climate of a college which suggests that scholarship is as natural as sunshine and as right as beans on a bush. It is the president who must create and maintain that climate.

Should the president himself be a working scholar? It is frequently suggested that he cannot be, for how shall a man whose administrative burdens beset him day and night find time to delve and read and so pull an oar in the research galley? Yet as a matter of fact some men have managed remarkably well. For example, I am quite sure nobody thought that Wisconsin's

Van Hise stopped being a fine scholar after he moved into the president's office. And a good president he was indeed. But admittedly the prognosis is generally unfavorable. Most administrators must be content, with as much amiability as possible, to observe the prowess of their colleagues, to savor enough of it to make a sincere compliment seem sincere, and to avoid the pitfalls which await those who view every bit of learned paper as if it had been autographed by the gods.

Finally, there is no getting around the fact that the front office is on the campus and that this swarms with students. These are never bees without stings. But experience leads to the curious observation that in some colleges the president is blamed for everything that goes wrong, while on others he is praised for all that goes well. Some men are accepted by whole generations as symbols of kindness, wit and integrity. Others get themselves written off as stuffed shirts, illiberal grouches, colorless nobodies. Yet I have known it to be a fact that some presidents at whom hardly an undergraduate looked while crossing the campus were men of stature and good will. Perhaps what one needs here also is a bit of good fortune. But it certainly makes all the difference in the world in the life of a president whether the ground he treads is warm earth or cold pavement.

In the pages which follow, I shall tell a little of what my own experience has been. They are not designed to provide a model for others to follow. Far, far from it. I can see more clearly than anybody else what during two decades I failed to accomplish, can sketch the dark places in which I fumbled badly for a light, and can summon up spirits I might not have alienated if the fire within me had shone more brightly. There were times when the weight of the enterprise sank down on me as if I had suddenly been buried under an avalanche. But at the end I find myself having liked very much what I was doing, grateful for a large measure of collective good will, and blest by the fact that the college grew like a young sequoia. It is perhaps a story worth telling because the time was of considerable significance in the development of higher education in the United States and particularly in New York. At any rate, I shall hope to have written a commentary which is only in a measure concerned with my own experience and a great deal more with a mighty city and one of the noblest endeavors.

Let me begin by calling to mind some of those who had been or still were ploughing deep furrows in the field of American education at the time I set out to cross the Hunter rubicon. During the twelve preceding years I had edited a weekly magazine, while keeping the doors to college teaching and scholarship partly open. The decision to continue struggling towards the doctorate at Columbia was taken with no thought of an academic career in mind. Indeed, though this is not the place to tell the story, I have always been convinced that editing an intellectual weekly is the most exciting and rewarding thing anybody could possibly do. Nostalgia for that task is still embedded in me as deeply as is a cave drawing in the Dordogne. Yet at the time I could not help feeling that being obliged as an editor to keep alive an interest in many subjects was a guarantee of being superficial in every one. And so I went to Columbia University and kept plugging away at a history of the English ode. This, and teaching done on the side, hardly constituted adequate training for the office of the president of a college.

In virtually no time at all I had made an important discovery. The Board of Higher Education was amazingly like the Board which had helped to shape the destinies of *The Commonweal*. Its members represented a variety of interests, clung to diverse and sometimes antagonistic points of view. But by and large they wanted the show to go on, and were willing to help. I found the Faculty hardly at all different from the authors who had come to the office of the magazine with their wares. Often they were quite cantankerous about each other. Most were eager to stamp a gold star on their personal products. They were sharply divided in their opinions of what the world needed most. Yet, like authors, they wanted very much to rivet their idea or discovery to the bosom of the public. In short, they resembled literary people rather than men of affairs. I shall confess that the student body was never really like the magazine's subscribers. For one thing, it was far more definitely a captive audience. You knew that the subscriber could toss aside your best editorial in disgust, and decide then and there not to renew.

But the student went on to the bitter end of his credits. In the early days I used to work very hard over my assembly talks, and was always cheered by a girl in the second row who seemed to listen with rapt interest. Years afterward she explained that she never paid the slightest attention to what I said. She liked the sound of my voice. It was a compliment at that, for this student, Regina Resnik, became a great opera singer.

Yet this was obviously far from being an adequate initiation. How could I find a pattern according to which my suit was to be cut? Unusual good fortune brought to my ken a number of amiable and distinguished men, two of whom will be remembered here. William Allen Nielsen, then retired from the presidency of Smith College, was a blend of Concord sage and ambassador to a royal court. Concerning his scholarship in English letters, some one has aptly said that it was as gracious as it happened to be impertinent—two admirable and quite compatible characteristics. In my judgment, he was one of the most sensibly liberal men the country has known—which means that although he sponsored many a good cause with abandon, he was always able to conjure up reasons why the enemy clung to his position and so to plan his conversion skilfully. Indeed, upon occasion he all but gave the impression that he stood quite ready to be persuaded of the error of his own ways.

His success at Smith had been legendary. The memory of it, and to some extent its secret, can be savored in the stories which have been told about him. Thus there was a mildly dismal day in the history of the College when student indignation rose high over an editorial in the Amherst paper proclaiming that the interest of the girls of Northampton in the arts of love knew no bounds. Everybody eagerly looked forward to the President's comment. He waited until the close of his assembly address and said, "I have just read the Amherst paper. *Gentlemen* never tell!" It was this ability to transform emotion into intelligence, with a barb that stung but did not hurt, which characterized his relations with human beings. He used to describe with a chuckle a train trip to Chicago during the course of which the big man across the diner table suddenly barked out, "I'm in underwear. What are you in?" Neilsen's reply was, "Skirts." This came to mind with a jolt some years later when I sat across a similar table from a square-jawed man as the train rumbled on to Omaha. He looked me over with some disdain and then said, "I'm in hardware. What are you in?" I took a cue from Smith College and answered, "Millinery!" It is a pleasant duty to report that on occasions when I was tempted to grow emotional or even phillipic in tone, the memory of a great liberal scholar stood over my shoulder like an angel and warded off a fate worse than death.

At least as valuable were Nielsen's views of education. When he spoke at the 1940 commencement of Kenyon College, he told the graduates that his generation of university professors and presidents had been guilty of "wrapping the young in romantic cotton wool." By this he meant that the prevalent temper of campus opinion had been formed by the belief that human society was steadily making progress in all directions, and that therefore nobody had much to do except serve by waiting. It was a soft and sentimental generation which all but held that good and evil were mere conjunctions of forces, economic or biological. Nielsen was honest enough to admit in retrospect that his own liberalism had not been free of this taint, but he would never have seen the matter so clearly if he had not been what William Ernest Hocking once called an "unimpeachable man." There was to be heard the hard ring of conscience in everything Nielsen said; and though he disguised it with memorable courtesy it was refreshingly there.

Henry Noble McCracken, who presided for many years over the destinies of Vassar College, was also a first-rate English scholar, but among the treasures which enriched his spirit was a noteworthy Scottish burr, which ground away at rhetoric and varied forms of sentimentalism with abrasive success. There happened to be no particular reason why he should have been immensely kind to me, but he was in ways he probably knew about and in other ways he did not. After all, Hunter and Vassar had been associated in one of the modes which history smiles upon. The gateway to the beautiful campus west of Poughkeepsie was originally capped with a cornerstone which read, "Vassar Female College." The formidable editor of *Godey's*

Lady's Book, then the most prominent magazine for women, organized a campaign to eliminate the offensive word "Female." It succeeded, and for a generation the gateway displayed a meaningful hiatus between "Vassar" and "College." Similarly the original name of Hunter College was "The Female Normal College." The editor of *Godey's* also saw to it that the term of opprobrium was deleted here. She likewise protested that the faculties of both institutions included not a single woman. As a result the ancestor of all deans, known as "the Lady Super-intendent," was appointed, first at Vassar and then at Hunter.

Of Dr. McCracken I shall say only that his disavowal of senti-mentalism in all its forms went hand in hand with as deep a commitment to spiritual values as I have seen manifested by any college president. He was a profoundly religious man who enter-tained a moving reverence for all peoples, nations and creeds. The entry of the United States into the Second World War greatly saddened him. I shall not forget the day on which he took me, with a sort of shy nobility which was characteristic of him, to a spot surrounded by campus trees where there stood a memorial to a Japanese girl who, years earlier, had been a stu-dent at Vassar and who had been so much beloved that when she left her American friends had wished to commemorate her presence. I did not learn from him that integrity is the only quality which those who aspire to lead young people cannot for a moment do without. But this was the meaning of his life. I am afraid that I do not resemble him in many ways, but when I look back I can only say that I am deeply grateful for his coun-sel and friendship at a time when I rather desperately needed them.

I remember these two men of genuine intellectual distinction because they exemplified so well the ideals which at the time determined the quality of American college life. As ideals they were lofty enough, but they were above all humane, based on a conception of higher education which was also fostered in Eng-land and Germany. Have we come down a notch or two in the scheme of things? I really do not know, and besides it ill be-hooves a man of my generation to write too many odes to the gods of yore. Perhaps life was simpler, and professors of English, or indeed of any humanistic subject, could without too great an effort suppose that the institutions over which they presided had nothing better they could possibly do than to let young people sense how greatly the reading of poets and philosophers could help them realize the beauty and meaning of life. As time passed and dictators were well-nigh everywhere, burning political issues, the nature of society and of what for some unfathomable reason we call the democratic process, came more and more to absorb our energies. Sometimes a strong man, Gordon Chalmers of Kenyon, for instance, held out against the tide. I myself (I say it with some nostalgia, satisfaction and reluctance) went from the teaching of English to that of Political Science.

But inevitably no one could have been where I have been without being very much influenced by a man in whose thinking that transition was clearly indicated and who was manifestly one of the most intelligent and skillful university presidents this country has known. Nicholas Murray Butler exemplifies to the full the glory and the tragedy of the educational builder. He surrendered very much of his initial personal scholarly concern as he moved on; and he stayed at his post too long past the time when he had ceased to be a dynamic figure and was bound to seem a dynastic survival. Nevertheless he brought into being a university of the highest distinction, so that there were decades when the stature of Harvard was manifestly lesser than that of Columbia. However critical some of us may now be of some of the men who taught in it, there can be no question whatever that, as American education went into a new age, its flag flew bravely on Morningside Heights.

It was an achievement to the realization of which Dr. Butler had to sacrifice a great deal of himself, so that upon occasion he seemed (and no doubt was) a promoter rather than a scholar, a man of unction rather than of substance, as well as, what is perhaps even worse, a man who staked off his educational kingdom completely from the great empire of the American university in its totality. At first it seems astonishing that a person so able and experienced should have left such little tangible written evidence of the quality of his personality. His autobiography is thinner in substance than even his worst enemies could have wished it to be; and I should not wonder if his accumulated correspondence kept no one awake. But these things should not deceive even those who are hardly of the elect. Had not Butler been the peer of the first-rate men he moulded into a Faculty whose inner worth was as signal as its prestige, he would have failed dismally in the attempt. What happened was that he submerged himself completely in the enterprise.

This is the supreme sacrifice which can be exacted of the president of an American university or college; and inability (rather, I think, than unwillingness) to make that oblation is probably the major reason why so many abandon the task prematurely. During his best years, and they were relatively many, Butler had a grasp of the structure and symbolism, the present character and the future possibilities of Columbia, which was in every respect phenomenal. The blueprints which became reality were scarcely less impressive than those which did not. Within the university he was the accessible center, not because he compelled others to recognize his presence but because they felt it was their privilege to seek him out. He established the principle that the country's institutions of higher learning were also resources for public service; and if by way of illustration he entered the political arena with a quite unique lack of success, this was no doubt because as a president he preached nothing he did not attempt to practice. We all used also to smile, a bit deprecatingly, at the array of foreign honorary doctorates he amassed, but this was after all merely the outer symbol of the genius he had for moving Columbia—and with it American scholarship—into the midstream of international intellectual life.

Noteworthy above all, it seems to me, was the skill he possessed for maintaining the dignity of the university through the squabbles which sometimes ruffled its surface—squabbles which are inseparable from academic life because this, like the world of opera and the theater, is not isolated from temper and temperament. There is an amusing passage in *Appreciations of Frederick Paul Keppel*, citing a letter Butler wrote after reading a report that a number of members of the Faculty were "disgruntled." "About all one can do for them," he wrote, "is to provide as much sweet oil as will suffice for a libation." That he had an ample supply of this balm on hand every one who knew Columbia can testify. Only once did he run out of it. During the curious waves of emotion which were rolling over the nation's sanity after the declaration of war on Germany in 1917, a brace of cantankerous members of the Faculty were alleged to have advocated pacifism. Both the Columbia Trustees and the press of the City were aghast at this manifestation of "treason." The men were dismissed and, in a hastily prepared speech for an Alumni luncheon, Butler proclaimed the doctrine that patriotic fervor, or something like it, would be maintained at the University. Thereupon Charles Beard, irascible, genial and unforgettable historian, resigned from his post. By reason of this error in judgment, Butler's name is still cited among the villains in some accounts of academic freedom, but the truth of the matter is that the concept of campus liberties owes as much to him as to any other man. It now seems incredible that Beard should have resigned for any such cause. But he was, during the course of his pilgrimage from Hegel to Marx, and from Marx to Hegel, often likely to dash too much pepper on his dissent. I recall one afternoon shortly after the outbreak of the Second World War that, as we sat chatting in his home in New Milford, he outlined his position as follows: "If the enemy attack the United States, I will not budge. If he enters Connecticut, I shall remain quiet. But if he approaches New Milford, I shall leap to arms." This was extravagant but it did manage to underscore his isolationist position. Noteworthy is that Butler did not defend himself in public or castigate his colleague. I know that to his mind the highest law of the administrator is that the institution is always supreme, and that therefore protracted controversy in which the man primarily responsible takes part must be avoided as if it were the Siren herself.

I shall confess that all this made a profound impression on me, though to be sure the part of the world which was clay in my hands was much smaller than his. If there be anything I did at Hunter of which I can be legitimately appreciative— and of which I must also say that it sometimes gnawed at the marrow of my spirit—it is that during two decades the college kept its potential scandals out of the newspapers. The worst of such scandals are of course those in which a president is found berating a member of the Faculty. Now and then a well-meaning but inexperienced member of the Board would say to me with some exasperation, "You have the biggest carpet and broom in town!" But as time went on he or she would agree that the lesson learned from the master of Columbia was good—learned from his success and failure alike. For nothing is so beneficent for the inner life of a college than is keeping its dirty linen off the clothes line. To this fact the president must pay his meed of tribute, however great the cost to himself personally.

My own relationships with the master of the University to which I owe a very great deal were not intimate but were diversified enough to provide a sort of all round candid camera view of his personality. Dr. Butler was one of the best friends *The Commonweal* had in my time, relying as it did to so great an extent on the judgment and imagination of one of the wisest and ablest of Columbia historians, Carlton J. H. Hayes. Irreverent folk used to refer to the President as "Nicholas Miraculous." Among the few miracles he did not succeed in performing was that of bringing in under the wing of the University the major religions. Just as he had a Deutsches Haus and a Casa Italiana, so there were to be seminaries and religious colleges, including a Catholic one. There came a day on which he almost succeeded, but the time was not ripe.

Among the many services which he rendered the magazine was acceptance of an invitation to preside over a luncheon tendered the English writer, Hilaire Belloc. Our editor, Michael Williams, had arranged for this great if sometimes bilious writer to visit these hospitable shores, and for a good two weeks the magazine's secretarial staff had done virtually nothing save attend to the business of our guest, who arrived when it suited him attired in a Napoleonic cloak and dictated letters to be despatched thither and yon, together with whatever chapters of books happened to occur to him. The luncheon was designed to be the culmination of the journey, and the invited guests were of the requisite distinction. But when the appointed hour came, everyone appeared save the lion. After an embarrassing period of delay, a messenger was despatched to Belloc's hotel to see if perchance he were ill. He was not. It had merely occurred to him that no honorarium had been suggested for his address at this luncheon, and why did British writers visit these shores if not to collect honoraria? Finally he was persuaded to come nevertheless, food was served nearly two hours after the appointed time, and Butler made a very gracious introductory speech. Belloc grudgingly got on his feet, said "Thank you!" and sat down. That was positively all the oratory he was prepared to deliver free of charge. I believe that Dr. Butler enjoyed the pageant very much.

He himself was never able to be as crotchety as that. Yet there were times when his role of university president did flutter about his spirit somewhat in the manner of *A Midsummer Night's Dream*. Paul Hazard, eminent French scholar in the field of comparative literature, used to relate with infinite delight how Butler was elected to membership in the Institut de France, surely a signal honor. He responded in French the like of which had seldom been heard in that distinguished hall, for his proficiency in speaking the Romance Languages was less than marked. He was followed by an eminent British educator, who likewise did not use the pure language of Racine. "How strange that the British have never learned to speak French!" was Butler's whispered comment to his neighbor, Hazard.

The last time I saw him is among the most poignant of my recollections of twenty years. Fiorello La Guardia, whose soul knew its moments of wistful tenderness for which it was not always given credit, decided that since Butler was old and ill the City of New York should confer its highest honor on him. Accordingly Harry Gideonse of Brooklyn College and I were bidden to be outside the Butler mansion at nine of a Saturday morning. When I arrived, a police band outside was playing the "Sidewalks of New York," and a few minutes later the Mayor drove up. We went into the house and into the gracious library, which will always seem to me—and no doubt to all who knew it—the most distinguished room ever associated with an American university president. The old man, blind and feeble, walked towards us on the arm of his wife. La Guardia read the citation in about the same reverential voice he might have used if perchance he had been able to grant an indulgence to the Pope. Butler responded and tears came from his old, tired eyes. I knew then, as my own were moist, that Columbia could not help waiting for the end of a great man's career, but that it might well be a generation or ten before it would see his like again. His great mistake had been that he knew not when the time had come to go . . . Perhaps this was only a last, tragic proof of how completely he had identified himself with the institution he served by making it eminently worthy of service.

The glorious feats of promotion are not as much in evidence now as they once were (though something must be said about their contemporary significance) because the patterns according to which the builders of our greatest institutions have cut their cloth are now so clear and basically fixed. But I should like to recall one of the most fabulously successful promoters in the history of American education, Father John Cavanaugh the first, of Notre Dame. What he had inherited was called a university but this it was not at all, but rather a random collection of undergraduate colleges which offered to a relatively small student body a bewildering variety of curricular opportunities—law, engineering, commerce, journalism, education, arts and sciences. But by way of assets it had the charm of a quadrangle which was almost a masterly collection of botanical specimens, amazingly beautiful at all seasons, and four or five buildings in which the homesickness of French religious driven from their country by anticlericalism had found expression—a chapel with the stamp of Anjou upon it, a main building capped by a replica of the dome of the Hôtel des Invalides, a residence hall which looked like a chateau in the Loire country and was almost as uncomfortable to live in. Moreover there were two small lakes, blue and fringed with trees. Until well past the first World War, old priests on the campus could remember that Indians had come silently to the emerging university, having forded the St. Joseph River at the same place where La Salle had once crossed. What more by way of rural peace and imaginative suggestion could have been offered than this place near enough to Chicago and Toledo to make it possible to forget for a time their turbulence and ugliness?

Over all this Father Cavanaugh was to wave a wand which made everything glamorous that was not, while drinking in to the full the flavor of what was. He was not a scholar but still a very good teacher of English literature who savored as well as any man could the headstrong impulses of youth. Once, having pointed to the Decameron as a Shakespearean source, he warned his roomful of Catholic boys that the luscious tales of Boccaccio had been placed on the Index of Forbidden Books. But he had taken the trouble to check in advance the number of copies available in the libraries of neighboring South Bend, and so was able to determine with a glint in his eye accompanied by a chuckle that every one had been borrowed the day following his advertising. Without this gift of worldly wisdom he could not have succeeded, but the impression he created in public was that of word-rich orator. He could weave round what was often a gossamer thin theme a great net of verbal satisfaction, and doing so gave him a meed of pleasure as huge as the wine-cask at Heidelberg. I remember that once he had delivered in Washington a long address every word of which he had memorized and adjusted to inflection and gesture. When he returned, he said with a gleam in his eyes which might have been that of John Drew in the hours after a very successful night, "There were thousands upon thousands of people there, and I had them in the palm of my hand!" I have never quite believed it.

But the university was something he was always taking out of his pocket and exhibiting as if it were the Kohinoor diamond. No matter how intrinsically devoid of value this or that part of the institution might be, he talked of it so reverentially and fulsomely that, when he had finished, one was hard put to imagine that this was not still another wonder of the world. Perhaps nothing could illustrate this better than does the unveiling of a monument to the battleship Maine. For quite some time there was talk of a day when this majestic memorial, hidden from view under a wooden frame covered with canvas, would be revealed to the world. It was announced that the Secretary of the Navy would come to deliver an address at the unveiling, the Governor and Senators of the State were to be present, and the cadet corps part of the student body was to be aligned in the nearest it could come to battle array. When the day finally dawned, Father Cavanaugh was for fifteen minutes at his mellifluent best. Then the monument was unveiled and stood naked before the world. It was less than three feet high, consisting of a shell reputed to have been found in the sunken hulk, squatted on the smallest of imaginable concrete platforms.

Give such a man something genuinely noteworthy to advertise, and the results are bound to be extraordinary. Fortune must smile, and in Father Cavanaugh's case it was covered with a great glow of benevolence. For years Notre Dame had, in so far as athletics were concerned, done what all the surrounding homes of education had done. Nothing more, nothing less. That is, wherever a big, mobile chap with an interest in sports could be uncovered, in large city or small town, he was gently induced to combine the quest for gridiron glory with the lore of books. But for a long time the results hardly seemed to justify the effort expended. There were games, but scarcely anybody came, the athletes were not notable exemplars of academic prowess, and above all the newspapers were chary of comment. But then one fine day Jessie Harper came to coach the football team. He had invented a new gimmick, the forward pass. Two agile and canny young men learned to handle it with dexterity, deadly perfection and abandon. They were, of course, Knute Rockne and Gus Dorais. There came a day when they humbled the mightiest teams in the East, and Notre Dame was off to a fabulous career as the exponent of a game which then glued the eyes of the nation on campuses.

But it might well not have risen above the stature of various other small institutions which have known their hours of athletic fame had not other marvels occurred. Perhaps Father Cavanaugh might not even have thought them possible during the years when he looked under every chair for something to drape in purple. There were a number of very able men on the Faculty, notably priests who had been trained in European universities and in some way or other had come to this Indiana campus. Among them was Father Julius Niewland, a fairly reticent, upon occasion rather droll and sharp-tongued scientist given to spending lonely and mysterious hours brewing concoctions in his laboratory. One day he emerged as the discoverer of Lewisite. Perhaps this was a somewhat un-Christian achievement, but it was an important one even so. Henceforth the university would have its genuine claim to scholarly distinction, and could set its sights constantly higher.

Finally, this Catholic center had a legacy of treasure gathered sedulously by one of the first lay members of its staff. He nosed about everywhere and hung from his belt an array of trophies which even today would make the fortune of a collector. Years were needed before the cases and boxes he had piled into storerooms—archives and libraries, works of art and mementos— could be opened and sorted out. What came to light was quite breathtaking. I shall not forget the day when I and another working student came upon a sheaf of letters written by George Washington to the Bishop of Vincennes. Few pirates ever brought together more gold than did this human ferret of long ago, but he came by his honestly and in a spirit of dedication to the future. When Father Cavanaugh dedicated the Notre Dame library, to the accompaniment of a torrent of resounding words by Bourke Cochran, he knew that it was to house collections of which any educational institution in this country could be genuinely proud. In more ways than one, that day of dedication placed the ultimate stamp of approval on the effort of a man who never lost faith, drive or the sense of glamor.

As I have indicated, the great days of promotion are probably over. The country has settled down, the grooves are in the wood. But good leadership is just as badly needed as ever, and probably harder to get. What it can accomplish may be seen, for example, in the fortunes of Herman Wells at Indiana University, under whom a good but rather routine institution has become in every academic sense a very distinguished one. The conditions under which such leadership must now be exercised are quite different from those of yore. Our larger colleges and universities today resemble those of Europe in the sense that the Faculties have become corporate bodies which are committed to concepts of stability and independence. It is everywhere necessary to work with them and to recognize that, as in the nation generally, the habit of security is vastly more dominant than is the spirit of adventure. The president, when he can function effectively at all, is the first among equals, the *primus inter pares*, rather than the commander of subordinates.

This limitation unquestionably adds greatly to a modern president's feeling that his is a divided personality. On the one hand, he is held responsible for financial well-being—which from the Faculty point of view is a synonym for security—but this chore is one in which the Faculty will only occasionally give him active support. On the other hand, the bed-rock on which he must build his appeals for money—namely the character and quality of his institution—is largely not any longer his to determine. The fact is that the money-raising and public relations effort which he must expend may, when added to the burden of every day administrative routine, diminish his stature as a scholar and a man concerned with the drift of the intellect in the nation and the world. It is, for instance, worth noting that not a few presidents take office as enunciators of ideas which are relatively new and significant. But as time goes on, they repeat these ideas over and over. The reason is of course that they have neither time nor energy to develop new ones. There are to be sure notable exceptions, among them the incomparable Henry Wriston of whom I shall have more to say later on.

It must be added that the rewards for taking on an assignment of this character are not significantly alluring. In general the difference between a president's salary and that he could have earned as a professor is not large, and even if it were the tax collector would pare it down. He has by comparison with most of his colleagues an added modicum of prestige. People know him, see his name in the paper, occasionally listen to what he says. If any glory attaches to his institution some of it will rub off on him. This would of course be very valuable if there were something he had to work for intellectually which would gain in resonance by reason of his position. Only very rarely is that the case. Dr. Conant, for example, has spoken very widely and effectively, even about education, before and after being president of Harvard. Robert Hutchins made his voice heard, but the price he paid was long and bitter warfare with a large segment of his Faculty. For my part, I have things to say upon occasion and have been listened to. But there was just as much to say and opportunity to get it said while I was an editor as there has been in my days at the helm of Hunter.

At any rate, the evident fact that so large a number of unusually able presidents retire from their posts long before age inexorably compels them to do so raises very serious questions. American higher education cannot continue to prosper unless its basic problems of administration can at least in a measure be solved. It is of course true that, despite all the study which has been devoted to it, the administrative process remains at least as mysterious as sleepwalking. The clearest blueprints imaginable will not help very much unless the man who interprets them knows precisely when not to do what they suggest. And who can tell him how to know? Academic administration is peculiar for many reasons, but above all because it is concerned with qualitative and quantitative factors difficult to bring into alignment. On the one hand, the goal of the college and the university is the training of the scholar (in my judgment, a brilliant engineer like David Steinman was such a scholar just as is a distinguished professor of English like Douglas Bush) who is by definition an exceptional human being. On the other hand, it must also seek to educate, in so far as their gifts and ambitions permit, a great many other young people. For if one were to say that only the elect should be chosen and retained, the enterprise would soon be bankrupt. It would also be rather unaware of the music of humanity, however still and sad. The tendency in this country now is, as it has long been in Western Europe, to isolate the elite from the mass. We seem to be moving toward a time when "honors" students, however one may define them or deal with them, will form a kind of campus caste.

If a president is chosen because he exemplifies the scholarly excellence which is the concern of this "caste," he will in most cases find it very difficult to develop a warm feeling of comradeship with the rest of constituency. And if he is not so chosen, the caste will very probably douse him with a contempt that will rub the skin of his psyche raw. The obvious solution of the problem is to find a man who qualifies for caste membership but is genially ready to devote most of his attention to "education."

Experience indicates that precisely such men are hard to find and to keep in office. Here John Henry Newman is a classical example. The great author of *The Idea of a University* was certainly one of the most eminent intellectuals of his time and yet was quite ready to devote himself to all the drudgery of an institution concerned with fostering the intellectual life. But he failed, and the reason was that the kind of "education" the community expected of him did not interest him in the least.

One can gain some insight into the dimensions of the conundrum if one endeavors to compare those who strip themselves of presidential dignity voluntarily and those who would like nothing better than to put it on. Quite a sizeable number of retired military men, for example, are being recruited for academic administration. Why? First of all, such men leave the service at a relatively early age because of the pension system. They thereupon look about for something to do which will be compatible with their rank and station. Secondly, they have certain manifest qualifications—social grace, usually enhanced by a charming wife; a measure of prestige, since we have become a country in which military men almost dominate the scene; and very frequently some valuable experience in the area of administration. But I sometimes think that the major underlying cause of the phenomenon is that the former general or admiral knows his way about in a hierarchical system. He will not upset the nice balance of the campus, as an intellectually distinguished academician might, both because he has acquired an instinct for the recognition of balances and because, while nobody would ever be tempted to confuse him with a scholar, his value has been proved in a way the average citizen even of the groves of academe respects.

If on the other hand one asks why some of those best qualified from the academic point of view abandon their posts, the answer can only be tentative because the motives of each would have to be known and considered. For my part I believe it is because the dichotomy described cannot be surmounted. A man who knows well, in humility rather than any kind of pride, that he could have occupied a niche in the building of scholarship is troubled by his conscience. This has prodded him from the days of his youth to go down the hard road of knowledge. He finds that as a president he is required to do much that is trivial and distracting. It is not its difficulty which degrades the presidential office in his eyes, but its incompatibility with what he had vowed to do with his life. This does not mean there is something radically wrong with the office as such. If there were all sorts of people would not gladly have given quarts of their blood to occupy it. The trouble is that it cannot for long tempt the kind of man I have described. And yet, paradoxically enough, he is the only kind that ought to have the job!

Now and then I have found myself wondering whether it might not help to do something akin to the practice of the Armed Forces. If a good university or college scholar were told that after he had been president for at least seven years he could retire if he wished on the salary which had been his as a professor or Dean, he could look upon his period of service as an administrator as a fruitful and stimulating interlude, and still have time and energy to devote himself to his major interest. Such a practice would of course cost some money, but the results might well amply justify the expenditure. It is very obvious that steps must be taken in time to correct a situation which could in the long run prove disastrous. In what has been said, there is no implication that the European system of university administration, which provides for the annual rotation of the rector's office among scholars of the several Faculties, should be imitated by us. That system has manifest weaknesses, which result in the transfer of administrative authority to a center outside the institution.

For my part, having made these comments, I shall quickly add that although there certainly were times when I would gladly have tossed the job overboard, I remain deeply grateful for every year I was privileged to spend at Hunter. A president has work to do in the secrets of which no one else can share. He is able to see the institution as a whole, in all its constantly changing parts. To him the human glories and weaknesses of his environment are touching, inspiring, comic, eccentric, as the case may be. There are times when he will feel like Stringfellow Barr (it is to be hoped not too often), and hours when he may be tempted to wax as sentimental as Thackeray or any other Victorian. Inevitably he becomes a sort of father confessor to his colleagues, his students, and upon occasion to members of his Board. He has an unforgettable opportunity to realize what the word "fair" means. If he can lick his wounds, he can sometimes rise above the common battle. To him the divers meanings of the word "freedom" can be no mysteries. He may become a deep well of silence into which the confidences of others are poured. And he will know at the end that an idea which came to flower because somebody else could be induced to believe that it was his or hers is the more beloved because, just as a child is a man's though born of a woman, it takes on life through another. Parting is here also sweet sorrow.

III.

"TO BE AT HEART ON THE SIDE OF TRUTH"

Hunter College, when I first came to know it, was as different from the genteel establishment for the training of lady school teachers which Thomas Hunter had opened in 1870 as the town of Bromley is from Picadilly. It was preparing a new manifestation of fidelity to tradition by awaiting the completion of a building on the old Park Avenue site. This had been quite bucolic in the earlier days, facing as it did on cow pastures and vegetable gardens. Indeed, when the chairman of New York's Board of Education spoke at the laying of the cornerstone of what was then called the Normal College, he felt obliged to justify the choice of so rural an environment. Taking refuge in prophecy, he said that within a hundred years the spot on which he stood would be the center of the city. Seldom has an oracle been more completely sustained by the progress of events. So urban had the neighborhood become after the turn of the century that a decision was reached to transfer the College to broad acres on the northern fringe of the Bronx, where its second campus is now situated. The initial plans for developing the new Hunter were nothing less than grandiose. But when four buildings had been completed, naturally in the gothic style, there was a change of mind and heart. The ancient brick building on Park Avenue, ivy clad and dear to the hearts of older graduates, obligingly burned down; the depression would seemingly never end; Park Avenue residences, built more or less in the style of the Renaissance, appeared to belong to an unrecoverable luxurious past; and, very conveniently, money could be obtained from the Federal Government for the construction of public edifices. It was therefore agreed to resurrect old memories by putting up on the familiar site the first radically non-traditional structure, of concrete, stone slabs and glass, to be erected in New York.

The great depression struck like a hurricane unable to discharge its sodden energy. On the farms it glued young people temporarily to the land. In a city like New York, it kept them away from jobs. Boys and girls who ordinarily would have sought employment in offices and shops now took shelter in the city's tuition-free colleges, filling the last available nook. Many of them were not prepared for higher education by awareness of intellectual objectives to be kept perennially in mind. Some were very poorly clothed and fed. It was not unusual to come upon a youngster who had fainted for lack of a meal. Inevitably these jam-packed groves of academe challenged every resource of educational compression. And quite as naturally they echoed the angry debates of the period. What was wrong with the "system" which had thitherto given form to the American economy? Why weren't there "two chickens in every pot"? On the one hand, spokesmen for Karl Marx, moving out of basement-level meeting halls where Leninism had for some years been touted as the gospel of social salvation, drummed up trade among young and old alike. On the other, rival doctrines ranging all the way from Father Coughlin's Social Justice to the New Deal, with Townsend's now forgotten ideas on the topic of money thrown in for good measure, marched out their own bands. On the Forty-second Street side of the Public Library, rival picket lines of "intellectuals" offered their wares and exchanged denunciations while the police looked on with the icy nonchalance which normally conceals their boredom.

Battle lines were drawn in the municipal colleges, too, just as they were on Morningside Heights and in Washington Square. As might have been anticipated, the apostles of Marxism were better organized than their opponents, and a good deal less finicky about what they said. The anti-Semitism of Adolf Hitler, running wild in Europe, helped to make Soviet Russia saleable as a land of freedom, employment and equality. In retrospect it seems remarkable that the number of Communists and their sympathizers grew no larger than it did, for the noise they made seemed at times to drown out the roar of the traffic outside. Hunter College, conservative to the core, was even so given a Communist coloring in the public eye. Solid citizens I met in the customary places looked at me with a blend of commiseration and suspicion; and hardly had I set foot inside the college door than the State Legislature established the Rapp-Coudert Committee to find out just how "red" we were. Meanwhile the institution was passing through some drab and trying years waiting for the completion of its new building. Many of the classes were held in lofts; assemblies convened in churches and synagogues. Under such conditions it was impossible to establish a sense of solidarity in either the Faculty or the student body. Hunter thought of itself as a "subway College," and thus qualified for the role it plays in *Marjorie Morningstar*. It is no wonder that being educated in this fashion left a bitter taste in many student mouths for years. It is an even greater miracle that first-rate work was nevertheless done.

Then in the fall of 1940 we moved, and 695 Park Avenue became a reality. It was almost too good to be true. Some of our neighbors viewed us with a measure of polite disdain, and we in turn were at times afraid to spill over into the fashionable thoroughfare. The president of the Union Club across the street generously invited me to lunch but complained that the height of the building shut out the sun and thus increased the fuel costs of winters. I retorted as genially as possible that the number of members who sat with their faces glued to the windows seemed to indicate that they were enjoying the scenery. But gradually we settled down and stretched out our legs. Here we were, with more than four thousand students in the daytime (not counting the Freshmen and Sophomores on the Bronx campus), and almost as many of evenings. How were these young women, for at that time Hunter was strictly feminine, many of them from homes which poverty held in a stern grip, to find their college experience worth while intrinsically as well as in terms of preparation for some kind of employment?

These were questions which jabbed through one's soul like

electric shocks. When at the turn of the century Hunter had become a college of liberal arts rather than a teacher-training institution, it accepted its new role with almost grim determination. Sometimes it suggested an intellectual fusion of John Knox and Carrie Chapman Catt. Not a few departments assembled remarkably able Faculties, profiting greatly from the fact that women trained for scholarly careers were then excluded from university teaching quite as if they were potential sources of malarial infection. Mistakes in recruiting were also inevitably made, but as the years passed the Hunter contribution, in several fields of study and inquiry, would prove as noteworthy as that of any other academic institution. In the Humanities generally it would make an enviable record. We had on the whole high standards and were proud of them.

Yet as a corporate body the College badly needed self-confidence. Students very often felt sorry for themselves. Had they not been cheated out of a rich college experience on some more pleasant and fashionable campus? Was not their Alma Mater a drab, proletarian place, which nobody knew about except when there was talk of "young New York radicals"? Likewise there were Faculty members who thought these students unattractive and vulgar. Some of them undoubtedly were. Not a few teachers had occasional class-room experiences which left a sour odor behind; and I think many arrived in the morning feeling as if they were to do another day's stint in a factory. And so, borrowing a leaf from Dr. Butler's book, I deliberately set out to give the College, the core of which was as fine in quality as anyone could have desired, as bright a coat of what is now called glamour as any of which Vassar or Bryn Mawr could boast. Looking back I must confess that possibly I spent too much time and effort doing so. But in extenuation it may be said that before very long the name of Hunter was identified at home and abroad with academic excellence and a certain point of view. These values were only to a very slight degree of my making. As the members of our family got around and saw that these things were so they became almost too appreciative of the virtues embedded in their collective identity.

It is with the Hunter point of view that I shall primarily be concerned at this time, because the story forms a page of the City's history having a significance far beyond any experience of my own. We were, as has been indicated, presumably wearing a little Communist button in our lapel. Undeniably there were three sources of infection. First, the Faculty had a "cell" of Party members. Everybody knew it was there, but no one could prove that it existed. Despite all its probing, the Rapp-Coudert Committee did not succeed. Next in the order of importance was the Teachers' Union, which the Party had successfully infiltrated. Sometimes it tried to make itself sound like Matthew Woll, but the attempt was hardly ever more successful than were comparable endeavors by Mephistopheles in Goethe's *Faust*. The Union emitted propaganda much as Old Faithful does spray (at intervals both regular and irregular), sponsoring every cause, unholy or otherwise, that had an appeal for less affluent members of the Staff. Initially a creature of the depression, the sounds which came from its drum were often those of perennial battle for battle's sake. And finally there was the American Student Union, a junior fellow-travelling affiliate of the Party, which exploited every legitimate student grievance and invented as many others as circumstances permitted. But it was above all an organization for the "political education" of the student body. Even when assembled, which seldom really seemed to be the case, this awkwardly disguised apparatus for the fomenting of trouble to bring about the "revolution" was probably not too formidable, but its nuisance value was by no means negligible.

The vast majority of members of the Hunter College Faculty viewed this tri-headed monster with a disdain which was infinite, though it was blended with a strange kind of anxiety. Often they were so conservative that they slept on spiritual boards to keep their inner spinal columns rigid and straight, but an integral part of their conservatism was an unflagging devotion to liberal opinion. It was not even good form to attack the Student Union in any overt and outright fashion, because the sacrosanct principle was that everyone had a right to his views, whatever these might be. This philosophy was shared almost to a person by the student body, regardless of religious or ethnic demarcations. During wartime the presence of a Nazi might have awakened collective indignation, but in every other respect freedom of speech and commitment was the order of the day. Overwhelmingly also the student body held its own Union in profound contempt. Everybody knew that while the public remained convinced that the College was dyed a deep pink, there might be trouble about jobs after graduation. But this was a purely practical matter which did not suffice to call a rival organization into being.

Accordingly it was obvious that the only way to offset the Party, as well as to thwart its efforts to win converts and to keep the campus in a state of upheaval, was to take full advantage of the climate of liberal opinion. (The word liberal is used here in its older, honorable sense. A conservative was somebody like Mark Hanna, and a liberal had, in the Middle West, some resemblance to Robert La Follette. In the East he was somebody who subscribed to the *New Republic* and felt certain that the young men recruited by George Croly had, if not the answers to questions, at least glimpses of answers. In the Catholic Middle West, in which I grew up, the initial impulse was given by an almost forgotten organization known as the Central-Verein, which sought ways in which to expound answers to Socialism and Capitalism formulated by German Jesuits. Of the work of this organization I knew very little, because my father and I were such ardent devotees of La Follette; it was only later on, when I came to know Father John A. Ryan, that I realized there were other people who counted. Certainly Father Ryan was as proud as a religious man can legitimately be of the label "Liberal." Nor do I employ it here in terms which might have been appropriate at the fag end of the Roosevelt Administration, when nobody knew who was secretly committed to the Communist Party. All I shall say in comment on that point is that when the Second World War ended, Stalin's best friends were not the intellectuals and clergymen who thought that if business were done with him all would be well, but the bankers and industrialists who were sure that Russian-American enterprise would pay dividends of the handsomest kind. This fact I shall not document here. But if perchance the nation is interested in evidence, it will be a pleasure to supply it. In the meantime, I shall wear the label "Liberal" with a good deal of satisfaction.)

Very likely I personally could not have lived happily in any other climate, but at any rate strategy demanded that it be done. At this point fortune smiled, as indeed it must if anything is to be accomplished in this imperfect world. The plans for the Park Avenue building had stipulated that a number of symbolic figures were to be erected on pedestals which one can still see by walking round the edifice. Provision had likewise been made for an inscription on the south wall, which is windowless because of the large Assembly Hall inside. The figures never came into being because the committee of experts assembled to determine who the sculptor should be and what he was to provide, could not agree. Night after night artists would appear with sketches of feminine or masculine figures in varying stages of abstraction. But for none could an affirmative vote be secured; and one member of the committee, Lewis Mumford, finally surmised that just as Chartres Cathedral had not been built in a decade, so also might the Hunter sculpture be entrusted to the ages. A fate equally dire seemed for a time to await the inscription. The Bible, Milton and Shakespeare were ransacked in search of a suitable text, but no words from any of them awakened more than a feeble interest. Then one evening, while I was skimming through Emerson's *Conduct of Life*, my eye lighted on the sentence, "We are of different opinions at different hours, but we may always be said to be at heart on the side of truth." The committee assented and breathed a memorable sigh of relief.

Bruce Rogers came and supervised the cutting of the inscription, for which he had designed a noble type face. Indeed, his genius would not have suffered him to do anything else. I am afraid, however, that he did not wholeheartedly approve of the text and might instead have preferred something from Shakespeare. Or maybe Alexander Pope. But the beautiful work was done, and we had hung out our banner. We had explained to ourselves and the world the things for which we stood. A Hunter student who knows nothing else about the spirit or the objectives of her Alma Mater does somehow lodge the Emersonian words in the back of her mind. In other ways it has become one of the best known characteristics of the college. It has been copied and placed on the façades of school buildings in Latin America and other continents. And of course it remains a monument to the genial, irreverent and greatly beloved artist who designed it.

Next, without at all realizing it, the Roosevelts came to our rescue. Eleanor Roosevelt we had come to know relatively early, because she had made the family home of her husband in Campobello available to house a summer institute for the training of youth leaders. In this work I shared during the two foggiest July weeks ever to befall me as a sort of elder and counselor combined, and twice we enrolled presidents of our Student Council. One of these girls Mrs. Roosevelt particularly liked and befriended. She was in due time invited to the White House, and of course will never forget having had dinner with the President and Winston Churchill.

My own experience as a guest at that hallowed mansion was one of an equally cordial welcome but of far less good fortune. Whoever was supposed to tell me that the invitation to dinner included a bid to address the large company on the subject of education forgot to do so. The audience was far too brilliant and intelligent for an improvisation, and so I decided to repeat a speech given a week or so earlier in New York. I was going along rather swimmingly when my eye suddenly lighted on Mrs. Winthrop Aldrich, who had sat almost equidistant from me when my remarks were first unveiled. There was a glint of tolerant understanding in her eye, which I endeavored momentarily to reciprocate. Then I went on doggedly to the end with a film of confusion on the oratorical part of my mind.

The major form of association with the Roosevelts came about in quite another way. We were wondering how we could create on the campus vigorous student organizations interested in doing more than looking askance at the Student Union. There was a Newman Club for Catholic students, but it had no identifiable place round which to build its activities. Only one other small religious club was in existence. We also had a number of sororities and a rival, presumably more "democratic," social organization to which the name House Plan had been given. But House Plan had no house! The YMCA to the south of us generously accorded some hospitality but this was in the nature of things an off-campus activity.

One day a representative of the Hillel Foundation came to inquire whether we would support plans to bring about the work of that organization among Jewish students. I then outlined an idea which had gradually been taking shape in my mind. Why not establish a center in which all three major religions had headquarters? Why not also make room for the principal social groups—Pan-Hellenic organization and House Plan—so that young people meeting separately for religious purposes could then join in the social activities of the others? Was this not conceivably a way of fostering spiritual tradition while recognizing as well the common social and civic ties which bind Americans together? The response to this idea was immediate and vigorous. Hillel also took kindly to the suggestion that the town house of President Roosevelt and his mother, then for sale, be purchased. It was conveniently situated within a few blocks of the College.

This was, I may say in passing, my first important money-raising experience and I still shudder a little at the memory of it. But in virtually no time at all we had formed a distinguished committee of New Yorkers—John Burke, Joseph P. Day, Aaron Horn and Charles Tuttle. It took quite a while to acquire what we needed, for cash was then hard to come by and it was certainly not thought good form to give money to Hunter, a socially ignominious tax-supported institution. But we succeeded and could open for student use a beautiful house which ever since has been about as busy a place as any in New York. Myron Taylor presented a matchless portrait of the President, who in turn went to Hyde Park, gathered souvenirs of his mother, and personally presented them at the door. They were small things, but they did help to create an authentic historical atmosphere. Many other people provided for furnishings, books, works of art. It was as if once having decided to give the college so agreeable a place, our friends were determined to make it as lavishly beautiful as at all possible.

We now had a solid core of student organizations with which the Student Union could not compete in terms of attractiveness and prestige. In addition, we had the magic symbolic value of the Roosevelt name. No one who did not live through that time can, I think, reconstruct the position which the President then occupied in the thinking of most young New Yorkers. He had been in office during virtually the whole of their conscious lives. To him they paid their meed of grateful, often touching tribute for efforts to take from their families the terrible burdens of poverty and joblessness. Of course there were people, also among those who generously supported our cause, who would gladly have consigned the Roosevelts to gehenna. So also beyond any question would the Communists. But again the College as a whole had made another impressive declaration of its purpose and outlook. It remained firmly dedicated to liberal opinion, but it had also manifested its regard for the great religious traditions. This was at the time not too easy. Many people, looking anxiously at the troubled world, preferred if not religious anonymity, then at least a tacit agreement that the matter would not be stressed publicly. Moreover, under the laws of the State of New York, a house according hospitality to religious organizations could not be a part of the College. But through the good offices of Charles Tuttle, and with the staunch support of Governor Thomas E. Dewey, we established an independent corporation through a special act of the Legislature. Even this action the State Department of Education felt obliged to oppose, though it made of its negation a mere formality. It should be added, perhaps, that at this time we were not sure that a Protestant student organization would come into being, since the various Churches had not worked out a plan for a common approach to the problem. But in a remarkably few months, owing to the combined efforts of Faculty members, student leaders, church women in the neighborhood, and a number of interested pastors, it had been organized and was flourishing like a cedar of Lebanon.

From that time forward Eleanor Roosevelt earned for herself a very special place in the annals of Hunter College. During more than fifteen years, she has been by ten furlongs the most popular speaker to visit the campus. On every occasion she talked memorably because she has a remarkable gift for directing the attention of young people to problems and attitudes which have meaning for them. Since it is still rather fashionable to assign her to the company of incorrigible radicals, I shall stress the occasion on which, during the 'forties, she drove a knife to the heart of the American Student Union. It was noontime on a late autumn Wednesday, and the great hall was packed with students all of whom had come of their own free will. Mrs. Roosevelt said that on this occasion she would prefer not to deliver an address but to answer questions. Realizing that our little group of earnest Student Union souls would doubtless load the queries they submitted, I asked whether she would like to have me screen the written questions as they came to the platform. "No," she answered with a smile, "let me take them as they are." I sat down to await the outcome with some misgivings. But in a few moments she was spreading light, if not sweetness, while the hush of expectancy which at first lay over the audience changed to a mood of excited participation. "That," she said emphatically, again and again, "is a question phrased by the Communist Party." In every case, she went into the matter carefully and deliberately, explaining why the Party line was devious and fatuous. On that afternoon the Student Union was unmasked on our campus. It wilted visibly before one's eyes, and never again managed to grow larger than the tiny group of the dedicated. No one else could have performed that deed. She had isolated the Communist movement within the framework of the liberal tradition.

This did not mean, however, that the Party was to remain inactive. The Hunter "cell" was never large. Perhaps at one time it may have mustered in a dozen souls, some of them clerical workers. The hard core was made up of four or five able members of the Faculty, and the others were lesser fry, proudly numbered among the "converts" but always expendable. Until after the widely publicized recantation of Bella Dodd (who had taught at Hunter prior to my coming) and the subsequent summonses issued by the Investigating Committee of the United States Senate, no one admitted membership but quite merrily resorted to perjury or solemn denials when pertinent questions were asked. It may be assumed that the abler founding members had originally signed up for divers reasons suggested by the structure of society in the 'thirties. But as time went on the sense of power, growing out of a strong, almost hierarchically organized solidarity based on secrecy, no doubt proved to be the basic attraction. My experience with American Communists is limited and I therefore do not wish to generalize. But I have never known a member who recanted so long as power was his to exercise. And power, though a college like Hunter offered limited scope for its use, could nevertheless be employed in attempts to create rifts between the officers of the Administration, the Faculty, and the student body. Sometimes the Party seemed to probe for weaknesses in the structure merely in the hope of having a curious kind of fun.

The years during which the Communist bid for influence was at its zenith are of course those associated in memory with the "Popular Front." In the United States they were roughly coterminous with the period between the dawning of a realization that the depression which set in with the Stock Market panic of 1929 was not a temporary slump but a major economic crisis, and the signing of the Stalin-Hitler Pact in 1939. I had an opportunity to sense the vigor of the Party appeal when, as an editor of *The Commonweal*, I honored a request from one of the agencies of the Archdiocese of New York to address a meeting of the Teachers' Union, of the nature of which I had at the time not the foggiest notion. At that moment quite a few people thought that a mission to the Communists would bear fruit! When I arrived at the place of meeting, a high school in Manhattan, a crowd of teachers was milling around. It could not be accommodated in a single auditorium, so that the speakers went from one place of meeting to the second. I found myself in the company of a bewildered young Protestant clergyman who also knew as little about the Teachers' Union as he may have of some forgotten Byzantine Heresy, sandwiched in between rambling discourses by Party stalwarts, Robert Minor and Earl Browder. It is to be feared that I made no converts on that occasion. But I am still glad I went, for it provided an opportunity to see the Teachers' Union in all its problematical glory. The trouble was that for years thereafter this expedition to the heathen cropped up every time my credentials were scrutinized by a Government agency.

In so far as the student body was concerned, the classroom was seldom used for propaganda purposes; and when it was, the pill was coated with so heavy a sheath of sugar that any objection to it would have been generally thought a violation of academic freedom. Other devices were, however, sedulously resorted to. The Party employed on the campus a fairly continuous squad of agents, some of whom could be identified. Now and then an occurrence lighted up the macabre character of the movement. Of these no doubt the most spectacular involved a girl who had graduated from a good high school in the Middle West and then come to New York, during the worst period of the depression, looking for employment. Somehow she became the mistress of a Communist agent and carried out as best she could the missions assigned to her. Apparently the ardor of affection cooled, or it may be that her usefulness was questioned. She was left stranded and penniless. A member of the Hunter Faculty befriended her and offered hospitality for a time. It was then agreed that the girl should return to her home. She set out for the railroad station but, incredible as it may seem, disappeared on the way and was never heard of again. This sort of thing seems luridly melodramatic now, but in those days an event of the kind was greeted with a shuddering shrug of the shoulders.

It was quite impossible to map the gyrations of such agents or to diagnose their psychology. One did, however, obtain interesting glimpses. Shortly after the Stalin-Hitler Pact was signed (which of course was the first major propagandistic defeat suffered by the Party), I sat talking with a very gifted and serious young lady whom many suspected was an emissary of the "revolution." I remarked that it seemed difficult to believe that anyone could henceforth credit the Russian dictator with good intentions. "A defection from principle," she replied calmly, "does not affect the rightness of the principle." She was a dedicated person, all right. There were others who had obviously been paid for their services, in one way or other.

What finally more or less disposed of the problem was that as time went on student leaders belonging to population groups which were special targets of Communist propaganda acquired an uncanny ability to spot the enemy. This was particularly the case with Negro girls. Having been exposed to the Party's best infiltration efforts they had a sort of litmus paper built into their souls which changed color when a young Communist came near. I have often said that the people of the United States owe a great debt to the Negro for having resisted all Communist blandishments. His genuine grievances the Party did everything it could to exploit. That nevertheless only a handful of Negroes were induced to abandon a sincere hope in democracy as well as simple but profound faith in Christianity is a fact of which social historians should make due and ample note.

At any rate, two things were abundantly clear. First, the Party would balk at absolutely nothing to win adherents. Second, it could not succeed unless the College acted in some way which would arouse against its leadership the dominant liberal sentiment. We were therefore engaged in never-ending tacit conflict, during the course of which one had to try to out-maneuver the enemy in advance. But nobody openly admitted that a tug of war was going on. Perhaps I had been aided in some slight measure by my experience in Germany during the 'thirties, when there was opportunity to take a good, hard look at the Communist Party there. But often it seemed to me that I was playing poker with my eyes blindfolded. It was a matter of conscience not to permit, if it could be helped, the intellectual seduction of students. At the same time it was clear that if one resorted even to a sliver of what would have been called dictatorship, the liberalism of the environment would have served the enemy admirably. That was the way the country was as a whole. Until well past 1948, the majority of our citizens believed that a social democracy was evolving under Stalin, and that world peace could be assured by cooperation with the Soviets.

I did not agree with them and often enough said so. But unfortunately the skeptics were frequently unwilling to play by the rules which insure free rein for opinion. They wanted to browbeat the opposition, to resort to suppression by governmental fiat, or indeed to take the law into their own hands. In so far as the College was concerned, they were often eager to forbid what could not be forbidden. I had often to reckon with the startling fact that because Hunter maintained a free market for ideas while doing its utmost to take advantage of that, my alleged sympathy with Communism became a favorite topic of conversation in certain quarters. Indeed, there were times when the anti-Stalinists surmised that I was a proper target for almost any kind of abuse. I shall merely allude to an afternoon when I ventured to cross Brooklyn Bridge for the purpose of talking to a group of professional people. During the discussion hour a young member of some Veteran organization or other first ventured to call me an agent of the Kremlin and then engaged in such realistic threats against my person that he had to be forcibly constrained and turned over to the police. Ever since that time, I have been persuaded that the ground rules of democracy were not nearly as well established in our beloved country as they might desirably have been.

At any rate, despite the amiable opinions of segments of the Brooklyn population, fate decreed that during a little more than five years the Communist attack would be directed at me personally. It was not a unique plague or honor, since on the Brooklyn College campus all the guns the Party could fire were aimed at President Harry Gideonse, whose economic doctrines and liberal views it held in abhorrence. In order to understand what the situation at Hunter was, it seems desirable to bring to remembrance the rather unusual temper of public opinion during the second World War. This conflict the nation as a whole had certainly not wished to enter. Nothing less insane or outrageous than the attack on Pearl Harbor could have induced it to do so, and the necessity for settling scores with the Japanese was accepted, grimly enough, as the paramount national obligation. But in so far as the Germans were concerned, our overt repudiation of Naziism was counterbalanced in a way by an undertow of anxiety lest in the end the defeat of Hitler might mean the triumph of Stalin. This anxiety could of course not be effectively voiced in public, even though President Roosevelt is known to have shared it for a considerable time. That nobody should allude to these fears became the principal American Communist enterprise; and since there were enough good people who did not see the danger or else minimized it, the Party chance was rather a good one.

After 1944 Communist influence in Hunter College had dwindled to such an extent that only through assistance from without could anything important have been accomplished. Personally I had long been concerned with the situation in Germany and had written a good deal about it. In addition, conviction led me to join many of the most influential anti-Nazi groups, so that my position was quite clear to anyone who listened to the radio or read the newspapers. But I also thought that the danger of an overwhelming Communist victory in Europe was very real, and that steps must be taken in due time to prevent it. The Party was all in favor of my being anti-Nazi, and had indeed complimented me on that score not infrequently—after the Stalin-Hitler Pact was broken, to be sure! When, however, I began to point out how urgent it was to take steps to insure a peace likely to preserve the future of democratic institutions, the faithful were marshalled for battle.

Had my ties with two New York groups not been strong and of long standing, I very much doubt that I could have survived the subsequent battle-scarred period. These groups were the American Jewish Committee, and Sol Levitas and his friends of the *New Leader*. With some of the work of the first organization, so ably led and oriented, I had been associated prior to coming to Hunter. For his part, Sol Levitas had come from Russia bearing the scars of the struggle which the Jewish Bund had tried to carry on there against the rising tide of Bolshevism. But they did not affect his inexhaustible energy or the remarkable good humor which characterized his spirit. Behind him stood the genial figure of David Dubinsky of ILGWU, as well as the men and women who had, over a period of years, rallied round the banner of the Rand School. From the beginning these admirable people, whose views of life and the world were clearly different from mine, welcomed, aided and supported me. It may be true that my unhesitating readiness to help work for the Spanish refugees for whose welfare they were concerned was a minor service they could honestly appreciate. In virtually every other sense I was merely a friend whom, for some inexplicable but no doubt providential reason, they had adopted and would not abandon to the wolves. In this respect they were to differ notably from a number of other groups on whose support I might perhaps have legitimately counted. German American friends of stature remained loyal friends, for example, but in the circumstances it was no doubt inevitable that any corporate entity they represented should, as the phrase has it, have gone underground.

This is neither the time nor the place to discuss what happened in fulsome detail, and so I shall content myself with illustrating the situation in terms of my life at Hunter College. The outlook of such dyed-in-the-wool followers of the Party line who were then on the campus may be exemplified by an experience with a professor who was an able man in his field of study and whom I liked a good deal as a person. During the honeymoon period of the Stalin-Hitler Pact he had carried a placard in a demonstration which had been staged outside our building for the benefit of the Board of Higher Education, which was meeting there and concerning itself with some aspect or other of Communist activity. On that placard were inscribed the words, "The Yanks ARE NOT Coming!" This, as he was frank enough to indicate, was also a message to me personally in my capacity as a member of the major Committee favoring aid to Britain. Then, however, Hitler marched into Russia and we entered the war. It took the Party a few days to adjust itself to each of these realities, but at any rate the words of the formal declaration of hostilities were still ringing in our ears when the professor came to see me. "Mr. President," he said with a ring in his voice, "it is high time that you explained to the Faculty that a war is going on! They are apathetic. Sacrifice is a word they don't understand. They are entirely unaware of what we are up against!" His analysis of the dire morale situation proceeded at some length. When he had finished, I was moved to say, "Well, Professor, I think the trouble is that they have worried about this war so much longer than you have that they may have grown a bit tired." He smiled a little wryly, we parted company, and that was the last visit but one I had from him.

But forces outside were being mustered in. The trouble started modestly enough as a result of a little piece written for the New York *Times*. During a number of years I had reviewed countless books dealing with the situation in Germany for that illustrious journal and had greatly cherished the association. The piece in question had to do with a work by Heinz Pol, a left-wing journalist who had come to the United States in the wake of Naziism. It represented a form of historical writing then enjoying a considerable vogue, for the spirit of the thirties was polemical rather than objective. I thought the book stupid, and said so with a candor which left little to the imagination. Some days later there came a letter from a well-placed refugee which declared bluntly that if I ever ventured to write anything of the kind again appropriate steps would be taken to silence me. Naturally I shoved the epistle aside and did not bother to reply. It should perhaps be added that this refugee was one I had befriended. Little by little, however, news began to trickle in which I perhaps half-wittedly found amusing. Money in considerable sums—at one time it was as much as $200,000—had been raised to discredit me and to destroy my "influence." People had been employed to ransack my books and see whether passages could be found which, taken out of context, would make me seem to have said the opposite of what I actually did. The files of *The Commonweal* and other journals were gone through with scissors and paste. The *pièce de resistance*, I was to find out later on, was a garbled report of a speech which, ironically enough, I had made to a group of students at Hunter many years before I dreamed of being associated with it. Of course the idea underlying all this feverish and ludicrous activity was that a man deemed able to oppose what later on came to be known as the "Morgenthau Plan" for Germany had to be silenced as speedily and effectively as possible.

Soon a number of organs of opinion, here and in other countries, began to display the fruits of these endeavors. They were alluded to in radio talks by the right sort of commentator. The *Daily Worker* urged that I be hanged in Union Square. Then a magazine dubbed *The Protestant* (it had, of course, no affiliation with religious bodies proud of bearing that adjective, but the title had nevertheless been chosen with some clumsy cleverness, in the hope that readers would be deceived) not only published a series of articles in which I was convicted of diverse intellectual and anti-patriotic crimes, but advertised them throughout the more proletarian sections of the city on great posters bearing the inscription, "Shuster Exposed." The first of these I saw, ironically enough, when I had come out of the subway at Union Square to attend a meeting of an organization for assistance to refugees from Naziism. It was strange in all truth to find myself, after fourteen years of relentless campaigning against Hitler, suddenly unmasked as his best friend! I am embarrassed to say in retrospect that I chuckled, for a number of good people were misled. Some of my friends on the Faculty began to fear for me, and Charles Tuttle, staunch member of the New York Protestant Council, felt it advisable to explain to his colleagues of the Board of Higher Education what *The Protestant* happened to be. The *New Leader* published a derisory article by way of comment. But there was no genuine reason for serious alarm. Hardly more than a good-sized ripple was stirred in the mighty waters of Manhattan, nor would Ordway Tead have been the man to countenance an assault on academic freedom. The great city newspapers carried hardly a line about the matter.

What was odd about these developments was their preventive character. Until this time, except for paying my respects to Heinz Pol, I had said or done very little indeed to justify the existence of so elaborate an enterprise as had been brought into being. When the war broke out, our German-American anti-Nazi organization, Loyal Americans of German Descent, was dissolved, in spite of a personal appeal from President Roosevelt that it continue and support him in his fourth campaign. On this occasion he assured me of his interest in and respect for the German people, despite the necessary hostility to Hitler. But we felt that we could not put ourselves so blatantly into the political arena. Some excitement was caused by the publication of an advertisement to the German people, written by Dorothy Thompson and paid for by the American Jewish Congress. To the small committee sponsoring this I had belonged, and of course my name had appeared among the signers. But it must be admitted that neither this nor the anti-Shuster movement as a whole seems at that time to have seriously interested the Communist Party as an organization. At the request of the Office of War Information, a meeting was called in New York to draw up a similar appeal. To this august assemblage Communist sympathizers were invited; and I recall with some pleasure that Hans Berger, of whom more must be said later on, proposed that I serve as chairman of the meeting. Nor was any attempt that I know of made to circulate *The Protestant* on our campus.

But soon the weather was to change abruptly. On the Saturday after President Roosevelt's return from the Yalta Conference, I was one of two speakers at a Foreign Policy Association luncheon at the Waldorf. The audience of well over a thousand persons sat looking up at a speakers' table along which were seated not a few people whom up to that moment I had numbered among my friends. In the main, my speech stressed two things—first, that although the agreements to which the President assented might well have been unavoidable, they would result in the division of Europe into two parts, the reunification of which we should in all probability not see in our time; and second, that the only hope of keeping Western Germany (at the time German territory was not to be occupied by the Russians) lay in proceeding as soon as possible to work with reputable groups in the German population for the rehabilitation of their country. I added that there were certainly three such groups—Catholic organizations, the Protestant Confessional Church, and the remnants of the Social Democratic movement. Admittedly it was a relatively bold statement, in view of the time and its emotions. So far as I know, the only similar comment was that of David Lawrence, whose concern, however, was only with the Yalta agreements. What I said was in part as follows:

I shall confess that it had seemed to me that we should be happy to find in what remains of liberal Germany friends and allies. To me the thought that Americans, aware of what price has been paid throughout history for the privilege of commitment to democratic idealism, should not openly proclaim their kinship with Faulhaber and Niemoeller, who in the darkest hours of Hitler's assault upon our common civilization spoke words which rang round the world, against pogroms, against violation of family ties, against the taking of life by a fanatically tyrannical state, was as inconceivable as the thought that I myself should surrender jot or tittle of that American creed. But it is necessary to say—to say not in criticism but with calm regard for the clear truth—that the Yalta Conference has doomed these hopes to extinction. For what this Conference has accomplished is to endorse a division of Europe into two spheres of influence, the one of which, namely the Russian, is to include a large and populous section of Germany, as well as nearly all the nations of Eastern and Southeastern Europe, and the other of which is to be subject to Anglo-American domination. In the second place, the only realistic international organization which has so far been established is an organization which is to determine what drafts of labor and materials are to be exacted from Germany; and the headquarters of that organization are to be in Moscow. For the first time in the history of free America, we shall have to look the issue of slave labor squarely in the face. In the third place, the kind of government to be set up in the Russian part of Germany has already been created. It is a government such as Radek dreamed of in 1919—a union of generals and Communist Party functionaries.

Under these circumstances it is futile to debate the future of Germany as that has been debated hitherto. Now Germany has been divided, the division will in so far as we can foresee remain, and there is nothing we can do to alter the fact. We shall therewith inflict not merely upon the Nazis, for whom no punishment could be too stern and no deprivation of liberty adequate, but upon a large section of the German people, even those who may have survived the torments of Dachau and Buchenwald, a fate in which freedom certainly has no place. Moreover, there has never been any difference of opinion in this country about the Prussian military system. But at this moment there is no guarantee whatsoever that what can be salvaged from that system will not be incorporated into the vast Russian agglomeration of military strength which may henceforth rule the world. I know that future discussion may soften some of the stark contours of the present picture. But I know also that only in so far as Yalta made provision for conference and discussion does it offer anything in which we may decently rejoice.

It proved to be a painful hour though, quixotically enough, I thought it not untinged with glory. A very few people in the audience applauded when my address was ended. One was my wife, another was a feminine stranger in a blue hat, and some were my loyal friends. Otherwise a hard wall of angry negation rose round about. Trumpets of jubilation rang out for every point the other speaker on the program made. When the meeting was over, a well-known engineer seated on the dais said to me as his voice trembled with indignation, "That speech of yours was nothing less than an act of high treason!" They all wanted very much to believe that when the struggle was over and both

Hitler and Mussolini were no more, history would usher in a regenerated Kremlin. The reaction might have been local, however, had it not been for the broadcast of the luncheon discussion to what must have been a very sizeable number of listeners. The response to this was by no means one-sided, for public opinion throughout the nation was far more troubled than it appeared to be on the surface. Many were anxious about what the world's morrow might bring, and more still had no desire to erect a stockade around Germany once the Nazi pomp had crumbled.

But there were those who wondered whether it was necessary that I place myself in so exposed a position, and the odd rumor was abroad that my address was an outline of Vatican policy! No such honor could of course be claimed for it, though it was true that during nearly two years spent abroad prior to coming to Hunter I had been initiated as fully into the counsels of the German resistance to Hitler as any foreigner could probably have been, and that meanwhile I had also come to know well the men who were then shaping Vatican policy in Central Europe. Some interesting and upon occasion mildly perilous adventures had befallen me as a result. Thus I had gone incognito into Nazi Germany during 1938 and had had the experience of an after-midnight rendezvous with Konrad Adenauer at his Rhoendorf home. But those met and known were by no means of one faith or political party; and not a few of them had meanwhile lost their lives in the wake of the abortive uprising of 1944. Could I have done treason to their memories, sacred and dear as they were, by not indicating my solidarity with them in a decisive hour?

Other things of moment seemed to me at stake, too. One had of course to be prepared for the realities of the situation. Just as the collapse of the Austro-Hungarian Empire had hollowed out the core of Europe and prepared the way for aggrandizements to follow, so also would the reduction of Germany and Japan to impotence very greatly affect the world situation. For this change everyone had to be prepared. If now the United States went blithely down the road to sheer emotionalism, the resulting effects on the future of civilization might well be utterly disastrous. Many men saw this clearly. The Council of Foreign Relations, with the informal assistance of the Department of State, had constituted, under the leadership of Hamilton Fish Armstrong, a study group to consider what the contours of the peace might be. Despite the fact that I was a member, let me say that it was an able body which conferred during many days with well-qualified representatives of foreign countries and prepared memoranda with extreme care. No use was unfortunately made of them. The nation had committed its destinies to a President in failing health who at a series of "summit" conferences gave free rein to his righteous indignation. Was it then not a matter of honor to voice whatever warning one could, however ineffectual it might prove to be? At any rate, I believed that it was, so long as what one said did not profess to be more than scholarly or ethical comment.

Unfortunately many of those who would later on clamor most loudly for the maintenance of a climate of liberal opinion were now doing everything possible for its abolition. A day or two after the Foreign Policy Association luncheon, there came a letter from Hans Berger, soon to be unmasked as a major Communist agent. It was a short, curt note which vowed that he and his "friends" would soon see to it that I was driven out of Hunter and indeed of New York. Today one can hardly persuade oneself that men of his stamp once had a fabulously powerful influence. But they assuredly did then. It was clear that the "preventive campaign" which had been launched earlier would be resumed and that in particular an all-out effort would be made to identify me with Naziism. Once again good fortune—perhaps my good angel—came to the rescue. Ruth Fischer, who had been the editor of the *Rote Fahne,* Berlin's Communist newspaper in pre-Hitler days, arrived in New York. In a series of articles written for the *Journal-American,* she revealed that Hans Berger was in reality her brother, Gerhard Eisler, and went on to make clear what his role in the Party had been and was. These revelations were so damaging that the offensive he and his "friends" had promised to launch never got off the ground. Instead his days in our midst were numbered.

Nevertheless the flame which had been kindled smouldered on

and sometimes flared up brightly. Doors closed softly or loudly, as the case might be. It began to be bruited about that I, one of the founding members of the National Conference of Christians and Jews, had long since been an anti-Semite! No longer did I review books about Germany for the New York *Times*, though it must be underscored that no blame for this is associated in my mind with that great newspaper. Nor was the cordial friendship which Iphigene Sulzberger had shown me and my wife in any way affected. As soon as the flurry was over, I did again write for the *Times*; nor did my friend Irita Van Doren of the *Herald-Tribune*, in whose mind I was of course not associated with German affairs, even for a moment flinch. It was just that in general the platforms on which my piece could have been spoken disappeared one by one. I made a last try and made a few speeches before small forums about the urgent necessity for seeing to it that Czechoslovakia did not fall into Communist hands. This seemed to me vital democratic terrain which was also the gateway to Berlin and Vienna. A few people listened skeptically, but any thought of making a dent on public opinion had clearly become utopian.

My reputation as an evil and reactionary emissary of the Vatican spread far and wide, but so did unwillingness to believe that it was based on fact. The resulting tug of war was never a source of comfort, but there were times when it was almost amusing. During the summer of 1945 I was asked by Secretary of War, Robert Patterson, to head an Historical Commission to be sent to Germany to interview Nazi officials and German army officers then in custody. I accepted the two months assignment and was duly briefed in the Pentagon. But on the day when passports for the group were due to arrive, there was an awkward pause. There was none for me. A high official in the Department of State—he was, it must be added, not a career man—had issued a caveat in my case on the ground of my pro-Nazi past; and it was only as a result of a strong personal intervention by the Secretary that my passport was at the last moment extracted. When we were abroad, duly conversing with Goering and others, I received a troubled letter from Washington reporting that General Mark Clark, then in command of American forces in

Austria, did not wish a man named Shuster to come to Vienna. That city was not included in my itinerary, but for once I was genuinely annoyed and protested to Mr. Patterson. By this time he was doubtless persuaded that his Commission should have had another chairman, but he nevertheless promptly and effectively expostulated. A cordial letter came from the General, to which the offer of transportation by his private plane was appended. It has always been my conviction that this strange caveat originated with some canny person in his entourage, and that he himself never had the foggiest notion of who "a man named Shuster" might be.

Probably the most bewildering but likewise most heartwarming episode in this story took place as a sequel to an invitation to participate in a symposium arranged by the University of Minnesota in honor of the inauguration of its new president. No sooner had the program been published than a member of the University's Board of Trustees protested against my being on it. He announced that I was a notorious pro-Nazi! There was a considerable amount of fanfare about this in the press of the Twin Cities, during the course of which a nun teaching at a Catholic college proved herself an expert in the field of public relations as well as the most assiduous reader of my writings so far unearthed. Yet even without her kindly ministrations, the University would never have thought of buckling under. Dean Theodore Blegen, as staunch and untiring a protagonist of free speech as even this nation has known, replied to my offer to withdraw by saying promptly and resoundingly that the University had no more ardent desire than that I come. The red carpet spread on my arrival was at least several inches thick.

The final act in the drama struck, however, very close home. During the early months of 1950 John J. McCloy and Dean Acheson urged the Board of Higher Education to free me for a period of service with the High Commissioner in Germany. It had seemed to me highly improbable that I could leave for so long a time, but the Board sacrificed me on the country's altar with pride and jubilation. It may be interesting to recall in this connection one of the most illustrious anecdotes in my career. I had thought that the College would profit if during my absence

Harry Carman, then retired from the Deanship of Columbia College, could serve as acting-president of Hunter. Dwight Eisenhower, then President of Columbia, received me with great cordiality, but said that he needed Dr. Carman badly and just could not let him go. Then he said to me, "Doctor, what's the matter with you anyhow? Here you are with as good a job as anyone could want, and yet you let yourself be talked into going over there for the Government. If they ask me to leave here and take on some assignment, I'll tell them where they can go!" Six months later, he was in Europe heading the SHAFE operation.

For the first time the Communist Party went into operation directly. There was on our campus a professor whose feet were frequently in water which I tried to make at least tepid. It had long been obvious that he was ardently committed to Leftist causes, but his frequent denials of Party membership had been accepted, it is true with a measure of skepticism. He now appeared with a mass of typewritten analyses of my "position," the purpose of which was to reveal my identity as an anti-Semite, a foe of the Negro, and an apostle of Fascism. There is good reason to believe that this somewhat hastily written document had been whipped into shape by the collective efforts of the Party "cell," still more or less dormant on the campus. (Later he would call on me to say that I would surely understand that, although he had not personally credited what was in the sheaf of denunciations, he was under moral compulsion to "act politically"!)

During the night, with the help of a pro-Communist person then employed in one of our administrative offices, he violated the rules of the College and placed copies in the mailboxes of all members of the Faculty. The document was likewise distributed to students. Simultaneously a picket line was thrown round the college building. Dozens of placards advertised my alleged sins. I was, of course, anti-Semitic, anti-Negro, anti-Labor, and pro-Fascist. It was a bitter experience to walk in and out of the premises wondering what effect this lampooning would have on young people who certainly had no way of knowing whether what they read was true or not. Still more acrid in the mouth was the realization that we had in our ranks men who did not shy away from callous deeds of character assassination when the political creed with which they were secretly allied demanded it of them.

Because the violation of the College rules had been discovered through a rather fortunate chance, everybody knew who the instigator of the action was. The counter-attack left little to be desired. At the time the Student Council president was a determined and intelligent girl with eyes like those which Homer attributed to the Goddess Athena. Certainly she marshalled her forces with the same efficiency as characterized her Greek forebear. The Faculty, with the merest handful of exceptions, stood firm; and one of our veteran feminine professors, a tiny authority on Shakespeace, routed the picket line, which turned out to be the same as that which had paid its respects to General Lucius Clay, when on his return from Germany he had spoken at Carnegie Hall. Wherever she appeared, the professor was seen wearing a flowered hat and carrying a dainty umbrella. On the third afternoon of the picketing, she came out of the building, shook the umbrella fiercely, and demanded of the Police Lieutenant who was keeping an eye on the picket line that this be removed forthwith. To the surprise of everyone, the highly irregular order was obeyed, after three hectic days we had a measure of peace, and I went off to Germany, where I was greeted on my arrival by denunciations by Gerhard Eisler, alias Hans Berger, then in charge of Communist propaganda over the Leipzig radio. He had originated the famous East German potato bug scare and thought up the legend of germ warfare in Korea. From my quite personal point of view he reached new heights by declaring that Hitler had authorized me to prepare the American edition of *Mein Kampf*. The basis for this noteworthy addendum to history was that at the insistence of Dr. Alvin Johnson I had written the notes for this edition. These Hitler had been the least likely person in the world to approve. Meanwhile the American Jewish Committee had done its valiant best at home by causing to be published in the New York *Post* a series of articles about my career, refuting one by one the charges which had been echoed in a short-lived journal known as *The Compass*.

The last act in this sordid and trying play involved the dismissal of a small number of members of the Faculties of the four municipal colleges on the basis of their continuing allegiance to the Communist Party, proscribed by the Board of Regents after the passage of the Feinberg Law by the State Legislature. The legislation provided that anyone committed to the overthrow of the Government of the United States by force and violence could not be employed by any public agency; and in so far as the teaching profession was concerned, the Board of Regents was called upon to determine who was so committed. The Communist Party was the only group designated. It was therefore incumbent on the Board of Higher Education to proceed with an investigation. During many months a relatively few persons, some innocent, others demonstrably at one time or other associated with the Party, were questioned on a strictly confidential basis. Fortunately only a very few persons at Hunter were involved. But it was nevertheless a harrowing time, for many of those interviewed, particularly those who at some time had been drawn into the Party net without realizing it, were naturally frightened and rightly expected assistance from the President.

I am very glad to say that the College did everything it possibly could to help even those who were more deeply involved. Watching a man being sundered from his academic lifework, even for good cause, is a very painful experience. Still more fearsome it seemed to me was observing men and women who could not bring themselves to break with finality from an organization in which they no longer fully believed, because the long-established secrecy of conspiracy had exacted of them a discipline they could not abandon any more than alcoholics can give up drink. With one or other of these we wrestled for days vainly. I am afraid in retrospect that our eagerness to save brands from the burning for a time persuaded the then Chairman of the Board that we were less than adequately patriotic. But the Board as a whole, despite one or two costly mistakes made at the beginning of its acceptance of the mandate from the Board of Regents, gave an excellent account of itself in terms of the climate of liberal opinion. The trials and hearings were conducted with scrupulous fairness, erstwhile membership in the Party was not considered a cause for recrimination, and the odious business of being asked to implicate others was abandoned.

On the other hand I must say frankly that those who feel that democratic institutions cannot be successfully maintained unless full freedom is accorded to Communists do not realize what the Communist commitment involves. Personally I have never been able to endorse Sidney Hook's thesis that the distinction to be made here is between heresy and conspiracy. There are some "heresies" which seem to me to have no place on a college campus; and there are some "conspiracies" which would not bother me greatly. Nevertheless I agree that Hook's views are tenable in so far as Communism is a conspiracy. For this has for its goal the subversion of youth in the interests of a foreign power. More than that. We at Hunter were reluctantly compelled to conclude that an otherwise amiable colleague, had he been named Commissar, would have stood us against the wall without a qualm and cheerfully ordered the execution squad to fire. That sort of person is not committed to anything in which the American college believes.

Nevertheless it would be quite incorrect to say that these proceedings did not disturb our students, or that clouds did not appear in the sky of liberal opinion. We accorded our young people every opportunity to discuss the problem frankly and fully. I felt that the general assemblies in which we talked about the situation together were, while they did not dispel every doubt or answer every question satisfactorily, productive of a meeting of the minds. Our students did not go away from Hunter College feeling that the bidding of Senator McCarthy or somebody else had been done in the dark, or that their views of the principles involved were considered inconsequential. We did not assault them with harangues about the views of the Party, but we tried to help them understand for themselves what that Party really and truly was.

In the final analysis the motto on the south wall of the College, which we owe to Emerson, was kept alive for us all, just as I am certain that the American people emerged from the ordeal of the great debate about security as the first one in history to have a theory and practice of civil liberties which makes sense. We seemed for a time to have become a flock of sheep scared by rather rabid hounds. After that it was almost true that we began to magnify every one of our minor infractions of decent procedure into the stature of glamorous vice. But, on the whole, we are remarkably sound. That I believe is a verdict I have the right to offer after the various experiences to which this chronicle has been devoted. Of course we have in our country a bevy of little groups which fish in waters not those of liberal opinion. Among these is the hard remnant of the Communist flock. This still exists in New York. It would be fatuous to assume that the conversion could ever have been complete. But I am sure that it will remain a splinter in the thumb of America. Let us merely remember that splinters can fester; this is not the wisdom of the FBI, but of John Donne.

IV.

EDUCATION IN OUR TIME

This has not been a very happy, urbane, or comfortable period, but in several ways it has been kind to the American college. As a result, this is quite a different institution from what it used to be. One source of improvement has been the relatively paradoxical circumstance that even while intellectuals were objects of public derision, they were nevertheless also models whom many people secretly wished to emulate. Max Beerbohm once characterized a critical essay written by a friend as "written somewhat in the tone of a young man defending the character of a barmaid who has bewitched him." I suppose that the typical American has often thought of higher education in some such way.

The opposite poles in our educational enterprise have, I think, been these: on the one hand, a constantly increasing and historically unprecedented demand for schooling, and on the other a widespread, often startling unsettlement of youth. Sometimes I think that, from an intellectual point of view, the nation has been like a man trying to pull himself up by his bootstraps, while standing on an escalator. It would be folly to suppose that the portrait which not particularly delinquent younger generations have drawn of themselves in literature, from Morley Callaghan and John O'Hara to the Beat Generation is not authentic. On the other hand, Thomas Merton is in a Trappist monastery, Robert Oppenheimer is at Princeton, and countless young men are flying jet fighters to safeguard the nation. Perhaps one can make the point more clearly with an anecdote of relatively humbler import. I know a Hunter graduate who put herself through college by doing all sorts of odd jobs after hours, and meanwhile enjoyed four years of Latin and similar subjects currently deemed erudite. After graduating she found herself teaching a class for the first time in a rather typical New York City school. A young candidate for honors in hoodlumism threw a blackboard eraser as her and scored on her ear. With unerring aim she rifled it back squarely on his nose. Class discipline improved for some time thereafter, though of course the method adopted for enforcing it does not appear on the list of approved pedagogical procedures. Of such contrasts is our educational scene compounded.

For a long time it was also believed that those employed in education were self-sacrificing human beings who could be expected to flourish on the outer fringes of society at low rates of pay. The older among us will remember that the school ma'am was presumably a paragon of virtue living in splendidly isolated genteel poverty. No educational institution suffered more by reason of such assumptions than did the college. The local Mr. Chips, beyond any question an amiable soul, was patted on the back at home-coming time by auto salesmen who wondered why the old boy couldn't find anything better to do. Not infrequently he was the son of an abstemious minister or rabbi who, as a result of having sat at the paternal knee, became similarly addicted to the training of the human mind, including of course his own. There has been a notable change. In many areas school teaching now offers pay checks, security and vacations which are making what is known as the American middle-class wonder why it did not take a few courses in pedagogy. The college professor has likewise been substantially upgraded. Government agencies, the various Foundations, and a number of other organizations now view his pilgrim's progress with such concern that only with difficulty can he ward off grants for research or travel abroad. At the more affluent institutions, he is believed to work under conditions akin to slave labor if he toils in the classroom for twelve hours a week during nine months of the year.

Entering the academic fraternity at the college level once often was difficult at best and not infrequently harrowing. A good college not only wanted men and women with doctor's degrees, but subjected those it could persuade to come to a sort of internship which, while possibly not as rigorous as that insisted upon by the medical fraternity, was from several points of view beset with far greater peril and anxiety. The young instructor had no way of telling whether he would be kept on after a period of probation. He was expected to manifest some awakening or continuing concern with productive scholarship, to prove that he was a teacher whom students considered a communicative oracle, and to assume his share of academic chores often inflated out of all relationship to tasks which any human being in his right mind should be asked to consider interesting or rewarding. But above all he was expected to impress his colleagues of the department, primarily the chairman, with the fact that he was a congenial companion who could be relied upon never to mar with laughter the decorum of a meeting called to discuss a matter of sovereign importance, namely whether a course hitherto labeled "Arabic I" ought, for the benefit of mankind and of course the institution, be dubbed "Introductory Arabic." Any young man who succumbed to a spasm of hilarity at this point could survive only if, having graduated from one of the more renowned universities, he was handsome in a notably masculine way and known to be engaged in writing a paper on some such topic as "Advertising Copy in Pre-Mohammedan Syria." The plight of women was as usual even more dire. Today, however, the scarcity of legitimate doctorates is becoming so pronounced that a mighty tide threatens to wash the ground from under the period of probation. I surmise that the day is just around the corner when a fledgling Ph.D. from Harvard will be escorted to the classroom of mornings by the President in person, in the hope that the young man will like what he sees.

This is from several academic points of view a blessed Macarian situation, indeed, as Abraham Cowley would have said in his commendable seventeenth century way. Meanwhile the colleges have collectively lost sleep trying to upgrade the student as well. Can one ward off the threat of Russia more effectively than by chaining the Sophomore to a library chair for additional hours? It is at the moment also surmised that an injection of analytical geometry and calculus into the veins of as many American youngsters as can be made to sit still long enough for the infusion will erect a mighty intellectual bastion round our imperilled nation. Just what the young person, having presumably survived, is expected to do with this knowledge has never been made clear. It may well be that despite the mushrooming of laboratories, publicly and privately supported, not enough provision has been made for research as the core of a mightily expanding economy. I do not know, but conversations with a number of persons who seem to be qualified to express an opinion appear to indicate that competing research activities in various areas have already created a factor of frustration—that, for example, the quest for still another antibiotic involves a sort of hurly-burly race rivaling that of various armed forces looking for still another satellite that will inch its way into outer space.

But if one considers the study of mathematics in a different light and asks what the significance of a serious concern with it might be in terms of general education and personal culture, the landscape is suddenly bathed in the equivalent of sunshine. First of all, such a subject as algebra enforces the carrying to completion of a task (in older days it was called a *pensum*) which cannot be circumvented by any flight of the student's imagination. For example, one of the traditional problems encountered in modern teaching of the Humanities is that, if one excepts language instruction, it is difficult to be sure that more can be abstracted from the student than opinions, which Newman in his day called "views." These are often interesting but seldom difficult to come by; and so the instructor's immemorial resource in a recent frame of reference is to pad the reading list. Yet this usually leads only to more and more opinions of lesser and lesser value. Second, mathematical studies have now become indispensable prerequisites for any kind of realistic philosophical inquiry into the intellectual substructure of contemporary life. This was already true prior to the work of Whitehead and Russell, but it is as commonplace today as anything could be. In other words, it can be argued that mathematics constitute, at least for a sizable number of students, a necessary price to pay for a liberal education.

Therewith we have at least hinted at one major aspect of the revision of educational thinking which has been a serious topic for discussion, and which incidentally could not help affecting life at Hunter College. Stated somewhat extravagantly, the point is this: whereas thirty years ago everyone who took a course in something or other wanted to know of what "use" it would be to him, the promising student of today is expected to feel degraded if that course should prove to be of some practical benefit. Not that a good many are still not converted to this austere point of view. But there is abroad in the land the conviction that a properly trained intelligence can do almost anything—even, if the spirit so moves it, make a million dollars—while the lad who spends four years imbibing useful knowledge will probably end up by being a bookkeeper and a bore. Deeply embedded in these sentiments may be a desire to repudiate the favorite image of an earlier period in our history—that of the self-made man who groused over his dollars while his sons prepared to spend them on chorus girls. Anyhow the mood travels all the way from the Beat Generation to Jacques Barzun, from Whitney Griswold to William Benton.

More generally speaking, the principal characteristics of the upheaval seem to be three in number, which I shall list at this point and comment on later. First, the "private enterprise" educational system, under which almost anybody could open a pedagogical shop and proceed to do business in his own way, has met a serious challenge, not by reason of any kind of fiat but because the desire of an increasing number of students to go from undergraduate to graduate schools is compelling the "free enterprise college" to set standards of performance which will meet university requirements. Second, the decision to look at the college as a period of preparation has brought scholarship rather than teaching unbuttressed by scholarship to the center of the stage. This is an important way in which the university has imposed its view. In one sense it is a commendable change, but I shall have something critical to say about it. Third, the emphasis has shifted from concern with the group to concentration on the individual as a more or less self-propelling unit. It is now rather widely assumed that the "superior student" can get along better outside the classroom than in one. This may be substituting the abrasiveness of books for that of other human beings, but we shall know more about the results a generation hence.

It is on the whole a decidedly new situation, as befits a time in which every morning is an advertisement of change. For my part I like to think I see, though I doubtless do so with a measure of fairly grandiose nonchalance, four principal periods in our academic history. The first was fidelity to the once established English model, with variations introduced from other countries, notably France, with rote learning all the way from bottom to top. Against this Edgar Poe and Huckleberry Finn alike rebelled, as did Charles Dickens in the little island home. Then came the idealistic upheaval, with Emerson in the lead, ushering in a time when even the humblest teacher was, with the help of Mr. McGuffey, a moralist and a seer. Next we had John Dewey and the army of his followers, competent and scholarly, or incompetent and unscholarly, not a few of whom wore the master's mantle in ungainly fashion. Finally, we have entered into a time of revolt against Dewey.

Idealism was a many-sided thing. The powerful influence of Germany on it, though in part attributable to the development of educational psychology there, was largely I think not the result of admiration for Heidelberg or Goettingen as exemplars of academic organization or scholarly method, but rather of commitment to the highest good presumably to be fostered, namely guarding the human spirit against surrendering to the lure of crass material gain. That the aims of Emerson, or of Professor Longfellow in his more modest, reticent way, were cognate, needs little proof.

> Life is real, life is earnest
>   And the grave is not its goal.
> Dust thou art, to dust returnest
>   Was not spoken of the soul,

are hardly lines phrased as transcendentally or eloquently as is Emerson's expression of man's hope that he will see "the identity of the law of gravitation with purity of heart," but they proceed in a comparable direction. All this was probably too gossamery of substance and too confused in outline to provide a secure foundation for a long time to come; and though idealism would be buttressed by later distinguished thinkers, the noblest of philosophers, William Ernest Hocking, among them, it did not withstand the tide of change.

There was no holding up the assault of the Deweyites. This was in essence a two-pronged enfilading movement. The first was directed against the philosophic assumptions of Idealism, whether transcendental or traditionally religious of inspiration. I shall have little to say about it. My personal association with John Dewey began relatively late, when the pro-democratic Committee for Cultural Freedom was formed during the heyday of Marxist influence in American life. And so I have pleasant memories of a natively eminent man, grave and courteous, about whom our Communist brethren then made as many uncomplimentary remarks as his critics at the opposite end of the spectrum do now. His philosophy is in its broad outlines so alien to any which might possibly ever have gained my allegiance that any discussion of it I could attempt would probably be too devoid of objectivity to be of value. Of course his thought is significant, at least from the historical point of view, because it pioneered in the effort to outline a humanist position after acceptance of Evolution not merely as a biological hypothesis but also and primarily as a framework of cosmic actuality in which Good and Evil are embedded not as *hubris*, as they are with Augustine or Spinoza, but as attainable or obtainable products of Science. But whether it is any longer genuinely interesting, except in the area of logic, is another matter.

Certainly John Dewey was a highly successful reformer of education. He and his friends set out to formulate a theory of the teaching process in accordance with what they believed natural scientists had discovered about human psychology. Though one might not know out of what the psyche had evolved, the fact of evolving seemed of cardinal importance. Regrettably Dewey never made very clear what he had set out to do. Though he may have got rid of Hegel from a philosophical point of view, there was always a good deal of Hegel in his prose style, and a little of that German can cloud any window pane. And so

I for one have never been able to see just how he proposed to bridge the gap between the "liberal" classroom and his new way of looking at the world, in which Relativism had become the only Absolute and so made the past obsolete. This past was, indeed, to use Sir Geoffrey Crowther's phrase, characterized by the "wrong ideas of dead men."

The second prong of the attack brought vigorous pedagogical action to bear on the capture for education of the ground on which a new industrial society was rising in the United States. From the cultural point of view this was expected to till acres which sociological fiction writers of ability mapped out in *Sister Carrie, Winesburg, Ohio,* and *Main Street.* What could be done by the schools, Dewey asked, to help create beautiful communities in which ugliness of scene and mores would be no more? It was thought and ardently believed that making democracy interesting in school would also make it work outside of school. Therewith science and romantic messianism were associated in an attempt to transform the classroom into a social laboratory in which experience would be changed into the only truth held to be truth, namely the socially useful. Much of Dewey's criticism of older methods and conceptions of the teaching process nevertheless remains valid. I think that like most reformers he may well have seen the enemy in caricature rather than in the round. The pedagogue he so vigorously shooed off the premises was the product of very second-rate normal "colleges," and was certainly not formed in the tradition of Andover, Deerfield or the Benedictine schools.

Perhaps one could add in quite untechnical language that what Dewey managed successfully to insist upon was the partnership of the young in the business of education. This was good, but it is to be feared that his followers often badly overestimated the prowess of the junior members of the firm. After all, the world will have acquired a formidable bank-account of experience before any one of us comes into it. It is remotely conceivable that what went before will turn out to be just as valuable as what came after. Dewey's spirit was somehow blind to this rather rudimentary fact. He bequeathed to American education the notion that "generalizations" about the presumably right

kind of social progress need not be subjected to rigorous historical scrutiny. I feel sure that although he certainly did not wish
it he also left to his disciples, notably the undiscerning ones, the
overriding maxim that the easiest way out of an intellectual
difficulty is the best way.

We live in a time when the romantic tide is receding. All the
utopias dreamed up during a couple of recent centuries have lost
their appeal. As their waters move to their crest, they are colored
by moods inspired by Darwin and Rousseau alike. What will
remain? The prevailing answer at the moment is derisory, indeed more vituperative than anything Dewey said about the
enemy he wished to rout. An America which is persuaded that
its young people know nothing blames the author of *Democracy
and Education* (which it has not read) for its plight. Not a few
of our fellow citizens cannot see beyond Arthur Bestor's quota-
tion from the immortal words of a principal of a junior high
school in Champaign, Illinois, who said it would be necessary to
admit "that it is just as illogical to assume that everybody must
be able to read, as it is that each must be able to perform on the
violin; and that it is no more reasonable to require that each girl
shall spell well, as it is that each shall bake a good cherry pie."
The nation is now in a mood to demand of its young ladies both
cherry pies *and* spelling. A cynic might say that progress is being
made by taking off in all directions at the same time.

I rather fancy that, when the din subsides, it will be evident
that Dewey would have been amazed to find himself characterized as an advocate of illiteracy. Yet the emphasis he placed
on group activity—without making it adequately clear what he
meant by this activity, in terms of the mind's going from sensate
perception to intellectual or esthetic abstraction—all but made
him, in spite of his own dearest wish, seem the advocate of a
primitive educational psychology and an ethic of social good will
based on an absence of reasoned moral conviction. Still, it is just
as true that his utopia was productive of good results as was
that of Karl Marx. Though faith in the Communist Manifesto is
ebbing by reason of the totalitarian bondage to which it unexpectedly but logically led, one must none the less agree that
it greatly helped to bring into being, however involuntarily, a

powerful organized labor movement, a system of social security, and even worker participation in industrial management. And in a comparable way there survives, as a legacy of progressive educational messianism, the extension of advanced school experience to a very large number of people who would otherwise never have had a chance. This has been a signal service to American life. Emerson was certainly no snob or devotee of the old school tie. But after all what really mattered in his opinion was whether there would be a small number of Abelards to inspire a larger coterie of Eloises. Dewey overheard the factory whistles and whirring looms of his country. He wanted the children of parents who bore the burdens of industrialization to have an educational opportunity meaningful to them. That is why I am sure that he will be gratefully remembered when there is good talk about education, however marked our retreat from his views of schooling or of life may prove to be.

Finally we have been ushered into the era which had Robert Maynard Hutchins as its trumpeter. It was a time of conflict, some of it the product of social upheaval and some of a deeply rooted disagreement about the nature and functioning of the human mind. The former Chancellor of the University of Chicago, once as distinguished a center of higher learning as the nation knew, has already lived to see the disappearance from that campus of a very great deal he had established on it as a visible embodiment of his ideas. Yet there can be no doubt that these ideas created a ferment in American intellectual life which has leavened even the outlook of those who for one reason or other shudder when they think of them. Obviously the Hutchins challenge had both antecedents and consequences which only more research than has been done to date can adequately clarify. By way of somewhat indirect ancestry there no doubt was the Humanist movement sponsored by Irving Babbitt and Paul Elmer More, as well as, probably, a something in the climate of Yale at the time. For Yale, at that period in history, was of all our universities the one in which new ideas were rubbing the edges off old ones. The sequels in the direct line of succession have been many. I shall note only the books of Jacques Barzun, though these are more recondite, fastidious and no doubt also discursive than are the more programmatic statements to be found in Hutchins' *Higher Learning in America*.

Dr. Barzun and those who resemble him are critics, while the voice which spoke from Chicago was that of reform, as vigorous and uncompromising as Dewey's but on the other hand (from many people's point of view) exasperatingly lucid. Training in the law, which stresses evidence, gave Hutchins the forge on which he could hammer out his sentences. And no doubt, arising as he did from a stock of preachers, he came naturally by a desperate sense of urgency to save brands from the burning. Sometimes he appeared to smite about him without realizing how rude the blows struck were, and how as a result the smitten were bound to wince in resentment. War sometimes appeared to be the only part of diplomacy which Hutchins understood, and yet for those who could get into the field with him it was a glorious conflict. Personally I have often felt and said that if only he had been more like Sophocles and less like the mordant Aristophanes his achievement might have come to flower to the accompaniment of more sunshine and less lightning. Nevertheless one must admit that the enemy against whom he rode was so strongly entrenched that only an all-out attack would do, if one was persuaded there was no time to be lost.

It is significant that just as Dewey did not divorce himself from idealism, though he reinterpreted its meaning, Hutchins in turn cannot be fully understood outside the context of *Democracy and Education*. Both men have wanted learning for everyone, the fostering of community, and the formation of character. They merely differ radically about what they have thought these are. Learning is for Hutchins primarily two things—the mastery of a "common language" of the mind, which means in practice that everybody reads the basic literature of mankind; and the art of using that language in frank, well-ordered discussion. Its aim is to form a community of men and women who can talk together about things which matter, and who as a result of that comradeship develop a measure of nobility and forbearance, which is held to constitute the goal of education as an agent in the formation of a democratic society. It follows of course that certain other commonly projected educational goals are peripheral or meaningless. Vocational (as distinguished from professional) training can, in Hutchins' view, be provided far better on the job. In like manner expecting young people to develop notions of how governments are to be conducted or businesses managed is merely hoodwinking them. For they cannot have the experience which alone makes it possible to develop worthwhile opinions on these matters.

Such a view of education might run the risk of encouraging a benign and static intellectual stance were it not for the principles of continuity and freedom firmly built into it. These Hutchins had expounded with crusading zeal. First, a viable community cannot be one artificially created for a few years, but must live by a desire to continue. This means in practice that the life of the mind as developed in a man during the collegiate semesters must continue to flourish as a mature and unfinished enterprise. And since there is to be a community there must be liberty of thought if the assemblage is not to go to sleep. Two rules follow from this principle. The first is that there must be unhampered discussion of the past and of the values and insights by which it lived. And in practice this means that doctrines, standards and principles which the "progressive" climate of opinion in America considered outside the pale came to the fore again. Therefore the Hutchins outlook acquired a tolerance of Scholastic and even of Catholic thought which many of his more rigidly modern colleagues found quite shocking. But the second rule was no less important. Any intervention by the active society to curb the freedom of the intellectual community must be vigorously fended off. It has been cheerfully conceded by Hutchins that the active society must have its code of regulations. There must needs be, for example, an FBI and laws against obscenity. But if the code is applied rigorously to the intellectual community the result will be the stifling of discussion. Therefore Hutchins, possibly the most anti-totalitarian of educational thinkers, immsersed himself in tubs of hot water by refusing to admit that Communists should be barred from the give and take of discussion. This did not of course mean that he liked Communists, but only that he loved freedom more. And now, many Catholics, grateful once for the liberty accorded them in the Hutchins cosmos, were sure the Kremlin had made another convert. It may be that it was unnecessary, indeed imprudent, to take so uncompromising a stand, but reformers would not be reformers if they were always models of caution.

It is merely a truism to say that Hutchins is the first American educator to formulate a significant theory and method of what we call adult education. Of these one may approve or not, but the fact clearly remains that they have given reflection on this topic a new and mature dimension. For the ultimate consequence of Hutchins' philosophy of necessity was that formal education was deemed better in Europe than it is with us, but that we in turn were held to have an unparalleled, glorious opportunity to make adult education truly universal and continuous in character. He therefore attempted to re-fashion the high school and college experience in the likeness of the European *gymnasium* or *lycée*, while assigning to the University a role comparable to that of Cambridge or Oxford. Yet quite characteristically he insisted that the study plan of the college was to be shaped in the light of the values inherent in dialectical discussion and of a non-formalized integration of knowledge. All this of course meant that in his view the college as we have known it was out of date. In order to prove this with a dramatic gesture, he abolished the football team and replaced it with a nest of eggheads. Meanwhile he was leading adult discussion down new paths by creating a pattern for the study of great books and significant political issues.

The American opportunity in the area of continuing education rests, in his view, primarily on two things. First there is taken for granted by Hutchins (who, like Dewey, has always been in some respects a utopian) the average citizen's demonstrable interest in and endowment for learning and discussion in terms of the "common language." Second there is the leisure which a technological civilization makes available in abundant quantities, whether we know what to do with it or not. Another fruit of the technological society is, however, the "mass medium." Television, the radio, the press are admittedly even for those who disapprove of them in their present forms unimaginably powerful agencies for community building in the educational sense.

Upon what happens to them the character of continuing education in the United States must to a great extent depend. Hutchins early took an interest in this problem, and developed at the University of Chicago the Round Table which was by all odds the most distinguished program of its kind ever to be broadcast by a radio network. But his concern has been unflagging ever since.

I may add parenthetically that none of Hutchins' pleas and homilies have been more tragically verified by events than have those concerned with the "mass media." It is very much to be deplored that it had to be Charles Van Doren who supplied the most harrowing proof. What in essence happened in this instance was that a young man much better prepared than the vast majority of his fellows to share to the full the life of the intellectual society suddenly found himself in a world which outwardly resembled that community but was inwardly drastically different. In the twinkling of an eye he was in show business. Its standards astonished and overwhelmed him. Had someone offered him many thousands of dollars to go about the country showing off his ability to discuss Tennyson or Eliot, the financial reward would of course have been legitimate. It is not inconceivable that some one could have done so. But instead he was paid a large sum to put on an act—to make of question-answering a more exciting play than mysteries or westerns. At this task he was astonishingly successful. And if somebody could be lavishly paid to imitate a sheriff who never existed, why should not another accept a tidy sum for a different kind of make-believe? In other words, he was lured into a form of mimicry which revealed, when it was found out, that for the manipulators of the "mass media" education is an unprofitable farce. Charles Van Doren permitted himself to be tempted into going outside the company of educators and betraying their standards and traditions. Yet I am not at all sure that anybody who has not tried it can be certain that he himself would have been proof against this kind of seduction. The experience suggests that of a boy who is induced to go to bed with a harlot because otherwise he would be thought a prude. Let us not be led to believe that even a man of integrity like Frank Stanton can change the mores of the mass media. For show business will never be the same thing as education.

Well, you may say, not very much that is tangible remains of the Hutchins experiment. The Chicago University college as he conceived of it is no more, the forms of the American system of higher education have not changed, and the mass media do not provide continuity in education. That is all quite true, but it is also to be observed that schools as John Dewey planned them have likewise disappeared one by one. I do not think that a nation's basic scholastic pattern can be revamped in any other way than through a process of organic growth. But the pulse of Hutchins continues to beat firmly throughout higher education. For example, although nothing has come of the idea that the European secondary school system could profitably be adapted for use in the United States, the number of young men and women who today enroll in college with a year's credit earned in high school is constantly increasing. It is entirely possible that, within twenty years, the Freshman Class will have been shrunk, in the better institutions, to a mere handful. Vocational as distinguished from pre-professional training is gradually disappearing from college curricula. But above all the awareness of necessary standards which is now to be noted in large segments of the American educational fraternity bears tribute to the thinking done at the University of Chicago by a man who cannot henceforth be taken off the front page of the history of higher education in this country.

No doubt one of the most impressive though also visionary of Hutchins' ideas is his conception of how the university could be reformed by making it (as he writes in *The Democratic Dilemma*) "an intellectual community in which specialists, discoverers, and experimenters, in addition to their obligation to their specialties, recognize an obligation to talk with and understand one another." This longing for a community of culture to bridge over the inevitable isolation of scientists and philosophers is one which a great many observers of the intellectual scene share. In order to satisfy it in a measure, Hutchins has now created the Center for the Study of Democratic Institutions; by bringing together a group of consultants drawn from various fields, studies of the causes underlying basic contemporary situations can be discussed and refashioned. Elsewhere the desire has found expression in the advocacy of the *Studium generale* at German universities and in comparable proposals made in other countries. To a certain extent it has been formalized in the Russian Academy of Sciences. In this country it gave rise to the Conference on Science, Philosophy and Religion created at the Jewish Theological Seminary by its far-seeing and imaginative chancellor, Dr. Louis Finkelstein, and is of course not absent from the programs of the American Philosophical Society and the American Academy of Arts and Sciences. But the hope is very far from having been realized, because the men and women who would like to make it the principal concern of their lives cannot find time and opportunity to do so. They may never be able to find it. Alas, as a result it is quite impossible in terms of the intellectual community to maintain a genuine awareness of what education is for. It is held together by a name, a budget and normally a campus. But in all truth it has become an aggregation of intellectual cenobites. How can one talk seriously about a "common language" of the intellectual life, when at the creative center of that life no such language exists?

It is only after confronting this question, for which no answer is discernible either here or abroad, that I feel it possible to discuss the three characteristics of the now developing educational situation to which allusion was made earlier. The increasing desire to go from college to the university has compelled the first to raise the standards of performance; as a result the process of instruction is being viewed more and more widely as dependent upon the quality of the productive scholarship carried to completion by college Faculties; and, finally, it is believed that the major purpose of a college may well be the training of an elite of students which can in turn be expected to go on to research as a career. These are, one need hardly say, highly significant changes in educational orientation. When one reflects on how casual the relationship between scholarship and teaching was on many college campuses a half century ago, the manner in which younger men and women now find continued scholarly activity as natural as a martini before dinner seems almost the result of an intellectual revolution. But of course it is nothing of the sort. The climate in which we live is being changed nearly every day by important discoveries, by new trends in the arts, and also by world-wide shifts in the character of political and economic institutions. It is therefore quite inevitable that a man of some intellectual ambition should wish to share in the seemingly endless enterprise of pushing back the frontier of the unknown. In addition, as I have indicated, nothing can halt in the foreseeable future the trek from the college to the university, which means that acceptance of university standards must play a role in the formation of undergraduate minds.

While the changes indicated are in many ways beneficial, there are dangers implicit in them which need to be recognized. Is it not clear that they must serve not to create an "intellectual community" speaking a common language, which community seemed to both Dewey and Hutchins the highest educational good, however differently they may have conceived of it, but rather to foster at as early a date as possible the formation of specialists? For if one says that the brightest boys and girls on the campus are to be freed from the common chores so that they may proceed to find their way forward as "individuals," one is certainly making two things very clear. The first is that one does not think very highly of the common chores, deemed unavoidable for the blokes but not of any real use to the brains. The second is that the brains do not require membership in any recognizable "intellectual community."

In like manner, if teaching at the college level is to be a sort of appendage to research or "productive scholarship," rather than one of siamese twins, we are also saying that specialization is the highest good. One cannot anticipate that the political scientist whose endeavor is to know all that can be known about constitutional law in Latin American countries will have much time to sit down with students of Proust or Picasso for discussion of the way things are going. In the Hutchins educational cosmos the college at least, though deprived of half the time which would normally have been at its disposal, was akin to what Newman in his time thought the university ought to be—namely an institution in which an impression was to be formed of the knowable world as a unified whole. Now, by absorbing in part the function of the university as we at present know it, namely an assemblage of intellectual anchorites, we are well on our way to making the specialist still more specialized than he ever has previously been. Perhaps, in view of the present character of human knowledge, there is no alternative. But at least we should be fully aware of what we are doing.

I shall now proceed to review, on the basis of these reflections, what the experience at Hunter College has been. It had to come face to face with special problems, as we will see; it could not serve a chosen few. The task assigned was to make "mass education" as personal as circumstances permitted. Meanwhile, of course, it could not avoid being influenced by trends in the nation as a whole. In other words, in spite of its size, it was a small place in a large and confusing world. Let me add that I shall enlarge a bit on circumstances growing out of the situation described in the last chapter.

V.

NOT BEYOND GOOD AND EVIL

Perhaps those who read these reflections on the texture of American higher education during the time when I have had the feel of it will conclude that our kind of college was so different from other kinds that my snapshots of what went on add up to something like an album about life on the moon. The portrait will, however, have the advantage of candor, though you will not be regaled with the secret history of a Dean or led to believe that all our secretaries had lovers on the side. I think there may be some value in taking a hard look at what we were doing. Little good can of course come from staring at education as if it were some sort of machine which through a change of design can be made to improve the output. Education is always human nature trying to become more human, in the best sense of the term. Since it deals with people, it has to reckon with the sad fact that many have been making fools of themselves for a long time and that their example is contagious. Yet now and then somebody turns up who is a credit to the race, and it may somehow have happened that one or two did appear at Hunter.

The first ten years of my presidential experience were lived in the shadow of The Misfortune. This was the creature of the great depression which blasted a deep hole under the national edifice in 1929. The cavity went so far down that some careful observers have compared it with the trauma of the Civil War. People continue to be fascinated by that War—by what happened during the course of it in terms of tragedy and error, of grievous loss and bitter vengeance, of blood and mourning, of heroism and fidelity. Maybe we of the present are sometimes guilty of thinking about battlefield agony as if it had been the by-product of a game of chess. But on the whole the great struggle seems to be treated with the grim respect it merits. Very probably there will come a time when The Misfortune will stand out equally huge against the background of the imagination. For what happened as a result of it not merely redesigned America but had a mighty impact on the whole world. The wars through which we have recently lived and in some of which we have fought can well have been acts in the tragedy. At any rate, this may be how historians of the future will see the matter.

In retrospect, does it not seem that it should have been just as easy to prevent the orgies of speculation which during the Twenties led to the collapse, as it ought to have been to find a place for the Negro in our society without killing off a large and valuable part of the population in order to come up with a decidedly imperfect solution of his problem? Yet even when The Misfortune was upon us, few saw that a withering blight was spreading from it which would infect virtually the whole world. Today one can hardly reflect on recent European history without feeling that dealing with Germany in such a way that Hitler could not easily have come to power would have been relatively simple, or review the course of events in the Far East without concluding that what has happened there was the result of blunders huger than the crimes. Perhaps the most extraordinary thing about The Misfortune was that the diagnosis was so poor. Today we believe that some medicines have been discovered which can be administered to the economy before it collapses. They are expensive but they appear to work. But when the disaster struck it seemed at first that all one needed to do was put the patient to bed and wait for the fever to die down.

If this were all that had been involved, education would be a decidedly peripheral affair. But The Misfortune was not by any means just an economic debacle. It was deeply rooted in the quality of the American outlook and intelligence. Here I shall perforce over-simplify, but there are some useful clues which can be followed easily. Anyone who now reads F. Scott Fitzgerald's *This Side of Paradise*, which in 1920 tossed a boy writer of my generation onto the center of the literary stage, is almost certain to find it an astonishingly silly book, half-baked and flamboyant, about people who existed far from the domain of reality. It is as if the vacuum-cleaned fields of an Arcady on which Harold Bell Wright had caused little lords and ladies of the Fauntleroy family to walk about in seemly fashion to the great approval of a vast reading public, had suddenly been invaded by a young man in mauve trousers, rather fey, who felt that life was properly lived only by those young people who could be aimless about things because there was money in their pockets. But, whether we like it or not, the scale of values suggested in the book was akin to that secretly cherished by a literate generation which sought to escape from what was dubbed the surrounding Puritanism by being the least bit addicted to flirtations.

America was escaping from its alleged Puritanism, which had had two last great flings in the War against the Kaiser and the enactment of Prohibition. The first of these imprinted the seal of-frustration on the brow of a generation, and the second by being unenforceable pried public and private morals loose from the traditional moorings. Not that one can write off the period of the Twenties as especially bad. The mass of the people remained earnest and hard-working, very many of them were poor and troubled by their poverty, and a few were as bitter critics of the society as the nation has ever spawned. But those who ruled the roost—which means those who had been given a sizeable dose of education—had neither ideas nor ethical norms different from those on display in *This Side of Paradise*. Al Capone and the begettors of the Teapot Dome scandal were a little tougher than the characters in the book, but what they really wanted out of life was pretty much the same thing. All this constitutes less an indictment of education than of the people who profited by education, but it remains an indictment even so. For the truth was that, in so far as the mind is concerned, America was rudderless and vapid.

At any rate, when the disaster struck New York stood in the hurricane's dead center. Not merely were the houses of the masters of money and banking here, not only had the plummeting of the stock market wiped out a million dreams of affluence.

The whole city seemed to close down. A population in large measure still near to its immigrant origins had now added to its normal frustrations a bitter burden of poverty which the average victim could do nothing to shake off. The more apparent this helplessness became, the more alluring also were the nostrums advocated for the improvement of the collective patient. Even the reasonably intelligent began to cherish grave doubts that private enterprise any longer had anything in common with the general welfare; and the differences between their points of view largely grew out of the ideological and other component parts of the remedies suggested. Many who by reason of heritage remained close to Western Europe toyed with ideas tinged with Fascism; and some who instead were nearer in spirit to Eastern Europe began to think that maybe the Communists had discovered paradise. In between stood the great crowd which hoped, sometimes almost despairingly, that regeneration would come through democratic action.

As I have previously indicated, one by-product of the situation was that the City's public colleges became refuges for young people who had no other place to go. Of this development one may no doubt remark that it was a blessing in disguise. But from the intellectual point of view the swollen student body was a source of headache and exasperation. The Hunter Faculty, proud of the fact that the college had so few decades earlier been transformed from a teacher training institution into a habitat for the liberal arts, contemplated the scene with profound misgivings. The ablest of its men and women had set very high standards. What the Phi Beta Kappa key stood for seemed to them the best that had been known and thought in the world. Was it not that which human wisdom had decreed for the proper development of young minds? If these, having been adequately fed, then turned to school teaching or some comparably genteel profession, or of course married properly, all would be well with them. But now? Most of the men and women of whom I speak, devoted as they expected to be to the higher education of the gentler sex, had been recruited where such persons could then be found. That is, most of them belonged to the more urbane strata of American society and assumed that these had a sort of monopoly on good breeding. Not all were of course of the same religious faith. But it so happened that even the scholarly and literate Jewish population of New York, which greatly cherished intellectual ideals, did not at the time make ample provision for the training of women for scholarly pursuits.

Now several things happened all at once. A large number of the girls who came to Hunter had absorbed a variety of prejudices from their home environments, displayed only the rudiment of good manners, spoke English atrociously, and had as little use for honor societies as they did for Herbert Hoover. Indeed some of them were raucous, gawky and afflicted with acne, halitosis and deplorable hair-dos. It was quite impossible to wave the banner of the liberal arts before them with any hope of inspiring them to a frenzy of enthusiasm. They frankly expected education to be of utilitarian value, and so help them get jobs which would relieve the stark misery in which many of them lived. And why not? The population figures dipped as the depression continued. Teaching assignments in the schools had therefore become as scarce as leaves on a rose bush suffering from an advanced case of blackspot. The college was forced to begin thinking about what pre-professional or even frankly vocational courses could be built into the curriculum. But this was so deplorable from the prevailing Faculty point of view that conflict, sometimes bitter enough in all truth, was bound to be rampant.

Meanwhile, in order to provide college teachers in sufficient numbers, instructors had to be recruited wherever they could be found, often from among the more talented of recent graduates. Even though the salaries paid these upstarts were prevailingly very meager, jobs were so scarce that as a result of various kinds of pressures appointments were made which simply had to be anathema to the older members of the staff. At any rate, within a few years Hunter had taken onto its bosom a sizeable number of malcontents, often so for excellent reasons, who for the most part campaigned for a variety of boons. The Board of Higher Education faced the situation by being on the one hand strongly in favor of divine discontent and on the other the advocate of intellectual distinction. It closed the door to pressure groups by establishing above all the requirement that the Ph.D. degree was necessary for appointment of the teaching staff, thus sending assorted younger folk off to sweat in the graduate schools during their spare time while affixing to some older and genteel instructors the stigma of citizenship of the second class.

Divine discontent was, however, served by drastically revising the distribution of authority exercised by the Faculty. The "democracy" thus introduced had a variety of consequences, good and bad, but the principal effect was the remodeling of Departments of instruction. The regal mores of yore, which had given the chairmen almost autocratic powers (sometimes quite arbitrarily used, indeed), were now abrogated in part and modified in other respects by creating a network of committee responsibilities which the conservative dubbed the "soviet system" while others considered it blissfully democratic. So as to prevent Presidents or Deans from keeping their assumed lackeys in power, the Chairmen were now elected for periods of three years. This has always seemed to me a thoroughly bad procedure and I inveighed against it to no avail for more than twenty years. It is true that in stable Departments no great harm was done, since the chosen leader would have been selected anyway under a more rational system. But in others it led to political infighting, favoritism and acceding to majority or minority pressures which would have been amusing, perhaps, had they not been thoroughly unprofessional. When election time came round canny estimates were made of the fences which needed repair, and the President was relied upon to survey the scene with the judicious eye of one who stood above the battle. But having once committed itself to being the godfather of the presumably downtrodden, the Board bowed to the fact that the Faculty saw gold in these hills.

It was a turbulent time, indeed, and my unfortunate predecessor had come to grief trying to deal with the roaring battles it generated. When I look back upon the situation, it seems almost incredible that there was enough fortitude in my soul to undertake the task of attempting to cope with it. There was no reason at all for assuming success and quite frankly I started out uncertain as to the outcome. But as time went by it appeared that there were three quite fortuitous arrows in my quiver, and that if I shot them about with sufficient accuracy survival might be possible. The first was that coming from German Wisconsian stock, which had memories of 1848 in its blood, I believed with all my heart and soul that educating the children of the poor if they had ability was about as challenging a task as anyone could undertake. The second was that scholarship, good scholarship, seemed to me the very heart of a college's concern, so that what the Board had done to make this respectable provided a solid foundation for such work in higher education as I fancied. Finally, having been buffeted about a good deal outside academic life I found the slings and arrows which it manufactures with remarkable proficiency relatively easy to absorb.

Probably no one could have believed more strongly than did I in the values and virtues of training in the liberal arts. Since I had majored in the classical languages at college, my first address of any consequence at Hunter had to do with what one could learn through the study of Greek. But only a month or so after I had settled down a student came to see me escorting a distraught young girl who had graduated the previous June as a music major. She had been unable to find a job of any kind; and her family had, it seemed, notified her that if she could not contribute to its exchequer, now that she had a college degree, she would have to fend for herself. To such depths had the familiar loyalties descended! The girl had been seen on Brooklyn Bridge trying to screw up enough courage to jump off. Somehow we found employment for her as a file clerk. There were many, many such girls, even if few so dramatized their plight. I went to a Faculty meeting and insisted that training in typing and stenography must somehow be added to the curriculum, and succeeded in getting a modification of the City budget for that purpose. Three-fourths of my colleagues who listened to the plea felt that academic standards were being gravely lowered, and so for my part did I. It was then that I coined the phrase, "vocational inlay," which suggested that although we were not abandoning our allegiance to liberal training we nevertheless realized that we could not face the students we were educating during the time in which they lived unless we somehow helped them solve their most immediate problems.

On the other hand, I heartily concurred with the Faculty in its determination not to permit students who were preparing to teach to major in Education. We said that their principal concern was to be with the subject matter in which they were to give instruction, but that we would gladly offer them such courses in pedagogy as the State required. I happen to believe that it would be a serious mistake to send a young person into a classroom without some preparation in teaching methods, child psychology and the more or less philosophically construed history of education. But it was obvious that the fraternity had inflated methodology well past the point of no return. The standard flag-bearers for pedagogy therefore looked at Hunter as if it had turned the clock back to the seventeenth century; and I was no doubt often identified in their minds with Rip Van Winkle and the extreme right wing of the Republican Party. But of course in the long run the nation's Education Departments were given the drubbing they richly deserved, and we were in the vanguard, far ahead of the procession, when divers Foundations proceeded to endow eminent private colleges and universities so that they could append to the liberal arts curriculum the same training in pedagogy we had long since provided. Not that any Foundation thereupon pinned a medal on our chest for pioneering. To a very considerable extent they continued to believe, with a firmness worthy of better causes, that a proletarian New York college was not visible to the naked eye. For years I tripped round to one of them, hat in hand, to plead for modest grants. But what was asked for invariably went to some other campus interested in much the same things; and I am sure as I could be of anything that the major reason was sheer inability on the part of its trustees to believe that a place to which what they thought a mob went by subway might somehow be worthy of any part of the income from dollars which the once quite proletarian founder had set aside for philanthropic purposes.

Since candor is a great virtue—I have always been sorry that St. Paul, who possessed a good deal of it, did not list it after faith, hope and charity,—I must quickly add that it was the

Rockefeller Foundation which first opened the door and invited us to share in its largesse. Indeed it did so with the courtesy which has in my judgment always distinguished those in charge of it. The point is of some minor social interest because in my experience the farther removed from the social register of educational institutions the establishers and trustees of Foundations are, the more probable it becomes that no college outside the Ivy or similar Leagues will be greeted with a radiant smile. If one cannot secure an honorary degree from Harvard, at least one can frame its letter of thanks. There have of course been exceptions to the rule. Louis Rabinowitz, who made the grant which established our School of Social Work, dealt with Yale and Hunter on equal terms. He was an extraordinary man—it seemed to me not personally a very happy one, though I liked to fancy that his benefactions gave him pleasure, but one who clung to a genuine love for scholarship through all the bustling of his business career. And the Pickers, James and Evelyn, who though the major concern of their Foundation was the promotion of radiological studies, gave generously to us for a variety of purposes. Mrs. Picker happened to be one of our graduates; and of another, Jean Webster, I can only say that her Foundation was a source from which Hunter drew a variety of elixirs. There were others. To be sure, let it be said finally, I have always felt that private institutions should come first in the Foundation scheme of things. These cannot appeal to city governments or state legislatures for funds. No laws insure their welfare. Still a good idea is good regardless of whether the man who came upon it lives in Princeton, Baltimore or Forest Hills.

At any rate, we proceeded to make provision for "vocational inlays" and so eventually fostered both Home Economics and Nursing. Nevertheless the liberal curriculum remained our principal concern. But what was it to be? I have been persuaded that the ideal definition is this—the course of study which the Faculty is best equipped to teach, and that therefore, once the variegated vegetable cocktail known familiarly as "general education" has dutifully been swallowed by the student, the work in major fields of interest will quite automatically congeal, for the best undergraduates, round what the ablest professors make of their classes.

Perhaps the sole advantage which a large college possesses is that it can provide a measure of excellence in a greater number of subjects than a smaller institution can develop. Thus Hunter College had long been famed for the first rate quality of its work in teaching the languages. To the general amazement of observers, a Hunter student who had majored in French or German could actually use these tongues very well, indeed; and for years we went against the grain of American academic life by maintaining classical studies, with the result that from our halls there went to the graduate schools far more than our share of those who would prove to be good scholars in these ancient literatures. But it was possible as time passed to do well in fields not always in the center of things. The Hunter Art Department, having recruited teachers of accepted distinction in all forms of the arts, became a citadel of modern painting and sculpture. There was a laboratory for the study of anthropology, painstakingly built up over the course of years, which was a quite remarkable achievement. And there was much else with which to be reasonably content, especially the growth of our interest in Political Science and Experimental Psychology.

Yet the college was perhaps best characterized from an educational point of view by its two largest academic departments, History and English, which over the years demonstrated most clearly what can be accomplished—and what perhaps cannot— for undergraduates when good scholarship and good teaching are conjoined. There were admirable people in both departments. I shall content myself with a sketch of one who, since he has now retired, may duly be impaled on the pin of judgment. Hoxie Neale Fairchild decided to leave Columbia University and throw in his lot with Hunter at a time when this was, for the reasons indicated, still chaotic. For years he worked at a massive history of *Religious Trends in English Poetry*, the substantial volumes of which appeared one by one. When completed it will be an excellently written, often witty and mordant commentary on poetry in the English language, whether created by recognized masters or by lesser fry with whom, perhaps, only historians concern themselves. But it is far more than that. It offers an astonishingly complete account of the changes in religious thought and feeling which have taken place in England since the days of the Tudors, and from this point of view merits an acclaim which has never been accorded to it. For this aspect of the morphology of ideas did not interest the critics who in this country at least have pretty largely determined where the spotlight of attention is to fall. But no doubt another reason for the frigid welcome accorded his *magnum opus*, which Latin title conveys more than the English "great work," was that Fairchild's religious position, conservatively Anglican but with nuances difficult to grasp and tinged with austerity, demands of the reader an assent he is not likely to be able to give. It was at any rate comforting to know that this kind of delving was going on while the campus resounded with harangues and debates incident to the time.

It was a fortunate collegiate day on which I induced him, whom I had learned to know and admire while he guided my dissertation to completion, to throw in his lot with Hunter. His academic philosophy was professedly different from mine; and since he could expound it with wit, authority and a measure of unction there was never any doubt that our educational enterprise would be seen in some sort of perspective on a campus which too seldom had time or inclination for the task of probing more deeply into what it was doing. Fairchild argued that the hub of the college world was the "scholar teacher," by which term he meant someone who is sincerely, actively and effectively engaged in scholarship, but who at the same time believes ardently that teaching is an open sesame to a special kind of earthly heaven, however paved with flinty cobblestones. Having spent a good many years trying to develop just that sort of man on our campus, I was naturally quite strongly in favor of him. Nevertheless, though my colleague was himself an admirable teacher, I felt that there was too much Mohamet and not enough mountain in his scheme of things.

My view, which may have reflected Newman's as expounded in the *Idea of a University* but was buttressed by an uncorroded legacy from the Middle West, placed the student in the center of campus concern. No doubt also I had been so strongly influenced by Dewey's idea of the community, Hutchins' practice of dialectic, and Martin Buber's philosophy of the dialogue that a belief that college life could be exciting and worth while unless conversation was incessantly moving to and fro failed to seem captivating. Why had the student come to us? What could we and she do to provide a satisfactory answer to that question? In addition, was there anything in our view of her probable future that she might upon reflection wish to take into account? Finally, what in terms of enriching experience could she acquire from her association with other students? Was there any way in which the rubbing of young minds one against the other could produce fire, warmth, insight? Of course I was fully persuaded, and often enough said so, that of all we had to offer being for a precious few years in the company of good scholars was the best. But I also felt strongly that the student must find this out for herself, and that the only way she really could was to share in the dialogue.

We also participated for a time in the once popular concern with the probable biological future of these students. Many of them would marry and have children. Ought we not therefore help to make sure that when a girl had a baby she would know what to do with it, or that she had absorbed a score of dependable recipes with which to cajole her husband? But—and I say this primarily because the higher education of women was once entirely strange to me—it was soon apparent that if our young people had any major interest it was in their potential chance for matrimony and that as a consequence they reckoned with all aspects of it so effectively that the little we could have taught them would have seemed just more advice to the lovelorn. And so we offered courses in home making and family relations to those who wanted them and in other respects concluded that the best thing we could do for the feminine mind was to accept the obvious fact that the sciences and the humanities are fairly stable in spite of the always disturbing factor of sex.

Still there is no doubt that nothing plays as great a role in the experience of the high school and the college as does the fact that the formation of the scholastic life and of the love life coincide for most young people. Exceptions must be noted, of course. Some boys and girls postpone all serious reflection on their probable sexual future until quite late, and others do not bother about it at all. But for the great majority the circumstance that one is growing up in two directions at the same time is troubling and distracting. It can gravely limit the vocational or professional goals which young people have in mind—goals which are necessarily generally different for men and women. Thus undoubtedly one reason why teaching attracts so many girls is because tenure, maternity leaves and vacations promise greater security to a woman than do a number of other pursuits. I do not know whether coeducation simplifies or compounds the problem. No one does. The most completely unexplored field in American education is the realm of the co-ed. It may be that this is on the whole more tranquil and rewarding than is that of the segregated student. Perhaps the reverse is true. The time may have come to try to find out. I shall add frankly that I have not found the answer, even though the uptown Bronx campus of Hunter became coeducational in 1951, after the Security Council of the United Nations had left the premises. More horseplay and ogling were of course visible up there. But often one thought that in general the boys and girls walked past each other in a mood of calm indifference. But it would require much more than such a quite casual survey to come up with data of moment.

At all events, the world has greatly changed in this respect from what it was some decades ago. First, early marriage has revolutionized the scene. Boys and girls wed in their teens with an insouciance which would have been inconceivable to their mothers and fathers. Job opportunities and varieties of insurance seem to open up prospects for a measure of security undreamed of earlier. Some girls apparently think no more of going off and getting married than they do of taking a trip; and since it has become quite fashionable to have babies, pregnancy is a phenomenon akin to having measles. Nor can one forget that the practice of contraception as well as the knowledge of effective remedies for venereal disease have gravely undermined traditional standards of sexual morality. Syphilis used to be a formidable barrier between the boy and indulgence. It is now hardly more serious a hurdle than possibly catching a cold is a deterrent from going to watch a football game on a miserable day.

I am not suggesting that the younger generation is more dissolute than were those which preceded it. Perhaps because it does not surround marriage with as many tabus—fear of the child, insistence on a measure of economic security—it may actually be better behaved. But no one will make me believe that a society which encourages high school youngsters to go steady from the age of twelve, and which saddles a boy of twenty with family responsibilities, is likely to place intellectual pursuits in the foreground. I am not a mathematician, but I can add; and the sum-total of hours spent by a good-looking boy of seventeen in the company of girls is persuasive evidence that there just isn't time enough left to do the kind of mental exercises which the studious life exacts. We produce a bumper crop of dilletantes who as soon as their noses are taken off academic grindstones settle down with *Sports Illustrated* for the rest of their lives, certain that literacy was invented for this purpose. The reason is that they have never learned what the life of the intellect is. Having been carefully selected on the basis of a battery of tests, they were found to have brains enough to carry out the assignments insisted upon. And that is usually the end of that.

My conviction has been that until quite recently Americans expected their young people to assume that on the one hand they were more juvenile than the facts warranted, and that on the other they were mature beyond their years. That a mind was something one possessed prior to forty seemed a declaration almost as startling as would be the news that Standard Oil of New Jersey had gone broke. Yet the fact is, the intellect is never keener, perhaps never again as keen, as it is at the age of nineteen—a truth which the best European schools, and no doubt their Russian copies as well, take in their stride. On the other hand, our youngsters quite uniformly suppose they have a maturity of character and judgment rivaling that of their elders. They presumably know how to order their lives, how to express views of moment on weighty problems of government and mores, and above all how to choose from the cafeteria table of the curriculum items that will constitute a satisfactory intellectual diet. Of course if you stick a pin through their mental skins, you soon find out that you are dealing for the most part with troubled, uncertain, puzzled young experimenters whose "views" echo whatever slogans they happen, for a variety of reasons, to consider commendable. The alleged "authoritarianism" of the European schools has conjured up in our minds visions of class-room martinets who, if they existed, ought to do exercises guaranteed to bring some flexibility into their spinal columns. They probably do not exist. But what happens is that the youngsters they deal with are expected to use their wits on the intellectual tasks assigned, and meanwhile put most of their opinions into their hope chests.

As I have said, the wind has begun to blow in the opposite direction, at least in so far as our best students are concerned, but a long time will have to pass before the results will be substantial. Meanwhile we must see what is likely to happen at the other side of the educational table. How many Fairchilds will there be to pass round to colleges like Hunter? Above all, how well will the universities be prepared to exercise leadership? Let me deal first with the second question, because it is no doubt the more important. Colleges today cannot, except in certain very limited fields of inquiry, foster faculty scholarship of significance unless they are in one way or other associated with universities. The reason why this is so may in a rather rudimentary fashion be defined as follows: if the university is any good, the core of its Faculty will consist of scholars interested at least in a peripheral fashion in the training of other scholars. Some of this highly desirable disease they will communicate; and dots and pimples indicating that contamination has occurred will be seen on college campuses. At least this has been the case at Hunter. In retrospect I think we owe Columbia in particular some really formidable medal.

But what actually is the situation? There can be no doubt that unless one thinks in terms of meticulous scholarship devoted to minute parts of the intellectual scene, there has been a marked decline of excellence. I like to date the beginning of the debacle from 1933, when Rexford Guy Tugwell left Columbia to become Assistant Secretary of Agriculture. Not that I have any competence in Agriculture (though I worked my way through college in part by shocking grain and helping with the threshing during summers) or any very special admiration for Dr. Tugwell. But the date marks the start of a serious draining of Faculty strength by the Government, the Foundations, industry and assorted other enterprises. Anyone who contemplates, for example, what cream the Ford Foundation alone has siphoned off university milk will see at a glance what I mean. The basic phenomenon, however, is that the nation found the university a wonderful bank to borrow from, but hardly one in which to invest major human resources. Gradually the average distinguished professor accumulated so many irons that those he put in the campus fire could be heated only upon occasion. The underlying causes were many, ranging from minor ones of an economic character—notably the struggle with inflation and the income tax—to the fact that the business of the nation would have gone to pot far more noticably than it has, if trained and intelligent men had not been taken from the universities and colleges, on a full-time or a part-time basis.

Beardsley Ruml made a valiant effort to redress the balance in favor of the university by arguing that professorial salaries should be increased to levels equivalent to those prevailing in business. His campaign deserves respect and commendation, but I continue to feel that it would have been far wiser to emancipate the Faculty at accredited colleges and universities who are on tenure from the payment of income taxes, in the manner currently applied to our nationals who serve in international organizations. For what has happened in private institutions is that drives for funds needed have absorbed so much time and energy that presidents have been worn out on the more eminent campuses, while on the ones with less affluent constituencies the lag behind the procession has been like what the slow motion of an ox-cart would be on the Pennsylvania Turnpike. And in so far as the publicly supported establishments are concerned, the result has been heavy burdens on the state and municipal taxpayer which have not produced the desired results.

At any rate, I am sure that the balance between university scholarship and teaching cannot easily be restored, and that indeed when it has been the basic pedagogical attitudes may be quite different from those we have traditionally formed. The great teacher, as we have known him, has been identified with his classes. Preparing for these in a sense both broad and deep, giving instruction, conferring with students and in some measure at least supervising and judging their work—these have constituted a truly professional service with high if perhaps somewhat narrow standards. In colleges, at least, scholarship did not exist for its own sake. It was intensified preparation, undertaken both in order to maintain intellectual glow in the teacher's own life and for the sake of renewing and enriching his instructional material. To a considerable extent much the same thing could once be said of the university. It is impossible to think of Kittredge or Manley, to mention two notable Chaucer scholars, without knowing how intimately what they gave their classes was associated with their scholarly inquiries.

To be sure the academician cast in this mold was in some ways parochial. He did not take kindly to committee work unless it had a direct bearing on what he was committed to as a teacher. Going off to other campuses as part of a program of college affiliation or association, now coming to be widely esteemed, was likely to seem to him a needless and frustrating form of monkey business. Although he went loyally enough to the meetings of his Learned Society, he was apt to look at these affairs as a sort of sedate picnic during the course of which he could strike up acquaintances, compare notes and upon occasion "show off" his wares and prowess. The mere conjecture that he might serve on a government committee or travel to a far country in order to persuade it that America was the best of all possible paradises would have seemed to him ridiculous. This parochialism, I shall confess with sorrow, once troubled me; and I was given to enunciate the theory that everyone who planned to espouse a teaching career at a college should spend a year of preparation doing something quite different and more mundane —being a prison warden or a real estate salesman, if nothing better turned up. How primitive this notion was from a contemporary point of view!

Now the situation has greatly altered. Abler young men and women hardly sit still on the campus long enough to become thoroughly acquainted with it. They journey to foreign countries as experts, Fulbright lecturers, Foundation fellows, cogs in the vast networks of training services which Government agencies and industry have created in all parts of the world. The amount of time thus drained off from the college reservoir reminds one of nothing so much as an irrigation system. Whether the benefits which accrue to the institution as a consequence of this assumed widening of horizons are adequate compensation is a moot question, indeed. Obviously the college has become a much livelier place, much more deeply aware of the world in which student and professor alike live. The cast of social science which lies over the place is far from pale. Whether in addition to all our studies, monographs, opinion polls, et cetera, we plumb any notable depths of contemplation is another matter.

It is in the light of these developments that one should consider such phenomena as the use of television in college teaching. As the instructor tends to revolve less and less about the classroom, the difference between seeing him in the flesh and on a screen likewise becomes smaller. The older variety of professor was seldom a brilliant lecturer; and indeed what he did effectively could hardly be classed with oratory in any of its more rhetorical forms. He practised with diligence and effectiveness the art of the colloquium, and I think that any of us who have actually seen him do this with great skill know that he has been a master craftsman. But, and I say this with some regret, the chances are that we shall lack the time, ability and inclination to continue in this mode. Maybe we shall perforce come to adopt the European university system, whether the professor lectures to large groups or resorts to television. But, and I do not think this view necessarily attributable to the conservatism of age, we shall have lost something which was not only as American as a pawpaw or a Navajo blanket but which provided a precious and memorable educational experience.

Of course not every one at Hunter was doing these things with a notable measure of brilliance. There were instructors who had nothing specially interesting to talk about because they themselves were not in the least interesting. And I suppose that if one had looked about painstakingly one would have echoed student opinion that there were classrooms in which life stood absolutely still for an hour while the man or woman at the desk performed the variety of ritual known as exposition of an intellectual vacuum. But a surprisingly large number of instructors who had come alive and could help make others live were on the premises. For all the impersonality which the size and character of the institution imposed, here was a haven for the personal in the deepest and most valid sense of the term.

So much for these things. I have said that my first ten years at the College were spent in the shadow of The Misfortune. The second decade was lived during what could undoubtedly be termed the period of the most widely distributed prosperity the country has known. Our student body generally took on a patina of well-being, not evenly spread, it is true, but still very agreeable to behold. Sometimes we enrolled a very wealthy girl or two. But in general our students came from families of civil servants and divines, of small business people and members of the labor unions, of immigrants and the native poor. Most of them probably wanted an education because it promised to be an open-sesame to a better job than they could otherwise have hoped for, but they were also generally not averse to what we are accustomed to call culture. The number of copies of the *Times* and the *Tribune* one found in the waste baskets increased. I need hardly add that the hairdos and the complexions had improved.

And so one who witnessed the scene day in and day out has memories of very human things etched in sharp relief or seen in long flowing lines. Sometimes, alas, our young people were troubled and bitter. Some hated their shabby, often worried and quarrelsome homes, from which the only escape was by subway into what seemed to them, and of course often was, the crowded, combative anonymity of their college. It may be that some deeply resented their fate. But there were also young people, many of them as a matter of fact, whose lives were so heroic without heroics that one often said to oneself that Dickens must have invented them and postponed their emergence on the scene. Upon occasion I was invited to the homes of some of these students—the simple apartment house homes of immigrant America at its noblest and most warmly colorful best. There food would be served in the style of the country of origin; and nobody made me feel that I was a god straying from his appointed realm. The favored daughters of these families were fortunate, indeed. They had been reared with respect, so that they in turn would show respect. But I will confess that sometimes I came away a bit shamefaced at the thought of living in a very comfortable house on Shippan Point and grousing about nothing in particular.

For instance, there was the daughter of a man I had known in Germany, where before Hitler's time he had been the editor of a newspaper many thousands admired and read with care. Since he had arrived in this country as an exile at a relatively advanced age, there was little of a profit-making character he could find to do. When he brought his daughter of seventeen to me in order to find out whether she could be admitted, I thought her a frail child. But during the four years which followed she not only took all the academic hurdles in her stride with distinction but supported herself and for the most part her father by working in an office every afternoon from two to seven. Yet I never saw her indulge in self-pity or in hankering after things she could not have. When she came to class, she was as debonair as any of Herrick's lasses. Then there was a girl with a face like a cherub's who told me, as if it was not at all strange, that she came to the college of mornings and then spent the rest of the day taking care of a bedridden mother. Next I think of a tall, stately young lady now well on her way to success in a profession who not only worked long hours to put herself through college but also spent almost as many being a volunteer worker for the blind. Who that knew this part of the story could doubt that New York's investment in higher education, burdensome though it was, had proved an admirable venture not merely in terms of academic prowess but also in those of character and integrity? Why have we managed to paint a picture of youth from which glow and color are missing? Not to see how much of integrity hammered out on hard anvils there is, how resolute commitments to high standards often are, and how great a love sometimes warms the houses of the poor, is surely to possess a quite distorted picture of the world around us.

The list of such young women I could provide would be a long one, indeed. But, alas, there was a good deal to see of the other side of the coin, too—of warping that came from warped and broken homes, of character which would not grow straight in spite of the ceaseless, genuine affection lavished on it, of stumbling and groping, sometimes in the long labyrinths of unsettled minds. A man who sat where I did had to realize that, whatever he and his colleagues might try to do to brighten this part of the sad music of humanity, would in large measure be wasted effort. Many of the city's pastors, physicians and psychiatrists helped us quietly and unselfishly. It is all very well to say that higher education ought to be concerned with the training of the intellect and have no other purpose. In theory I agree. Yet I am as certain as I could well be about anything that a man who, having ceased to be young, deals in turn with young people will never succeed in living up to that lofty doctrine. You cannot train the intellect of a boy or girl living on the verge of agony by assuming that this agony does not exist. And then of course one comes to realize sadly that however valuable the hand held out under the rubric of guidance may be, there can in the end be no answer to this problem save affection, which even in being rebuffed is holy.

And so we tried to make our pedagogical task one of realizing what the education we offered was to be as a whole—the kind of whole which, as I have said, had been seen clearly by the great teachers of the Western tradition but had sometimes been lost sight of. This we could not perform by preaching, though upon occasion we preached, too, but by trying to create a climate in which the essential things would be felt—generosity, freedom and the nobility which characterizes the mind when it wears fetters for the sake of a cause. There was a great deal of generosity at Hunter, as there is in any good college, whether it happened to be that of the Deans who in the first instance reflect in their attitudes and their work the spirit which breathes in the institution as a whole, or that of Faculty members for whom teaching was courtesy even as it was discipline, and of girls in the administrative offices whose task it continued to be, day in and day out, to meet the community on the level of commonplace abrasiveness about matters which may seem small but can upon occasion loom up big as storm clouds. Of course it was not omnipresent. There were hearts and minds into which no warmth entered. Some held jobs, and that was all anybody could say for them. But on the whole it was a reality manifest in professor and elevator operator alike; and it came to be, I think, what students in the succeeding years most deeply appreciated. For they had seldom expected to find it, coming as they did so often from neighborhoods without any personality other than a dreary sameness, in which an individual remained only a face or a name.

Freedom we cherished also. No doubt we of the Faculty as well as the students were often limited in outlook, cribbed and confined by prejudices of assorted kinds, and given to thinking that the world would be better off if it saved time by agreeing with us. There was also evident a widespread inner instability, resulting from the lack of a reasoned and satisfying way of life, which dearth sapped the strength of many and in particular, in so far as we of the Faculty were concerned, left the commitment to teaching curiously unrelated to the personality of the teacher. In extenuation it may be said that the spiritual environment in which we live is characterized by turbulent stresses. Does it not often seem as if our culture were one in which canny men carry on and on so that they may keep up and up? Wallace Stevens asked:

> Who, then, are they seated here?
> Is the table a mirror in which they sit and look?
> Are they men eating reflections of themselves?

We, too, did not always sense that man, as a creature wedded to flesh, is a great and shadowy mystery, and that therefore art, poetry and thought have been gravely unsettled by reason of a recent sharp awareness of this mystery. No farmer in the dell is any longer conceivable without his complex. And of complexes there were hundreds on the campus.

Yet I believe that on the whole we somehow felt that we were free. There were tabus. We did not assail one another's races or creeds. Sometimes the grim shadows of conflict were flung across the campus, but we did not take them too seriously. One after-noon in Paris, when more earthy autumn shadows were being flung far across streets, I happened to be in a taxi riding down the Champs Elysées when the tall figure of General De Gaulle, flanked by a small group of men who probably belonged to the Sûreté, came walking along. My driver said very simply, "It is a good thing that that man's head is not in the clouds. For there would be no place for his shadow to go!" I am persuaded that whatever else a college president may or may not do, he must keep his head out of clouds. It is immensely tempting when one is beset by problems of freedom created, for example, by brash young campus journalists, to come down from the equivalent of Olympus and, having mounted some kind of charger, lay the enemy low. But ears are more effectively boxed when one meets the victim on his own level. Upon occasion, marveling at the public clamor over something silly and offensive penned by a student editor, I wondered whether these sensitive outsiders really wanted a college to arrange a public ceremony at which, against the background of a stage draped in black, the gawky offenders would be ecstatically hanged in effigy.

Here of course was only one of the seams at which a student body and a college administration are conjoined. And seams can split wide open. It is impossible for a president always to keep the flimsily sewn garment of campus unity from coming apart somewhere. But it may help him to bear in mind that his princi-pal duty is to think twice about everything and three times about this. There are assigned to him many of the functions which Benedict, author of the most memorable of monastic rules, wisely imposed on the cellarer. Gradually acquiring with the passing of years avoirdupois and unction, he is expected to commit him-self to nothing which might glue a potential donor's dollar to his wallet's lining and nevertheless to sprinkle the after-dinner landscape with wit and sage eloquence. He must be concerned with the broad acres of the campus, the size of its laboratories and of budgets to maintain them, the number of articles pub-lished by the Faculty, and the approachable prosperity of its alumni. But his most difficult chore is to be courteous to all and sundry, and beseech the Lord to make it possible that every instructor speedily becomes a dean. Only seldom can it be hoped that he will have a moment to consider what Benedict wrote concerning the Abbot of a monastery: "Let him always bear in mind what he is, and what the name is that he bears. . . Let him reflect on how heavy and troublesome a task he has undertaken." He will have no time at all if he gets himself needlessly embroiled in controversies with students.

Hunter, of course, was not called upon to solve a number of problems commonplace elsewhere. Since there were no dormitories, it was unnecessary to worry about whether students had been safely tucked into bed. I probably could never make anyone understand how very glad I was that it happened to be so. Nevertheless the college had a variety of special concerns. Our young people left home, wherever that might be, and came to us. I am afraid they did not always receive a very warm welcome. New York, if you know it well, is not nearly as icy as it is reputed to be, but there are times when one must turn the heat up high to take off the chill. Then the warmth does wonders. For some time I had asked myself what would happen if a random citizen said "Hello" to a subway conductor. One morning, after having arrived at 125th Street via the New Haven at more or less the customary time, I descended into the Lexington Avenue Subway inferno and greeted a little man in saggy blue trousers who then, at the given hour, invariably stood on the platform in front of the first car. The shock of my "Good morning!" was almost more than he could bear. No doubt for the moment he fancied that he was back in Rumania or Ireland or Belgium or wherever he came from. He stared at me in utter astonishment. But during weeks afterward he used to hold up the train, if perchance I happened to be seconds late, so that we could pass the time of day. Then he disappeared from the scene. One afternoon more than a year later I was being jolted uptown from City Hall when I heard a voice calling to me over the din of the crowd. "Doctor! Hey, Doctor! How are you?" my friend asked. How he came to realize that I was loaded down with an academic title I shall never know. But obviously the hand of friendship had been extended all the way from Harlem to Brooklyn Bridge.

There are a few things to which I never became accustomed

during all my years at the college. The most important of these had ethical implications. Whoever is responsible for the saying that there are no morals save mores has created incredible havoc. Difficult though it may be to anchor ethical postulates in the waters of any Absolute, one can hardly think it so impossible that generations have grown up, are still growing up, which believe that moral conduct is something very like English usage. That is, whatever the majority of people decide to do is necessarily right. This majority may only be approximate, but it must include the proper people. Well, we have pretty generally come to hold that there is no such thing as correct English—that all the ancient caveats hurled against such misdemeanors as coupling singular predicates with plural subjects are out of date. What if standards of conduct were to suffer a similar fate? They already have. I do not wish to imply that the human race has suddenly gone to pot, or that it was a model of good behavior at some time in the past. To be saved from such errors one need only read the Book of Kings, or indeed the Gospel according to St. Matthew. Nevertheless it does unfortunately seem to be true that in the United States the sense of personal commitment to norms of ethical practice has badly faded under the impact of moral relativity. Many of our youngsters are canny enough to see that the color has gone out of the cloth.

Here I am not referring to sexual behavior, or indeed to the whole cluster of social causes and consequences which are conveniently though inadequately summed up under the rubric of juvenile delinquency. The concern is rather with everything meant when somebody says he is not for sale. We shall further restrict the discussion by ruling out as irrelevant the cases in which human beings alas prove that they are not insulated against temptation. A politician otherwise reputable lets himself be talked into accepting a "loan" from a contractor doing business for a city or a state. A business manager or a cashier diverts a trickle from the stream of funds which pass through his hands into his private irrigation ditch, knowing full well that what he is doing is evil. Or a middle-aged man who has hitherto led a blameless life kills another in a fit of belated romantic love. These are sins and are understood to be so, by whatever code a man or woman accepts; and the only things humanity has ever known how to do about sin are called forgiveness and atonement. What is under discussion is quite different and in a sense new in our society. It is a belief to be defined as follows: everybody knows that there are shortcuts to take to get ahead, and so if I slip down a few myself I am merely living up to the rules of the game.

Of course students have cheated in earlier times. It was almost always part of the educational process to look at the instructor as the enemy; and outwitting him in any manner that came to hand was a phase of the combat. But if one looks at some aspects of the current scene the change in outlook will be manifest. New York City, like many other places, makes a practice of raising the pay of teachers when they have earned a number of credits for additional advanced study. This is of course in itself not a thoroughly reputable practice. It is resorted to for two reasons: first, the organized fraternity will not permit the system to make advancement and promotion depend on quality of performance; and second, it is manifestly impossible to maintain that teachers should be steadily paid more unless there is some justification for assuming that by reason of training and other qualifications they are entitled to preferred treatment in the society. Therefore a balloon-size bag of tricks has been devised in order to make getting the additional credits as painless and, one may add, as aimless as possible. What I am saying does not of course reflect on the core of well-educated, wholly honest and in more ways than one distinguished people in the school system.

And one of the results? The discovery that despite all the carpets spread out in their honor, a surprising number of teachers have paid somebody to write their term papers and dissertations, and that the great mechanism devised to insure their progress would not have found out what they were doing had it not been for the ingenuity of reporters, paid very much more poorly, in ferreting out their iniquity! I wonder if we have as yet realized what this means. Here are the teachers of youth who, despite all their clamor, are often paid better than are people with the same personal qualifications outside the school system, who are nevertheless ready to violate the most sacred canons of the academic profession for further gain! What an example to set before youth! I am reminded of a Sholem Aleichem story. A rabbi in Kiev was visited on the eve of the Sabbath by a man who asked him to keep forty thousand roubles for him over the holy day. This substantial sum was duly locked in the rabbi's cupboard. When the day of prayer had ended the stranger called to collect his money. The rabbi professed to know nothing about the matter. When the poor visitor expostulated, he merely said that it would be necessary to summon the trustees of his synagogue to consider the problem. When they arrived and listened to the story, they unanimously declared that the stranger was an impostor and should be thrown out. Thereupon the rabbi went to the cupboard and produced the roubles. "I merely wanted you to see," he commented, "what sort of trustees I have." I should have vastly more respect for the teachers' organizations of New York if their indignation on this occasion had equalled their wrath when the salary increases they desired were not forthcoming.

In the circumstances one could not marvel at the sympathy manifested by students generally with those whom many of them considered the "victims" of the TV scandal exposures. I found that they were not experienced enough to know that the advertising and public relations people who had resorted to such practices were the shysters of their professions, just as crooked lawyers and venal physicians long since have been of theirs. How were they to know of the many men and women who work hard to make the business of merchandising honest? And what shall one say of conformism among young people for the sake of conformism? This is in my view only a subtler, deadlier way in which the gospel according to which mores equals morals has corroded the spirit of youth. Its cause is, in terms of ebbing conviction, the radical belief that what most people want you ought to want. Your substitute for a conscience might feel guilty if you didn't. "I never read the *New Republic*," the possessor of a Phi Beta Kappa key said to me, "because most people I know think it is too far to the Left."

More generally the proper thing to do is considered to be locking yourself up with the group to which you happen to belong and then pretending that this isn't really very different from other groups. The trouble with most inter-group and inter-faith movements therefore is that the aim is not to learn what steadfastness of purpose and commitment the others enshrine, but to realize how "unessential" the differences are—and of course how "unessential" nearly everything else is. Why should anybody wonder, then, when brainwashings of our young men captured in battle reveal a flabbiness of moral substance and a lack of brute physical courage which alone justify fears for the future of the Republic? It is as acridly ironical as anything could be that, in discussing free elections to determine the fate of Eastern Germany, Khrushchev said that he did not believe in the democracy of the majority but only in the democracy of those who are right. How can we respond effectively by saying that we have no recourse to anything save the views of the majority because we cannot see how righteousness could be established on any other basis? What if the majority were to say that Khrushchev was right?

Could anything be done to counteract the trend? Like American higher education generally, we had emphasized the scholar's dedication to truth, regardless of where it might be found or to what conclusions it might lead. It is a noble ideal and there can be no doubt that as an example it has an effect upon a certain number of young people. The difficulty is that once the discussion has proceeded beyond the realm of dedication to accuracy of perception and judgment, it becomes necessary to say what one means by "truth." And arrived at this juncture the normal response will be that "truth" is what the evidence establishes; and since the only kind of evidence for which we have respect lies wholly outside the realm of reflection on justice and ethics, nothing has happened save that the basic issue of personal responsibility has been still farther removed from the realm of actuality.

Obviously the sole possible recourse must be to a long line of followers of Socrates who can hammer out the case for the Good through discussion. And therefore like many another American educator I thought that maybe the disciples of the great Greek might be found among the custodians of the religious clubs.

Good men and women were among them, to be sure. But in general they were so deeply concerned with the lines of demarcation which set one of them off from the others that any chance they might have had to help students probe to the hidden wellsprings of moral living seemed identified with China. They could get into a fearful dither about whether Hannukah candles were to burn in the same room which housed a Christmas crib. They could mount a virtual crusade if something or other occurred which seemed to them, perhaps with some justification, an affront to a faith, a tradition, or even a custom. They could go into mourning for the College as a whole if an instructor "endangered" or "insulted" the group to which they belonged. So far as I could tell, and my survey of the scene was hardly unfriendly or disinterested, they rallied those who for one reason or another needed no rallying and otherwise affected the moral outlook of the students very little, indeed. As I have said there were exceptions. But whenever I tried to help make the whole enterprise more significant, all I actually accomplished was to evoke a stony, upon occasion a hostile silence. Reluctantly I came to the conclusion that the average American cleric does not comprehend the intellectual temper of the age in which he lives. When one summed up his ministrations, one knew very well that he had lost more sheep than he had saved. It was often almost heartrending to realize that young people of genuine quality were being swept away from their traditional moorings, not because of some kind of carefully thought-out aversion but simply for the reason that the cult of the here-and-now seemed to them more beguiling and more easily reconciled with the standards of the society in which they were to live.

Of course there were in New York religious men and women who could have helped us a very great deal if we could have brought their influence to bear—men like John LaFarge, Louis Finkelstein, Reinhold Niebuhr, John Bennett, to mention only a few. But hard though I tried to enlist their counterparts, the results were less than negligible. Sometimes one or the other was brought in, but they seldom had time to leave more than a trace of their passage through our midst. Thus one day I had a visit from Mrs. Lecomte du Nouy, widow of the author of *Human*

Destiny, which book marks a cleavage between older scientific conceptions of man and newer ones. She wished to foster the writing of books discussing the relationships between religion and science: and for years the committee she established for the purpose met at Hunter College. It was quite non-denominational in outlook, and honored men like William Ernest Hocking and Michael Polanyi. About such activities our students, alas, knew little if anything. It seemed to me that religious leaders who did not get out their young people to stand in line to catch a glimpse of Hocking were singularly ineffectual. So far as I could tell, few of them would have known who Hocking was; and, if they had, they would probably not have cared enough to bother.

Perhaps I should add, in order to be quite fair, that the efforts of religious counselors necessarily reflect the long isolation of theology from the university which tradition has now made virtually sacrosanct. As things are at present the theologian serves not the "queen of the sciences," or even a science more democratically envisaged as one of several, but a corpus of commitments to which homiletic, moral or apologetical purposes are appended. He is a missionary, a pastor, a confessor (all of which are noble parts indeed to play in the drama of life), but only very rarely a scholar with a scholar's interest in question and hypothesis. I am afraid that until this basic fact is changed, as it has been altered abroad, the religious leader of good will on a campus will remain a kind of addendum to the proceedings rather than an integral factor in their development. At best he will be, in so far as public education is concerned, the custodian of his own orthodoxy and an exhorter to moral conduct. A distinguished Irish Catholic professor, who spent a summer teaching at one of our best universities, told me that he was bewildered by the fact that all the sermons he listened to in the campus Catholic chapel were exhortations against fornication. He was not in favor of fornication, but he believed that if young people were to be weaned from indulging in it the reason would definitely be that they had arrived at spiritual insights and commitments which would make weaknesses like sexual promiscuity unthinkable. And he feared that in the absence of these the advertising done from the pulpit might very well produce unwittingly results akin to those which follow from the Kinsey Report—namely, that something so socially important that every Sunday morning had to be devoted to its consideration might be well worth trying. I am not necessarily agreeing with the professor's critique, except in the sense that the chaplain was merely carrying out his function as he had been trained to think of it, and that a change would be possible only when he had been trained differently.

There were moments when I almost fancied that what bright young sociologists were saying about "religosity" in the United States was true, and that all it probably meant was a coveting of respectability through some kind of church membership. But having got into such a mood I thought of Father John LaFarge and immediately saw that I was playing the role of man of little faith. For so probing and yet so serene was his view of life in the United States, of the spiritual tides which were moving underneath the surface, and of what might happen if the good in diverse points of view could be brought to converge on the central issue of strengthening and cleansing the nation's spirit, that when I thought of what it meant to serve as he was serving something in which there was at least a semblance of humility rose up within me. For it was clear that the work to be done is ontological rather than homiletic in character—that is, one has to try by being something to wield a pedagogical influence more profound than one could exert by saying this or that. John La Farge was for years a sort of candle I carried about in a twilight which was sometimes almost darkness. His is the kind of light for which one could not properly be grateful, because thanksgiving would do it an injustice. One had rather to accept it as one does sunshine, or the fact that the harvest comes when all goes well.

One other twinge of conscience afflicted many of us. We knew that the Negro was amongst us, that until he had come out of bondage something would be radically wrong with American life, and that above all his children must feel that we drew no line of caste between them and our own. For his sake some of us at Hunter had to root deep prejudices out of ourselves. Naturally there was no overt discrimination of any kind on the campus. Quite an effort was made, as a matter of fact, to see to it that Negro students were included in the leadership of student organizations, and after a while we also appointed Negroes to the staff. But such things were only bits of make-believe as far as meeting the situation as a whole was concerned. Although the end result was as far from having been planned as is the distance from the Empire State Building to Sirius the dog-star, Hunter downtown and uptown is the City Negro's gateway to higher education. It is virtually a step to either campus by subway. Nevertheless we had to concede that only a pitiful fragment of the total number of Harlem's young people eligible for college availed themselves of the opportunity. Doubtless the majority could not have qualified, but I am sure that one principal reason for our failure was that the parents did not have the necessary confidence in the ability of their children to rise from a relatively low level of social effectiveness.

We were unable to deal with the problem in a systematic way. Perhaps we should have managed to put on some kind of intensive campaign; but a college which always had too many students and too much to do could hardly embark successfully on so flamboyant a pilgrimage. A number of things we did attempt, the best and most successful of which was my wife's mustering of gifted Negro women for service to our student center at Roosevelt House. Many of the baited hooks which I dropped in the figurative river of Harlem landed no fish. But in the end I think we had come up with a program which seemed to promise more success. I am certain that in the long run Negro youth must take its rightful place at the educational table, and in so far as New York is concerned this means that Hunter College will write another great page in the annals of its service to the city. It would be a waste of time to look at the future of the Negro in America with any sentimentalism. In the North, which so often prides itself on achievements in the field of inter-racial cooperation which do not exist, there is no gainsaying the fact that by and large the Negro will probably play in his own yard. Perhaps for a long time to come he will keep his doors locked in every meaningful sense to alien whites, not because he has anything in particular against them but because they do not seriously interest him. Going his own way, he will be quite proud of his ability to travel. It seems to me, much though I desire it did not, that his interest in desegregation is a passing phase and that a generation hence the Negro will be seeking support for his own educational institutions even as some religious groups now do for theirs. Meanwhile Jim Crow cars will have faded into history. No Negro visiting a place like Stone City in Chattanooga will be ordered to drink from a different water spigot than whites do. Hotels and restaurants throughout the country will hardly recall that once upon a time there were mandates which made it necessary for the Negro to go elsewhere. We of the different races will work together or for each other with the same relative nonchalance as do Texans and the sons of Maine. But unless in the interim the Negro succeeds in taking advantage of his educational opportunities, his share in the partnership will be a disadvantageous one.

I shall end this chapter on a more theoretical note. When my own college days were ending, young men who took education at all seriously were reading either the philosophers or the social reformers. The more conservative-minded were rediscovering Aristotle. Nietzsche was no doubt the hero of the radicals—H. L. Mencken in particular was carrying a lantern for him—the era of burrowing into *Das Kapital* having not yet dawned. More professionally there were Harvard's William James and George Santayana to reckon with, and at Columbia Dewey and Woodbridge were forming a generation. From the point of view of social reform, one could sit up all night talking about people and ideas, ranging from Jane Adams and her then new settlement house plan, or the movement spearheaded by Woodrow Wilson, or the litmus papers slipped in the soil by Thornstein Veblen and the New School of Social Research which to some extent at least had been fashioned in his image, or the debates between John A. Ryan and Morris Hillquit about the lot of the worker, in which an emerging evolutionary democratic doctrine was pitted against a well-presented version of Socialism. And if one wanted to go farther afield there were always the Fabian Socialists, the early *New Republic*, and maybe a French syndicalist writer or two.

What now shapes the outlook is the tremendous impact of science and its offspring technology on the contemporary scene. For my part I have often said that a man of the generation to which I belong can visualize this most clearly if he thinks about the fact that the animals which so shaped the contours of his more or less rural youth have steadily become more useless until they are dead. For amusement, such as that which brings countless thousands to Yonkers or Louisville for the races, is hardly utility. Even the cow has become the target for abuse due to the effect of her fatty legacy on the heart, and it is evident that margarine could easily supplant butter. How great a revolution this is one cannot even imagine. But sometimes one can visualize it rather well if one observes the effect on simpler things, such as human locomotion. It seems to be a fact that young football players now suffer most generally from weaknesses of the knees, due to the fact that walking has become a lost art. Only in remote areas do farmer boys still plod behind the plough, or strut about fields tossing hay into racks. Thus the mechanization of the human body has become a fact. The little peninsula on which I live is now virtually surrounded by boats, to which one drives by car. An occasional maid takes the dogs out for a walk, and now and then an old timer will saunter around looking at views of the Sound. But the rest of the world is motorized. When I become genuinely reminiscent and therewith a bore, I recall that once I arrived in Wisconsin on a snowy winter night to find that the connecting station wagon had departed and that the only way to get home was on foot. And that is how I got there—doing twenty odd miles with a suitcase in my hand, despite the snow. The anecdote has an antediluvian quality for youngsters, one of whom said to me quite frankly that I ought to have had my head inspected for signs of serious disorder.

If the change through which we have lived is so marked from the physical point of view, what shall we say of the human mind and the human outlook? The shift which has taken place in the Western world, to which I also attach Russia, has been so staggeringly swift and complete that it has altered almost every mode of thought and feeling. How queer it seems that not many years ago William Jennings Bryan opposed during a famous trial a Tennessee statute which permitted the teaching of Evolution in the schools! For today an educated person, however religious he may be, simply could not if he would rid his mind of concepts which have their origin in the study of morphology in Nature. But vastly more important from the average man's point of view is the change in the character and tempo of his labor. The man with a hoe has been transformed into a man with a cultivator. Laborers who once carried hods of brick and mortar up ladders now operate cranes or elevators. Gradually the citizen whose principal asset is a strong back is becoming almost as outmoded as a beast of burden. However incorrect it may be to use the term social science, it is plain as day that one can no longer sunder the study of politics or economics from the machine. And it may well be that the principle that leisure is the dominant force in urban sociology has become elementary. There is nothing for small boys to do but to run around the streets looking for the kind of venturesome releases for their energy which express themselves in breaking windows and writing signs on walls. There is nothing for their elders to do but look at television.

I have sometimes thought (and said) that sex has become such an obsession in our culture because sex is almost all that remains of Nature in the ordinary life of the city dweller. Here is still something of the animal, though it is encountered only in the consciousness of man. And it may well be that forms of sadism and perversion which spring up all about us are rooted in the too abrupt concentration of the whole world of the natural in one function and action. Of course these things are shocking, and sometimes so steeped in disgust that one can hardly contemplate them without a sense of foreboding. But it is even more important to realize that in such trends there may well be present a kind of misunderstood urge to mechanize even this last vestige of the pre-scientific world. We may see a time when young love, of which Shakespeare and Spenser wrote with so much rapture, has become little more than the first stage in a process of experimentation which in the end must be hardly more or less than a kind of automation.

That this mighty revolution should have evoked abstract art

and verse is not in the least surprising, for the arts can be honest only when they mirror man as he is becoming. But vastly more impressive, it seems to me, is the fact that the notion of freedom is now also largely an abstraction. Just as it is difficult for a young person to conceive of himself in society unless he is to do whatever that society does, so also is it rapidly becoming impossible to think of power and influence outside the limits of the concentration of power. All of us must live in constant fear of the weapons of incredible destruction which can be wielded by men at the various summits of political might. It is a two-fold fear, lest on the one hand our own free world lag in the race, and on the other that in spite of everything these weapons will be used and make all of us helpless victims. But the dread is much broader in scope than that. What can a labor union any longer do to slow down the race to machine domination, so that the worker can preserve some liberty of choice? And what power does the citizen retain over economic mechanisms which are now grown so vast and complex that even those presumably in charge no longer understand them?

An older person, having his store of images by which the mind lives and his recollections of things as they once were, can still live in two worlds—the one which has irrevocably passed and the other which is being born. Pasternak was one of the elders. So to some extent Albert Camus was by anticipation. But young people cannot do so. They have a choice between acceptance and rebellion. They can take off for Alaska and live in cabins, or they can write beatnik verse. Or they can, if they have some money, buy an old New England house, with fireplaces and a grandfather's clock, grow herbs and chickens, paint landscapes and go to town meetings. But the great majority will have to live in the world science has made. I think it has now become the major business of education to help them do so well. This is perhaps the most difficult task the schools have ever faced. A gifted college lad once told me that when he first read the *Odyssey* he thought it silly, because he just could not visualize being out in the kind of ship which Ulysses guided home from Troy. And yet another told me that her greatest experience in life was walking through an Egyptian pyramid in which time stood still because the artist had stopped painting when his mistress died. If one puts these two side by side, perhaps a kind of key is provided. For it may be that the life of the mind is satisfying when one has found the experience of others, however strange, significant.

At any rate, it is for different men, different from me, to go with young people down the vistas which are thus revealed. But I hope they will remember that the bliss of man is compounded of a zest for comedy and an acceptance of the tragic in life. These are the twin compensatory movements which give history significance and stature. By comedy I mean the source from which laughter wells up, kindly and healing, gracious though mordant. And the sense of tragedy is that which, because it has the smudge of our mortality upon it, suggests that upon the tomb it were better there be enscribed words suggesting nobility rather than remorse.

VI.

PEOPLE WHO DROPPED IN

The great hall of Hunter College is a rhythm of arcs, simple in outline and yet adroit of construction, so that as a result there is symmetry but also an appealing absence of geometry for its own sake. Building it into a structure occupying roughly three-fourths of a city block was a not inconsiderable feat of architectural skill; and the design itself, over which Louis Harmon presided with the deftness of a Stokowski concerned with spatial harmonies, has the best characteristics of a time when there was no money to waste but when the resources of functionalism were not yet being fully utilized. Every inch of Harmon's not too ample body was of the most authentic urban vintage, but in his eyes there was the whimsy of the country, reminding one more than a little of Robert Frost. He was not, like Marcel Breuer, the other great architect in Hunter's history, a genius half of whose nature is that of a German *Privatdozent* digging with rigorous research into the heart of every problem. But even so he was genuinely an artist whose vision of the whole was associated with an almost passionate concern for every part. It was an unanticipated joy to confer with him about each detail of the great hall. Of necessity my knowledge of his art was slight, indeed; but since my father had been a builder and contractor (he put up among other things the first structure on the campus of the University of Wisconsin), I looked upon what was in progress from much the same point of view as that with which a Paris seamstress might have regarded the prowess of Christian Dior. This is, I think, not without its rather special value.

At first nobody thought that the hall would serve any other purpose than to provide a setting for student assemblies. Members of the Board of Higher Education were, as a matter of fact, committed to letting the general public see as little of the inside of 695 Park Avenue as possible. This attitude was by no means unbuttressed by reasons. The time was, as I have indicated, one in which the Communist brethren were eager to squeeze through every door which stood the least bit ajar; and the thought of fellow-traveling mass meetings, held under more or less camouflaged auspices, was not likely to be comforting. There also existed at the time little awareness of what a metropolitan center of community education could be like; and I shall confess of course that at the outset I also had no clear notion of what might happen, for good or ill, if one set out to create such a center.

It was merely evident that student assemblies and other academic functions would fill the hall on only a relatively few occasions. Could this be thought sufficient to justify its existence, particularly in view of what property values were on this segment of Park Avenue? To be sure, we were developing an adult education program; and while it would remain necessary to foster this with every resource at our command, might it not be worth seeing what the community could devise on its own responsibility? After all we were in New York, and this had its causes and concerns, not to mention its unflagging desire to create a semblance of community in what would otherwise remain a vast expanse of anonymity. Gradually, as the Board overcame its reluctance to embark on so imperilled a sea, we drew up a caveat which excluded all partisan political activities and announced that any group which applied for the use of our facilities would be judged by its ability to sponsor a program meeting college standards.

The success proved to be genuinely phenomenal. Hunter College on Park Avenue is beyond any doubt the greatest college community center to be found anywhere in the world. To some extent this is of course due to the fact that it is the only place where such a center could be created on the east side of New York north of Cooper Union (which has also served the city admirably) and south of Fordham. But in far greater measure the success is due to the initiatives taken by a large number of groups and institutions. These have, as time went on, used not merely the great hall but literally every facility which the college can provide. They and we have made mistakes, inevitable mistakes, but on the whole it seems quite amazing that things should have gone so well. In broad outline the story is one of the unsuspected creative energies of the people of New York: its municipal agencies, its educational systems and establishments, its groups of men and women interested in schools both public and private, its volunteer music organizations, and its philanthropic associations. Sometimes the narrative must be concerned with professional skills, as when the Little Orchestra Society presented its concerts for children on Saturday mornings (the aftermath, it is true, was a mass of scattered paper and innumerable wads of gum under chairs). But often enough there lay about what went on an aura of improvisation. This last was, I frequently thought, particularly treasurable and memorable because it revealed the true life of a city which is normally identified in the public eye with what goes on in the narrow rounds of its theaters and concert halls, or if you insist its night clubs and sporting arenas.

In what follows I shall try to conjure up moments in which the turbulent history of the period was reflected, and some others in which the slower pulse of art was felt. It is well that a man should pay tribute to his time while remaining aware of what was sordid and silly. You may perhaps find it odd that these things should have happened in a college for the people, of the people and by the people, rather than under more fashionable auspices. Let me quickly add that the educational confraternity in New York has long since lived down any such distinctions. My admirable colleagues, Grayson Kirk of Columbia, Henry Heald and Carroll Newsom of New York University and Father Lawrence McGinley of Fordham among them, were as eager to see progress in my institution as I was to note the same in theirs.

The time which ushered us into Park Avenue was a period of Naziism and war. Round about us in New York then were many men and women I had known abroad, and very many others whom I would now be privileged to meet. Some of them would not emerge from the unexpected obscurity into which they were cast. I recall the publisher of a leading German newspaper, forced to leave his native country because his mother was a non-Aryan, who looked like a portrait of Bismarck, mustache and all, and who eventually by sheer dint of homesickness fell out of a fifteenth-story window; a poet who arrived with a precious cargo of three pictures by Emil Nolde, expecting to learn English and begin a new literary career, and who eventually did manage to have a few things published in a magazine unable to pay him more than a pittance for his services; a banker who escaped with a suitcase full of stocks and bonds, a suspicion-arousing circumstance which caused his temporary arrest when war broke out, though he had for years financed the principal European anti-Nazi journal edited by exiles; and another banker, considerably more fortunate, whose gift for making money did not desert him in the new world and whose apartment was blanketed with masterpieces by French Impressionists. Doctors and scientists generally had an easier time of it, but for some of them also the transition meant mortal wounds.

There was a man in New York for whom the coming to this country of European intellectuals meant a challenge worth walking the floor at night to meet. Alvin Johnson, founder and then President of the New School of Social Research, had inherited serenity, doggedness of purpose, and a zest for intellectual pioneering from his Scandinavian ancestors. His School was, intellectually as well as in the physical sense, a place in which there was a surprise round every corner. Thus the room in which meals were served had been festooned with frescoes designed, in my judgment, to deprive anyone not actually starving of an appetite. It was in a secular way like a monastic refectory in which pictures of the scenes in Dante's *Inferno* which reeked most of brimstone and despair would greet the monks when they filed in for lunch (there is, so far as I know, thank God, no such refectory). On the other hand Dr. Johnson's own ramshackle office, where he sat tugging away at a pipe from early morning until late at night, was something akin to a snug and sunny cabin on a Viking ship. So also was it with the procession of ideas which moved ceaselessly to and fro under his tutelage.

Dr. Johnson was perhaps the first American educator to assert that freedom was queen in his establishment, and that anyone was at liberty to teach in it as he would who had not tied him-

self to a totalitarian chariot wheel. The doors of the New School
were therefore opened wide to able and learned victims of Naziism, Fascism and Communism. He happened also to be one of
the first to recognize that religious faith was the supreme barrier to the onward march of Naziism. Accordingly, at a time
when it was still not very fashionable to think that Christian
belief was an intellectually viable enterprise, he welcomed with
genuine cordiality distinguished men and women who professed
that faith. For a good while the Faculty of the New School was
staffed with the finest flower of German and Austrian universities; and though not every one of them fitted into this somewhat
nonchalant environment as neatly as does a pin in a cushion,
on the whole it was a decorous and studious assemblage. The
President was often casting about for enterprises on which these
colleagues of his could sharpen their wits. With one of these I
was associated, namely in preparation of an American edition
of *Mein Kampf*, to which allusion has already been made.

Alvin Johnson's traits of character and his scholarly bent were
never more clearly reflected than in his desire to make this
strange and sinister book available to the American reader. How
could this country, he asked himself, really come to know Hitler
unless it read his own exposition of the social and political philosophy he professed? At the same time it seemed imperative
that some commentary be provided; and since I had just returned
from Europe after the Austrian *Anschluss* with a few bucket-
fulls of experiences and notes, he cajoled me into supplying the
desired comments on the text. A distinguished advisory committee was assembled, and all went well until an unexpected snag
was encountered. The publishing firm possessing the copyright
was an old and extremely reputable New England house. Not the
least taint of Naziism was associated with it, but its editor-in-
chief felt it his duty to protect the character and reputation of
his client. I had written a note about the strange death of Hitler's
niece, in circumstances which certainly reflected no credit on her
uncle. This, said the editor, was calculated to besmirch the good
name of his author and so he could not sanction its publication.
For the moment it appeared that we might be asked to remove
every indication that we considered Naziism at all disagreeable

but Dr. Johnson argued so tenaciously and skilfully that in the end the reference to the niece was all we had to sacrifice.

It seems strange in retrospect that at the time a great many people were not only ignorant of or indifferent to Hitler's purposes, but quite favorably impressed with him. Anti-Semitism was widespread. When the book was published, a good many circulars distributed by the firm were returned with remarks in pen or pencil to the effect that the writers wished Hitler the best of everything. Since it was easy to trace their professional associations, we noted with some consternation that the remarks did not emanate from a submerged tenth of the population but from clergymen, lawyers, doctors and professors. Indeed there was a small but impressive intellectual cult which festooned Hitler with a special kind of incense. One professorial member of it, whose name I have kept to myself because he later on fully repented, I had encountered a few years earlier in Berlin, where he addressed a small luncheon group. To the great discomfiture of the German who had invited me, the speaker told of a very agreeable visit he had paid to Hitler in Berchtesgaden. He entertained, he added, the greatest respect for the man who had clearly recognized the three evils which beset our world—Judaism, Bolshevism and Catholicism. But there were also Christians in number who for a variety of reasons subscribed to the Protocols of the Fathers of Zion, that strange forgery which proclaimed that Communism had been devised by Jews so that they could conquer the world. Others were merely emotional. When my wife and I were in Europe during 1937 and 1938, we rented our house in a small Connecticut town to a reputable and sedate young Jewish merchant. When we returned, we found the sidewalk painted with swastikas and Heil Hitlers, put there not by some German-American crank but by a quite indigenous New Englander who considered it a disgrace to have a Jew living in his neighborhood.

Just as Alvin Johnson had unfurled a flag for German freedom undermined by Adolph Hitler, so also was he one of the first to welcome intellectual exiles from Italy, some of whom I also came to number among my friends. Max Ascoli, fiery, ingenious, righteous, went from the New School to found and edit

The Reporter. But it was Count Carlo Sforza who probably loomed largest on my horizon, if I except the great founder of the Christian Democratic Movement in Italy, the unforgettable Luigi Sturzo. Both were associated as contributors with *The Commonweal*, and some of the best pieces we published about European affairs were written by the Count, who unquestionably would have been one of the most eminent statesmen of his country had it not been for Mussolini's triumph. Sforza was anticlerical but in his own way. After the signing of the Lateran Treaty in 1929, which ended the conflict between the Vatican and the Italian State, I was one of three panelists assembled in Buffalo by the Foreign Policy Association to discuss the issue. Another was Sforza and the third happened to be a fairly uncompromising foe of the Church of Rome and all its pomps. For a moment I fancied that my lot would be a difficult one. But it was hardly possible for me to get a word in edgewise. After our colleague spoke, Sforza bristled with several kinds of indignation; and though he did not desist from attacking the Treaty, he made so eloquent a defense of the Catholic contribution to Italy's prestige and welfare that Dante himself could hardly have ridden to battle with greater zest.

Finally the hour struck, alas, when France in turn would lie prostrate; and once again it was Alvin Johnson who made room for noble intellectuals from that country and gave them a home. The French University-in-Exile which grew out of the initiative he took was never large and influential enough, perhaps, to justify being christened so glamorously. But in my judgment it remains, despite all the other good deeds done, the most signal contribution made in our time to Franco-American amity and understanding. To house under a hospitable roof men as distinguished as Focillon, Maritain, Laugier and others was to have more than a symbol of France beside one's heartfire. It was to possess a vial of its most precious essence to mete out drop by precious drop in a dark time. This achievement was from my personal point of view just another but possibly specially stirring act of lighting up the scene which came from the heart and conscience of a great American. Dr. Johnson never made anyone feel humble in his presence, for he was far too droll, too slow of speech, in a certain amiable sense too down at the heels for that. But it is not at all strange that the farther away from him one went the shorter also the distance became between him and that eminence scholarship can claim when it is associated with the love of justice and a genuine goodness.

In this work Hunter was to have its part, particularly perhaps by reason of its great hall. We have known our professors in exile too, good men, but of them I shall not speak here because a book like this cannot be the roster of a Faculty. Memorable indeed were the lectures by Thomas Mann which crowded the hall to its rafters, though the discourse was in German delicate of nuance and elaborate in the phrasing. It was thus I came to know rather well a writer who was perhaps as thoroughly, representatively German as anyone could well be. In his written work he was all artist, but when one actually confronted him in person he was oddly prosaic, putting one of the feet of his mind before the other with the precision characteristic of a rather provincial Hanseatic town like his native Luebeck, quite ready to talk about anybody and anything with candor mingled with curious but I always thought delightful prejudices. I shall confess that his family, exception having duly been made for the exquisite and brilliant daughter who became the wife of Professor Borghese, seemed to me to drape his melodic line with a variety of dissonances, but possibly that is what the line required.

Thomas Mann had entered the United States very quietly. He loved to tell how upon his arrival he had received a letter inviting him to address the Elizabethan Club at Yale University. Fancying that thus a great seat of learning had extended a cordial welcome, he accepted, made the journey to New Haven, and found himself being greeted not by the President flanked by senior professors, but by two undergraduates in casual attire who took him to lunch at a place they affectionately referred to as Morey's. This reeked with tobacco smoke, the aroma of beer, the clatter of dishes, and the brisk chatter of collegians. It was a bit as if Tennyson, thinking himself invited to the Académie Française, had discovered instead that he was the guest of young poets in a bistro on the Left Bank. The subsequent lecture was also a model of informality. But for all that Mann enjoyed his modest introduction to American intellectual life and was wont to speak of it with benevolent malice. Most of his later life was spent in an atmosphere of adulation which ought to have turned anyone's head, but he was like Goethe insofar as he did not permit it to make him feel he had been seated on a pedestal—at least not on one more than a few inches high.

Like most authors, he wanted above all to be read by people who could understand what he was saying, and by others if that ideal was not attainable. His ventures into political commentary cannot, it seems to me, be understood if one does not recognize the extent to which he had identified himself with his German audience and with the roots of thought and feeling from which its outlook sprang. During the First World War he was as ardent a patriot as the Fatherland knew and made a spirited defense of its viewpoint. It likewise took him some time to grasp the meaning of Naziism (in which, of course, he was not alone), probably because he could not believe that this deformation of the German character would be dominant for any length of time. Then, just prior to the outbreak of the Second War, Dorothy Thompson persuaded him to direct an appeal to the writers and artists of the world for a clear, unified repudiation of Hitler. This I had the privilege of translating into English. The response was lukewarm and indeed sometimes hostile. A large number of the confraternity then considered Naziism a purely political question into the discussion of which they did not wish to be drawn.

When the conflict was over, Mann embarked on that odd campaign for friendship with Russia which cast a shadow on his final days in the United States and for a time deprived him of influence in his native country. Acting in behalf of a group of intellectuals, I had urged him to throw his strength fully to the side of the West, but instead he accepted an invitation to speak in Weimar under Communist auspices, without seemingly bothering about inquiring into the notorious concentration camp at Buchenwald, just a few miles away, where a new totalitarianism was flailing about as cruelly as had the one it supplanted. To many the action seemed callous and unperceptive; but in extenuation it should be said that Mann simply could not conceive of a permanent division of Germany and that he no doubt wished, through a symbolic gesture, to usher in hope for the future.

One of the last letters I had from him was characteristic and very moving. He had gone back to his native city and learned that its beautiful ancient cathedral, having suffered grievous war damage, would have to be restored quickly if it was not to fall into utter ruin. Thereupon he had given the royalties which had accumulated, in Germany, to the cause and was eager to know if assistance could be obtained in the United States. At any rate, his work is proof against the emotions aroused by Naziism and war. With its virtues and faults, it is the most effective expression of Germany as it was in essence in our time.

Heinrich Bruening, ill-starred former Chancellor of Germany in Weimar Republic days, lectured at Hunter once to a large audience, but his scrupulous avoidance of the political situation he had left behind in Europe disappointed most of those who came. It has lately become the fashion to deny stature to the man who in 1931 was almost single-handedly trying to ward off disaster. This verdict has, however, recently been submitted to scrutiny by John W. Wheeler-Bennett in *The Nemesis of Power*, unquestionably that British historian's most significant book. Certainly Dr. Bruening was a public servant of great intelligence and nobility of character, who stood as firmly for human decency and the cause of peace as any man of his time. I think historians may well decide that the remedies he proposed for the ills which beset his country were too drastic, but desperate ills they were. In Germany, exasperated by a severe depression, the inroads of an inflation carried to utterly fantastic extremes, the spread of Communism, resentment of the Peace Treaty, and constant minor attacks on its dignity, the tide of militant nationalism was foaming to a crest while in Great Britain and France the paralysis of defeatism had set in, undermining readiness for combat even though the façade of preparedness seemed intact.

During a number of years I doubtless saw as much of Dr. Bruening as did any American. We had first met while he was Chancellor; and during the months which followed Hitler's seizure of power I often visited him clandestinely, always aware that, outside, an emissary of the secret police was grimly watching. It was possible to persuade the Oberlaender Trust to offer him money for a trip to the United States. He entered this country incognito, under the name of Harry Anderson, after having effected his escape from Germany just prior to the political murders of the summer of 1934. The stay was relatively brief and proved to be an exciting blend of incognito and discovery. I recall taking him to dinner at the Players' Club, only to have a drama critic who passed our table stop to inquire, "Sir, has anyone ever told you that you look like Dr. Bruening?" "Yes," was the reply, "there seems to be a resemblance!" Then came the night when his presence was discovered by the press; and my poor wife, home alone, was kept up until dawn answering the telephone.

At the time, for reasons of state, it was not thought desirable that Germany's ex-chancellor should emerge as a public figure. But when he returned later, to accept an appointment to the Faculty of Harvard University, he likewise did not speak out strongly in any political sense, did not publish his memoirs, and did not assume the rank which might have been his as a leader of the German Resistance. These failures were often taken amiss. In part his reticence was no doubt due to characteristic shying away from any role that seemed to him journalistic. But it was attributable in large measure to a realistic appraisal of the chances for success of the opposition in Germany, served as this was by not a few of his dearest friends. He considered Dr. Goerdeler, who became the chief civilian conspirator against Hitler, lamentably indiscreet; and from the beginning the only military leader in whom he reposed any confidence was General Kurt von Hammerstein, a general who might indeed have seized and removed the Fuehrer, had it not been for the quite incredible good luck which so consistently smiled on that evil genius. The abortive uprising of July, 1944, cost Bruening very dearly, leading as it did to the execution of several men he considered his closest associates.

He was at the time a resolute, uncompromising German patriot, who avoided as if it were the germ of some bubonic plague any action or statement which might somehow have added to the plight of his friends at home. But that he failed to do whatever he could to uphold their morale or indeed to advance their cause is as remote from the truth as anything could be. Often he remained in touch with them at considerable cost to himself, just as he assisted many a refugee with funds he could ill afford to give. I am sure that, when the full story can some time be told, the cloud which has descended on his name and stature will be dispelled. His greatest fault was an odd tendency to romanticize about the business of soldiering. He had, though physically never very strong, risen in the Imperial Army to the rank of captain and commander of a machine-gun company; and sometimes, listening to him, I fancied that he believed it could have staved off defeat unaided.

During 1938 we were in Europe together attending some clandestine meetings in which Germans participated. One day we sat on the bank of the Rhine in Basel, looking wistfully over at the Baden landscape from whose placid delights we were both at the time barred. Indeed it often seemed that neither of us would ever cross the River again. Then my wife and I drove him to Laon, cathedral city the austere beauty of which he particularly admired. On the way we talked a good deal about the stark and bloody battleground of the Chemin des Dames, where the opposing armies of the First World War so long stood each other off at a fearful cost. We decided to visit the scene. But every trace of the grim encounter had disappeared save one battered and decrepit road sign, left over from war days. We could find no resident of the area who had the foggiest notion of the whereabouts of the Chemin des Dames. After having vainly trudged about trying to reconstruct the landscape, we gave up and returned to the car. This had been registered in Poland, since we had landed in Gydnia, and bore on a rather large license plate the initials PR. As we started up, French lads on bicycles followed us shouting, "*A bas, les Prusses!*" (Down with the Prussians!) No bleaker finale to an old soldier's dream could, I think, be devised.

During the course of the inevitable trek of Naziism to War, Dr. Bruening had not infrequently been asked for his opinion and advice, in Great Britain as well as in the United States, and among those with whom he conversed was President Roosevelt.

But as the conflict dragged on, the President became more and more violent in his antipathy to all things German, while Bruening grew steadily more bitterly critical of what was being done in Washington. Indeed his hostility seemed upon occasion almost an obsession. This eventually led to a cooling of his relationships with my family. But I none the less continue to be quite certain that, however different the part he could have played in the post-War era had he wished it so, he deserves to be remembered as a man of sterling nobility.

We did not quite succeed in having Dr. Adenauer speak in the great hall, because at the last moment his plans had to be changed. But there is a story about one of his visits to the United States which I think deserves to be told because it lights up an aspect of his character too frequently ignored. He was staying at the Greenwich home of David Heinemann, the engineer; and for the guests Rudolph Serkin played Schumann so delightfully and brilliantly that one thought of music in the old days of princely houses. There was present that evening a somewhat talkative photographer, an acquaintance of ours, whose wife had died shortly before after a long and painful illness. As he busily snapped pictures, he engaged the Chancellor in conversation on this mournful theme. "The thing for you to do, my friend," said Dr. Adenauer, "is to marry again. Indeed, I know the very woman for you. She has recently come to the United States, and I will send you her name and address." And shortly thereafter the promise was kept. The photographer's curiosity was aroused, he got in touch with the lady, and was triumphantly married in a remarkably short span of time.

I had my first opportunity to meet Adenauer during the early thirties when he was the tireless and imaginative Mayor of Cologne. A German Herr Oberbuergermeister was then a very impressive blend of city manager and statesman whose position was so important from a number of points of view that a man seldom moved from it to a political post, though the attempt to pry one loose was often made. Indeed, history might well have been different if in 1932 Von Hindenburg had followed Bruening's suggestion that he be succeeded by Karl Goerdeler, then Mayor of Leipzig, and later on, spearhead of the attempt to supplant Hitler as well as one of his victims. In his spare time Adenauer was a very active member of a group which was then trying to lay a foundation for Franco-German understanding. Thus he was, though I did not know it at the time, already working for what would later be a functioning community of West European peoples built on solid friendship between Paris and Bonn.

Then Hitler came, Adenauer was of course ousted, and a long period of durance began. The former mayor was in and out of jail, but for the most part was confined to the house he had built on top of a steep hill across the Rhine from Bonn. It enjoyed a good view but by 1938, when I saw him again, the trees and shrubs he had planted gave it above all an air of seclusion.

We were in Holland during the summer of that year and attended a conference on social problems to which some German guests had also been invited. It was a meeting the prelude to which was relatively amusing, though the aftermath turned out to be far more venturesome than I had surmised. In order to shield the Germans from contagion by a "bad" American, I was registered as Dr. Sutorius, which is of course the Latin form of my name. It had been suggested that we stay in a pleasant little town not far from the place of meeting. But not one of its dozen hotels had either a reservation for us or a room. Finally, I asked why so many people were staying there. The hotel clerk in question drew himself up to his full height and replied, "Sir, this is Holland's mountain resort!" I went out and was overawed to find that the town actually stood on a little plateau about a hundred feet or so higher than the surrounding plain. It became apparent once more that all things human are relative.

During the three days of meetings, one of the German guests virtually challenged me to come to Cologne for a few days in order to meet friends who belonged to the German underground. But how carry out such a feat? I had had a transit visa but this had expired and the likelihood of being able to get another in Holland, where I was at the time well known, was so slight that there was no point in considering it. Finally my prospective host decided that I should go part way on a train which Dutch workers packed on a daily trek across the border, and which was seldom if ever controlled by the customs police. If the worst came to the worst, I could fall back on my expired visa and pretend not to have noticed the passing of time.

All went well. I rode the crowded train to Muenchen-Gladbach, and there suddenly met my German friend with feigned surprise at seeing him again after many years. On to Cologne we drove in an Opel and entered a large house where, unbeknown to the police, I was to spend a few of the most interesting days of my life. Person after person came by day or night, notes and experiences were exchanged, and I could piece together a picture of what was building up inside Germany in terms of potential resistance. Had any one of those who came been caught talking with me, off to a concentration camp he would assuredly have gone. Today at horrible moments my blood still freezes when I recall that only a few of those who came to that house escaped the executioner after the attempt on Hitler's life failed in 1944.

The climax of the visit was a nighttime call on Dr. Adenauer. Three of us went by car to Bonn, which was having its first blackout on that night (the Nazis were already preparing for the worst), and drove thence shortly after midnight to a maternity hospital across the river where, the chauffeur was told, one of my companions was to visit his wife who had suddenly been taken ill. We left by the rear door and trudged through the darkness until I was asked to follow over a fence and then go on hands and knees up the steep hill through a maze of trees and bushes. One of these last was, I cannot for ample reasons forget, very thorny indeed. Then we saw the lights of the house. Adenauer received us in his living room with great cordiality, though the hour was then past one. Again there was conversation, for the purpose of informing me what the situation in Germany was actually like, and what could in strict confidence be said about the plans of the opposition. Two hours later, we crawled down the hill again, went back through the hospital, got into the car and returned to Cologne. There the dawn greeted us.

A few hours later I was off again to Muenchen-Gladbach to catch a similar train which was taking German workers across the Dutch border. In an old bag on the rack above the wooden seat were documents which I was expected to give to designated persons. Having provided myself with a Dutch newspaper which I could read only with extreme difficulty, I thought my pose would deflect attention. But suddenly I heard a harsh voice say, "Secret police. Show your passports!" In five minutes or so he would have reached me, and the border was still a few miles away. It now dawned on me that I was in quite a fix. For how could I explain getting into Germany, and where had I been? Why on earth could I not have thought of these things before? The green-coated policeman was now standing over me. I looked up and pretended not to understand a word of German. First I got down the bag and proceeded to fumble about for a key. Then I got out my wallet and displayed a few guilders and a pound note. His impatience waxed steadily and my inability to understand what he was saying got on his nerves. But since all he knew how to do was keep on saying, "*Geheime Polizei. Paesse bitte!*" little progress was made towards mutual understanding. Then I looked out the window and saw that we were across the border and pulling into Venlo station. My wife was waiting there, as it turned out she had been during an agonizing hour; and I shall confess that I had never been happier to see her in my life. Later on I would ask myself why I had risked such a trip, but at least it gave me one last chance to meet with brave men.

Though I have been privileged on some occasions to discuss affairs of state with Dr. Adenauer, my most precious recollections antedate his rise to political power. Arriving in Cologne on a military mission during July of 1945, I paid my respects to the British commandant, who was at the time a man of great personal charm and marked efficiency. Then I went to the City Hall, oddly enough ensconced in the only building which stood relatively intact in the midst of a sea of rubble—the former office of a Fire Insurance Company! Dr. Adenauer received me with a cordiality which seemed to indicate that he had practically taken the office in order to extend a friendly welcome to old acquaintances. That night I went to visit him at the apartment he was then occupying in St. Elizabeth's Hospital. My colonel friend and I had taken cans of rations with us, and as a result the nuns prepared as festive a repast as the household had doubtless seen in a long time. Dr. Adenauer's beautiful wife, grave and already stricken, was there. We talked of his plans for the city. It was to be rebuilt in part as a center for the arts. He did not appear to believe that this would be at all difficult, nor had it seemingly occurred to him that he would ever hold any office other than that of Lord Mayor. It was an evening of quiet talk about the past and the future of Germany; and I who had stood with tears in my eyes looking at the ghastly ruins of the city—there was a great hole in the roof of the cathedral, all the windows were gone, and through the space where the door had once been one saw only a heap of rubble—could scarce believe that a man could be so confident about what the future might bring.

Shortly after my return to the United States in 1945, I received a letter with which Dr. Adenauer enclosed a copy of a lengthy memorandum he had addressed to the British commandant—the successor to the man I had known. It was exceedingly critical of the way things were going. The letter asked me to call this memorandum to the attention of the Government of the United States. This, alas, I could do only in the most perfunctory fashion, since at the time I was so much under fire from a variety of directions that any sound I might have uttered would have been thrice discounted in advance. But the memorandum remains one of my most precious possessions, since it seems to be the only copy still in circulation. The British understandably did not like it, Dr. Adenauer was removed from office, and thereupon the fabulous career of the builder of a great German Party—the Christian Democratic Union—and of the West German Federal Republic began. I often enough think of the disservice I might have done my country if perchance I had been able to persuade some one in Washington to insist that the Mayor of Cologne retain the insignia of his office, no matter what memoranda he might compose.

Many more occasions in Hunter history were associated with the German emigration, some of them moving and even tragic. We opened our doors to Dr. Manfred George and his friends of the *Aufbau*, the newspaper published for Jews to whom German culture remained indispensable. Two occasions seem specially memorable. The first was an invitation extended to the great actor, Alfred Bassermann, to read from the plays of Goethe and Schiller. I shall confess that I looked on this enterprise with some misgivings, for it did not quite seem reasonable to believe that a sizeable audience would assemble. But on the appointed evening the hall was packed, and as the stirring lines of *Egmont* and *Maria Stuart* were read, tears were in hundreds of eyes. So difficult it is to eat the bread of exile, particularly when the reason for enduring that bread was only the weird magic exercised by a little man from Braunau, with a mustache and a diseased brain. The second occasion came later and the audience was smaller. Years ago there was stationed in New York a German Consul General whose name was Karl Kiep. More people liked him than have probably ever been fond of a man in his station. He returned to his native land, took part in the conspiracy against Hitler, and fell a victim to the subsequent purge. I persuaded his wife Hannah to come and talk about the German Resistance. An old friend, Iphigene Sulzberger of the *New York Times*, introduced her. When she had finished, there was not a person who did not sense that he had lived to the full during an inspired hour.

Free France was, in so far as the United States is concerned, almost born in Hunter's great hall. Night after night this was where the flags were unfurled, where the vows were made and the pledges were taken. I sat again and again listening to men whose words came from them in incessant torrents, distilled from agony and remembrance. I shall say no more here than that throughout the time a man whom I have every reason to call my revered friend symbolized the glory and the tragedy of France as no one else could have done. Jacques Maritain has always been for me a person with a halo about his head and a comprehending smile in his eyes. Perhaps I should have been intellectually more hospitable to his philosophy than I actually was, for I am not even now a dedicated neo-Thomist. But there has never been the slightest doubt in my mind that in him our age, so distraught in many ways, has reached a peak of luminousness and integrity.

Although we had first met in New York, our first real confrontation was in Paris, where I was trying to represent the Catholic Bishops of the United States in a study of the German refugee problem. But previously we had discovered a sense of solidarity because our publicly expressed attitudes toward the Franco uprising in Spain were comparable. Maritain, avoiding the bitter indignation of his notable contemporary Georges Bernanos, urged caution in thinking that a new crusade could be undertaken, this time by Moors. My views on the thorny issue, as published in *The Commonweal*, brought down on my head the angriest tirades through which I had until then lived and led indeed to that sharp change in my professional career which brought me to Hunter College. Neither Maritain nor I, it should be quickly added, favored the Loyalist cause. It was clear that this was fanning into a giant conflagration the scattered fires of persecution which the Spanish Republic had been unable to suppress, and that priests and religious would now be hounded with implacable fury. But was it not also apparent that General Franco's mutiny against what was after all his rightfully constituted government bore part of the responsibility for the fact that the issue would now be decided by sanguinary fanaticism? The outcome, I thought, would have to be a further cleavage between the Church and the working classes; and as the struggle progressed it likewise became evident that the Falange would lay a heavy hand on some of the most staunchly Catholic groups in Spain, notably the Basques. Above all it was certain that Franco's action would greatly strengthen Naziism and the movements allied with it and that, as a result, the conflict could not fail to spread throughout the whole of Europe. But there were many who quite understandably did not place the religious struggle in Spain against the larger background. I have never criticized anyone who did not do so; but it is saddening in retrospect to realize how angry and partisan even some of my friends had become. One prelate who had long been rather intimately associated with me said, with a fury he could not restrain, that "Hitler is on your brain," and that this monomania had brought my usefulness to an end.

Jacques Maritain was likewise to find that doors which had

otherwise been open were now closed. Some of them would indeed never open again. But at any rate, we met in Paris. Raissa, Jacques' wife, sensitive, intelligent, spiritual, was then a center around which a world of the intellect moved. Marc Chagall was among the guests in the cheerful suburban house on that sunny afternoon—Chagall, each of whose paintings I have dearly loved and none of which I could ever afford to own. Thus there was formed an association which would mean very much during all my years at Hunter. It began with the gracious address with which Maritain honored my inauguration; and it ended with the research professorship which friends established for him at the college. This brought him to Hunter several times during each semester for lectures, usually dealing with philosophy but once at least, and very memorably, with the cultural life of the United States. Thus we were given not only glimpses of work in progress but above all the presence of a great and good friend, frail in his old age but radiant also and, in an unmistakable way, holy. Still he was never without a bit of the spice of that malice about human things which is always a part of the treasure of the French genius.

No one will expect that I should try to give, in a few words, a convincing indication of the reasons why Maritain has been so greatly esteemed among us. His philosophy, which is above all an attempt to use the method of Aquinas in the discussion of problems which concern the modern time, follows that method with fidelity and yet also with an imagination not hidebound by literalism. For Maritain as for his mediaeval master, philosophy is the "servant of theology" but never the slave. It has its own status and freedom. For all that, I have never believed that Maritain the philosopher is the image we conjure up in the first instance. Rather we think of him as the layman who more than any other has represented all aspects of the life of the Catholic Church in our time. He has understood and reverenced the mystics, being in that sense as much concerned with the "basic reality," the *Urgrund*, as any Existentialist. To the problem of knowledge he has devoted one of his best books. There is a whole shelf of essays dealing with aesthetics, poetry in particular. Finally, there is a long list of books which discuss problems of social ethics—the nature of human society, the authority of the state, war and peace, cultural pluralism, the totalitarian challenge. If ever a Catholic has endeavored to live intelligently but always daringly, unselfishly, in the modern world, Jacques Maritain is that one.

No doubt he would not have been so greatly beloved if he had not also been human, however completely emancipated from the baser urges of the time. I who am in essence a German and therefore made of grosser fibre to which the smell of the field clings, can therefore sense the quality of his personality with a certain awe, even as a man living close to nature may discern the verve of a disciplined prince. Once when I visited him in Rome, where he was then the French Ambassador to the Vatican, I was amused by the quite frankly amorous frescoes in the waiting room of the old palace in which he lived. I ventured to jest with him about them, but he smiled and said, "In this place I always walk about with my eyes modestly cast down." But for all that, one could be certain that he was fully aware of the quality, or lack of it, in every painting in that weirdly grandiose domicile without for a moment having been affected in the least by what was wanton in them. From a totally different point of view, he was well insulated against what is menial in life by the sister-in-law who served so long as the Martha in his household. To this straightforward, noble and unselfish woman all of us who cherish the work of Jacques Maritain owe a great debt. One could but hope that she would continue to care for him always. Once when he came to the college he was suddenly taken ill and could not lecture. Having seen that he was put to bed, I went to tell the audience and was so overcome by the thought of what would be gone from the world when he was no longer there that words all but failed me completely. Later on, after a long and harrowing illness, she died; and it was quite as if a pillar had been taken away from the building of his life. Age cannot wither the spirit of a man like Jacques Maritain, but the penalties it exacts are grievous, in lopping off the friendly branches on which the spirit has rested during stormy and fair days.

How heavy the burden was to be became apparent only during

the long last illness of his wife, Raissa. Together they had gone back to France for the summer. But in Paris she was stricken; and during many months she lay without the power to utter a word or give a sign. So long was this illness and so harrowing her plight that the great old man was distraught. The letters which came from him were brief and terribly poignant. But in my view this long silence into which Raissa's spirit was dropped as into a great plummetless sea had a strange, almost eerie mystical significance. Like other great women who were converts to Christianity from Judaism—Simone Weil and Edith Stein among them—Raissa had experienced the terrible persecution launched by Hitler in a way which was not that of the world generally. It was a repudiation of what was most Christ-like in Christ—not His humanity merely but His transcendence also. The Beatitudes which he had added to Jewish tradition—the meekness and the love of mercy, the love of justice which could never be hatred—were for the warlike Nazi leaders major reasons for treading the Jew under foot. In their eyes, as they prepared to trample over peoples and subject them to a planned rôle as menials, there could be no room for a creed which held all these things in abhorrence.

Was not the silence of Raissa a mirror of the doom of silence which had been meted out to millions of men, women and children in the dreadful slaughter camps? May one not see in it a kind of participation in their martyrdom—one of those strange and dreadful boons given to a soul not for its own cleansing merely but for that of mankind as well? At any rate, when I came to Paris and learned that she had died, I summoned up in my mind the mysterious history of the women referred to, in which Raissa had the last and, in some ways, the most tormented place. And it seemed to me that some time a young man or woman might wish to write a book about it, which would not be history so much as an evocation of the evil our time has seen —the truly ominous evil. But for Jacques life had now come to another place. Henceforth he would devote his last years to working with the Petits Frères, a new religious organization that would seek to serve the poor of France.

Hunter's relations with France reached a kind of dramatic climax when Georges Bidault, then Premier, came to New York. At first it seemed that Jacob Greenberg of the Board of Education and I were only to arrange a small reception at which the cross of the Legion of Honor would be conferred on the State Commissioner of Education. What more convenient site than Hunter could be found? But within a few weeks the affair had expanded like an atomic cloud at Bikini, until it was announced that Premier Bidault wished to make a major policy statement in the great hall. The guests now included all the dignitaries of New York, with Cardinal Spellman and the French Ambassador leading the procession. The time happened to be one in which Governor Thomas E. Dewey and Mayor Vincent Impellitteri were feuding, and it was necessary to arrange to have them in separate rooms. I succumbed to a mild version of dual personality shuffling from one to the other. But in the end everything went off well, though I fear that the audience focussed its attention on Madame Bidault, whose great beauty was more dazzling than her husband's oratory. And that, after all, was meet and proper in a college for women. Later on, when I glanced at the guestbook, one of the names inscribed was that of Pére Teilhard de Chardin, the great archeologist who was surely one of the seminal minds of his time. Possibly it was his modest, undemonstrative presence which most made that occasion memorable.

One other meeting with Mr. Dewey remains unforgettable. Henry Luce gave a dinner in honor of Winston Churchill, who had just come from Fulton, Missouri, after the grave speech in which he threw down the West's first great challenge to Stalin. As a result, a highly professional Communist picket line, well supplied with posters and chanted imprecations, had been thrown round the hotel; and it is interesting to recall that it drew not so much as an additional scowl from the intended victim. Since he had just before gone down to political defeat, there was a certain aptness in the fact that Dewey, who some weeks earlier had quite unexpectedly been nudged out of the White House by Harry Truman, was chosen to deliver the address of welcome. This was not one of his best efforts, for such a situation required a special kind of good-humored wit which was not native to him. When the affair was over and the guests were leaving, Dewey was left standing entirely alone; and so by reason of an urge in the making of which political sentiment assuredly had no part, I went up to say a word of appreciation to him. Never, perhaps, have I seen the ancient maxim that the glory of the world passes like a cloud spelled out in more Hogarthian terms. Just a handful of days earlier millions of people had acclaimed him as certain to be elected to the Presidency. And now it was quite as if he were a hardly recognizable remnant of the past, taking his place beside the shades that had been Wolsey and Chamberlain.

For the Austrians Hunter also had a warm place in its heart, in part because some members of the Faculty cherished intimate associations with the land of which Vienna is the glorious crown, and in part no doubt because of my own love for it. Vienna was, indeed, our most cherished city. And so it was natural that we should have worked there during the whole of the winter of 1937-1938, reading masses of material about the background of Naziism and the fatal weaknesses of German democracy. It was then impossible for me to go to Germany; and since also many of the pertinent documents had been destroyed at Goebbels' behest it was to the Viennese libraries and archives that we turned.

But the capital was from every other point of view a sorely troubled place. Kurt von Schuschnigg, a good and intelligent man though possibly more of a dabbler in the arts than he was a statesman, was holding his quasi-dictorial party government together under what were assumed to be the powerful and benevolent auspices of Mussolini. Unfortunately few then realized how thin the wall of Italian military strength really was. The Social Democrats for their part were in silent and sombre suppressed opposition—a fearfully stupid situation for a country to be in which was so manifestly living under a constant threat. Both sides were no doubt in a measure responsible and it is not for me to assess the blame. Austria also had its special variety of intellectuals, among them the then famous Othmar Spann, who believed that every idea about the structure of human society he deduced from premises peculiar to himself, was destined to become the magna charta of a new and more glorious time. Ideological battle lines were tautly drawn. Night after night a fearless German Jesuit, Friedrich Muckermann, used his extraordinary oratorical powers to persuade thousands of the evils of Naziism. At the same time, however, it became increasingly evident that youth groups in the secondary schools and colleges were badly infected. The spiritual soil on which the rising generations stood was being steadily eroded. Staunchly conservative, freedom-loving fathers would note with a helpless sigh that even their sons and daughters were eyeing the Nazi pageant across the border with envy. Meanwhile the opera houses, theaters and concert halls were scenes of performances which had never been more brilliant. On another level, masses of people would crowd the streets for miles to watch a favorite movie star ride to the Hotel Bristol. Viennese Jewry, which then constituted a sizeable percentage of the population, lived in a constant state of febrile excitement, veering as it did from breezy confidence in the way things were going to a quite overpowering sense of doom waiting just around the corner.

Then in rapid succession came the events which ushered in the end of Austrian independence and, with that, the beginning of the Second World War: Hitler's summons to Schuschnigg to attend a conference in Berchtesgaden; the admission of avowed Nazis into the Austrian government; the appeal to the Austrian people to support national freedom in a plebiscite organized in frenzied haste; and the march of German troops into what during the seven years to follow would be called the *Ostgau*. All the while we were living in the apartment of a distinguished physician who had accepted an invitation from King Zog to supervise the installation of hygenic improvements in Albania. The house was old fashioned and stood under *Denkmalschutz*. That is, since it had been built during the glorious days of the baroque culture, it could not suffer so much as a change of one stone without the permission of the government. We were bequeathed an adequate supply of porcelain stoves, a series of strange convolutions for the heating of water, and a kitchen no doubt contemporary with the time when the news that Benjamin Franklin had invented the iron stove reached Europe. There were also four bottles of Scotch which we scrupulously avoided imbibing, thus meriting some special kind of award. But there were two notable treasures which seldom fall to the lot of wayfarers. The first was a priceless jewel of a cook, who had served prelates, ambassadors and others in the days of Emperor Franz Joseph and was now, her latest employer having migrated to alien parts, willing to assume that we were of the vintage to which she was accustomed. The only drawback (if indeed it can be called one) was that her fame had spread far and wide, so that persons of rank and station happened to arrive to see us at luncheon time and were as a matter of course asked to stay. In this manner we met poets and diplomats, politicians and journalists, artists and professors, who would otherwise have remained outside our ken. That apartment had what was in view of the time a more precarious advantage. Our living room had served as a doctor's library and consultation room. It was lined with books which, I discovered to my great chagrin, dealt exclusively with the liver, an organ which at the time gave me no special trouble. The room was also soundproof, so that persons of some eminence who did not wish to be overheard begged leave to converse in it. For these and other reasons we were, despite placid hours in libraries and archives, knee-deep in Austrian political affairs.

My personal contributions to these were two in number, both more than useless. One had in it the semblance of an idea, the other I shall confess now seems a by-product of irrationality. The first suggested a plea to such Austrian officials as I could buttonhole as the sky began to darken, to ship the country's sizeable gold reserves to a foreign country. Oddly enough the little Austrian republic then had larger supplies of these mundane but invaluable commodities than did Germany. Of course nothing came of this sage counsel, and we later on watched the Germans cart off in trucks the treasures of the Laenderbank, just across the street from where we lived. It still seems to me not inconceivable that faced with the prospect of a government-in-exile possessing such a bank account Hitler might have delayed the invasion. But as was so often to be the case, the impact of growing Nazi power on the outwardly and inwardly divided small countries of Europe was like that of a specially glowering tornado. France stood frozen in its tracks while Hitler marched his troops into the Rhineland. Czechoslovakia would surrender without firing a cannon. Hungary took the easy route—or what seemed so at the time—to passive surrender.

During the ominous final hours of the Austrian Republic, one of the most incorrigibly individualistic but still the most courageous of Schuschnigg's colleagues, Ernst Karl Winter, Vice-Mayor of Vienna, drew up a plan of resistance to Naziism. No doubt it was a hopelessly romantic version of possible realities, but at least some kind of action was suggested. Winter believed that as a result of a last minute reconciliation with the Social Democrats, Schuschnigg could mobilize the nation round its solid and dependable small army. The question was, would we make a loan of our Pontiac, believed to offer a measure of camouflage by reason of its American pedigree? Very rashly I agreed and accepted an invitation to go along. Provided with an Austrian chauffeur, we set out to have our first conference in the old town of Steyr with leaders of the Socialist opposition there. Bearing in mind that years had passed without an overture from the Catholic Fatherland Front, the discussion was by no means too acrimonious. When the hour came when it had been announced that Schuschnigg would address the Austrian people, the radio was turned on and we sat listening to the blood-tingling declaration that a plebiscite had been ordered to determine whether the nation wished to remain independent. It was a quixotic proposal which was soon to cost the Chancellor dearly in terms of imprisonment and torment, and which would also raise questions as to whether it had not precipitated the action by Hitler it was designed to forestall. At any rate, the Socialist spokesmen now resignedly declared that it was too late in the day for any thought of resistance, and I was reluctantly compelled to agree with them.

Nevertheless we went on to Linz and thence to Salzburg, where we spent the fateful morning of March 13th talking with a hard-fisted little group of labor leaders in a café up the hill just around the corner from the Hotel Stein. They informed us that Nazis were bubbling over in the old city of Mozart and Rococo, but that if there were any prospect of effective resistance they would join. We drove off across the mountains to

Graz. There was still much snow on the ground, and into it planes dropped leaflets urging citizens to vote. We reached our destination just after darkness had settled down, to find the city in a state of tumultuous uproar. Nazi banners and flags were flying everywhere, the crowd was dense, youngsters clustered round the car and daubed it with swastikas etched out with soap. When we finally reached the hotel, the porter informed me that Hitler had just arrived in Linz. I told him that it would therefore be necessary for me, as an American journalist, to leave forthwith. With my distraught companions, I set out for Vienna. At every few kilometers along the route, boys who could not have been more than fifteen or sixteen had formed barricades. They were armed with rifles and bayonets, indicating not merely the grip Naziism had on youth but also the dimensions of the illegal arsenal. Finally we reached Vienna. The Kaertnerstrasse, thoroughfare of fashionable shops, was already a shambles, but I reached our apartment and fell into the arms of my wife, who had witnessed the frenzied taking over of the city by the Austrian Nazis—worse just then than their German counterparts.

We had never before grasped the meaning of hatred, and above all had never realized the possible intensity of racial prejudice. For us too, who had always been friendly to the Negro but had nevertheless taken white superiority for granted, the three following days of tumult were above all days of soul searching. My wife and I considered ourselves tolerant. But we knew now that in our spirits there were residual places where race feeling was still very much alive; and looking about us in Vienna, where a trumped up commitment to biological supremacy was staging orgies of cruelty and venom, we saw clearly that the roots of the disease must be stamped out in ourselves, that we must henceforth differentiate between man and man not on the basis of color or any other physical characteristics but simply in accordance with individual worth. Up until this time, I shall confess, I had, despite all my experience in Germany, felt there was something ridiculous and unreal about Hitler's theories. But here in these old streets they were being spelled out in terms of naked horror.

We saw people drive knives to their hearts in those streets. Women were dragged along by the hair. The looting of Jewish shops ended with the crashing sounds of breaking furniture and fixtures. In the first couple of days 35,000 people were taken off to prisons and concentration camps. Others managed fantastic escapes, and some leaped to their deaths from windows. At the end of the time of visitation we had scarce a friend left. But I suppose that what most affected me was the slow moving out of history of everything that was gay, gracious and warmly human in the legacy of Habsburg culture. The bells of St. Stephen's Cathedral rang a welcome to Hitler and Himmler—to me a terrifying sacrilege, against which I later protested in Rome only to learn that there too it had been found so shocking that on the insistence of the future Pope Pius XII it was denounced over the Vatican Radio. We had been accustomed to going to Mass on Sundays at the Hofkapelle, where the famous Wiener Saengerknaben sang. But on this Sunday there was no choir. It had been forbidden. Outside, at the entrance to the palace, there had always been a tiny shrine of the Virgin where a candle burned. But now instead there was a picture of Hitler.

We harbored a few people for a while, until they could somehow manage to disappear. And then we packed our belongings and drove off to Prague, and later by a circuitous route to Italy. But the days were long enough to witness the pageant of the march of the Germans into Austria. First came Himmler, to set up the offices of the Gestapo and the SS—a curiously schoolmasterly figure in uniform, suggesting nothing so much as a cheap villain in a play about damsels tied to railroad tracks. Then Hitler arrived, to speak gloatingly to a vast throng from a hotel balcony. Slowly, efficiently the German army arrived, following a squadron or two of ominous black planes which swooped down over the city. There were battalions of quiet, ruddy, efficient young men whose conduct was above reproach. I never think of them without realizing that during the few years that were to follow most, who came so jauntily into Vienna, were to die on Russian battlefields or in Siberian prison camps. And finally there were buses, seemingly in endless array, filled with young girls mustered into the Nazi youth movement. They were blond and amiable as they piled into the square round the Votivkirche, belying all one had seen in the streets.

These experiences had a sequel which may shed some light on the mood of the time. I came to London in due course and was invited to address a quite exclusive group, which met regularly for luncheon at the Savoy, on the subject of Hitler's seizure of Austria. My description of what took place evoked some comment, and I was asked what conclusions were to be derived from the event. I said that in my opinion the only thing which could be done to prevent the outbreak of war was to introduce conscription immediately in Great Britain, and added of course that I fully understood the difficulties which stood in the way. Quite a furor resulted. Among the guests were some of Britain's leading bankers and business men. They assured the audience that there was nothing whatever to fear from the Nazis. The condition of the German economy was held to be highly unsatisfactory: one member of the group reported having been in Hamburg where he had noted that among the motley population which served the city's docks there was no one who smiled. How could a nation in that kind of psychological state be asked to fight a war? The verdict, insofar as my suggestion was concerned, was overwhelmingly negative.

It reminded me not a little of a journey made to London some years earlier. We were in Germany during 1933 as a result of a comfortable study grant made by the Oberlaender Trust, and the impressions gleaned were included in a book, *Strong Man Rules*, which was the first appraisal of Naziism to be published in the United States. A code of race legislation was promulgated at Nuremberg, in conjunction with the Party's earliest great jamboree which brought thousands upon thousands of Brown Shirts and Black Shirts to the then fabulous medieval core of that city. (Incidentally an incident took place there which greatly interested me. A tall pillar had been erected in the square in front of the Church of St. Sebald, and to the top of this there led a ladder. On the appointed day, Hitler climbed up and talked down to his faithful. But some twenty years earlier, a similar pillar with a comparable ladder greeted the German Navy at Kiel when it assembled to hear a speech by Wilhelm II. He too climbed up and delivered his harangue. Only then the Navy thought it rather funny). I thereupon journeyed to London at my own expense in the hope of inducing a segment of the British press to start a campaign against the Race Laws. At that time what was said in English newspapers and periodicals had a good deal of influence in Germany. But, alas, the only editor I could interest was Father Joseph Keating, S.J., who presided over the destinies of a small monthly periodical, alas without influence on any but a handful of scholarly readers.

It was therefore wholly out of the question that we should forget Austria and its people once our European adventures were over and life at Hunter had begun. The Austrian-American Friendship Association, in the activities of which a great variety of people joined, moved for a time round the person of the Archduke Otto. I had first met him during the course of studying the refugee situation, and had driven out to Steenockerzell, the Belgian castle in which he and his mother, the Empress Zita, were living at the time. It was never possible for me to believe that restoring the Habsburgs was a practical enterprise, but it was nevertheless a fact that if you were going to have an Emperor you would have been hard pressed to find a more appealing one. Otto was a young man of great charm and very considerable intelligence, whose optimistic estimates of the opportunity before him were not without a measure of political good sense. The Crown of St. Stephen, Hungary's greatest treasure, had not been left with his father by reason of an Allied fiat at the close of the First World War; and Admiral Horthy had in a sense been its custodian, presumably until such time as the situation would change. If one supposed that after Hitler's defeat a decision was reached not to place Hungary in peril of Russian domination, why might it not mean a restoration of the Monarchy? And if there were a Habsburg on a Budapest throne, why not, if the Austrian people willed it so, in Vienna also?

In the end nothing came of the dream, but for a time it captivated not a few Americans. As always the realists had their way. Communism was bound to be so powerful in Eastern Europe that few really thought it could be staved off save with defenses on paper, such as peace treaties which carefully but futilely de-

limited Russian rights and powers. It was Tito who triumphed
in Yugoslavia and not the King. Hungary was slowly forced to
groan under the Communist yoke and finally to try to throw it
off in an hour of heroic frenzy. And Austria, after having lived
for years under a four-pronged occupying power, had the unparalleled good fortune of watching the Russian troops depart.
But of these things the Association had no premonition. The
meetings were repudiations of Naziism and nostalgic evocations
of Austrian culture. Some of them were very moving and, thank
Heaven, never bogged down in singing ditties about guzzling in
Grinzing. Nor did anyone talk about *schlagobers* and *schnitzels*,
or try to bootleg a waltz by Johann Strauss. And yet it does not
seem to me that we were too solemn. The mood appears to have
been one of Mozart, rather than of Mahler.

Perhaps the most memorable of our constant non-Austrian
guests was Sigrid Undset. We could not think of her apart from
the background of the great novels which had become a portion
of the world's literary patrimony. Yet she sat among us being as
enigmatic a person as ever loomed up in the sagas of her native
land. Having emerged from a spare little flat she occupied somewhere in the mazes of Brooklyn, she never spoke more than a
few words to anybody and kept doggedly on, when circumstances permitted, smoking cigarettes in formidable series. Having been deeply impressed by the little book in which she had
described her flight from Norway through Russia and Japan to
the United States—a book in which the contours, sounds, odors,
movements and domesticities of Moscow and Tokyo are set forth
with incredibly evocative realism—I never got over the uncomfortable feeling that this all-seeing, all recording woman, in whom
volcanoes of emotion were buried under a sheath of ice, was
noting every movement we made and every word we uttered, so
that we might emerge some time in a book not as wraiths which
had passed, but in all our real curves and angles, with not a wart
missing or a bald spot undetected.

In many ways, however, the most glorious Austrian day in the
annals of the great hall was that on which Dr. Leopold Figl,
then Prime Minister of Austria, made to a large audience the
first presentation of the spirit and purpose of the new Republic.

How could I forget the occasions on which I had conversed with this remarkably simple but gifted and straightforward man, whom Dolfuss had failed to recruit inwardly for his ideas of the corporate state, while the situation grew ominously darker. For him of course the coming of Hitler would mean years of duress in concentration camps. Yet these did not crush his spirit but enriched it instead with that deep awareness of the nobility as well as the tragedy of mankind which, to my surprise and awe, I was sometimes to find had been the legacy of Dachau and Buchenwald. Figl never learned how to pose for a moment as a victim or survivor. He went on being what he had always been, as the best of Austrians are, good-humored and matter-of-fact, doing his level best to piece together the details out of which the new Austria was to be built. It was an unexpected, unmerited but deeply cherished moment when, on a subsequent visit to this country, he conferred on me the Great Gold Medal of Honor of the Austrian Republic.

Nor can I forget, though her association is less with the great hall than with smaller spatial areas in the College, the untiring courtesy and affection of Frederike Maria Zweig, for so many years the wife of Stefan and the unselfish guardian of his spirit. For all of us who have been privileged to know her she has been an unfailing guide to the spirit of Austria, from the *Zwetschgenkrampus* to the nave of the Abbey Church of St. Florian, so dear to Bruckner, from Vienna's memories of Beethoven to its satisfaction in the flowering of literary genius. The rhythm of Austrian intellectual and cultural life, which was so constant that one was almost led to think that the coming and going of the Habsburgs was only counterpoint, one could learn from her if from anybody, perhaps but by no means wholly because an unfailing ear for that rhythm had been Stefan Zweig's precious secret. The *Zwetschgenkrampus* may need a bit of gloss. One afternoon in Stamford, while Mrs. Zweig was busily directing the activities of a conference organized by American-European Friendship, which she had helped to bring into being in order to assist European newcomers to our shores to find a richer life in the United States, I met her coming down a garden path and muttering the strange word to herself in a tone indicating profound disapproval. She was, I learned subsequently, applying it to a little professor who had in her judgment proved to be a nuisance of extraordinary dimensions. The term was, I shall confess, appropriate in the circumstances. It describes a dwarfish clown, fashioned of dried plums or raisins on a string, which half amuses and half frightens Austrian children at St. Nicholas time.

Hunter will likewise treasure its memories of Poland and Hungary. In the commemoration of the always transitory splendor of the first we had our share, as well as in the effort to awaken an interest in Polish culture. It so happens that although in my college days I thought the Polish colonies in Middle Western cities unnecessarily exclusive and hostile (as indeed they were), deep friendships formed brought me to a household where Paderewski was frequently a guest, stroking with debonair good will a piano that was far less well pedigreed than a Steinway. My preparatory school memories also include nothing more exciting, unless it be hulabaloo about championship baseball games between the Giants and the Cubs (neither of whom I had of course come within a hundred miles of seeing), than reading the Polish trilogy of Sienkiewicz; and I firmly believed that Pan Longin, who had cut off three enemy heads at once with his sharp sword, was quite the noblest hero in history. I rated him several notches higher than Odysseus, some of whose adventures I was then fumblingly extricating from the Greek, and whom I found guilty of having taken unchivalrous advantage of the suitors who craved Penelope.

Little did I surmise at the time how poignant the Polish tragedy would come to seem in my own experience. Two trips through Poland, the earlier one taken during the course of making a study of the Eastern boundaries of Germany as created by the Treaty of Versailles and subsequent rulings, and the second a lengthy journey by car from Gydnia through Cracow to Prague, had supplied a measure of insight into a culture which Miekiewicz and Reymont had celebrated in their own ways. It was in very large measure a world of peasants, sometimes quite unbelievably primitive, sad as the landscape which often seemed vistas of trees, fields and animals perennially emerging from mist, and steeped in the mystic pathos of a belief, tinged with messianism, which on the one hand was Catholic, ardently Catholic, and on the other Polish, built on the conviction, sensed rather than formulated, that in the country's future all care would vanish and glory come. Yet Poland was also its old cities where the humanities were taught and loved by some of the ablest scholars of Europe, and where the ease to be taken at inns was extraordinarily satisfying. Everywhere were memories of ancient battles and unhappy things. Here too was a land where, to borrow a poet's line, warriors had gone forth endlessly and had always fallen.

I came to find that deep draughts of the Polish experience thus taken in were enough to kindle an affection which was far more profound than words. And yet it always seemed clear that the country was ruled during that fateful decade of the thirties by the worst possible government. There was nothing noble in its chauvinism, which prevailingly seemed as stupid as it was pretentious. In the Eastern provinces Ukrainians whom heroic military action had prevented the Russians from annexing were subjected to quite intolerable and meaningless indignities; and in the Western ones crafty attacks on German territorial sovereignty, based on flimsy pretexts, could not fail to anger the great nation to the West and so fan the resentment which was one major contributing factor in the making of Naziism. But the government's domestic program was in many ways even worse. It was tyrannical, but in an oddly pompous and ineffectual way. Government buildings were erected as show cases, blending neoclassical architecture with corruption and inefficiency. No social problem was ever solved. And so in the end there was a blundering pact of friendship with Hitler and a stupid reliance on bravery and antiquated armament which set the stage for the tragic downfall and the dreadful years when the flower of Polish manhood was slaughtered by German and Russian as the spirit moved them.

These and many other things were memories, pleasant and bitter alike, when one morning in 1945 on an Army assignment, I was driving with a soldier from Headquarters of the Seventh

Army outside of Naples to Rome. We were approaching what was left of the town of Monte Cassino, below the vast gaping ruins of the Monastery. We had just passed a shack on which there was a sign warning that the water was polluted and before which squatted a boy down whose chin saliva was running, when a man in the uniform of a Polish officer hailed us. We took him in and soon learned that on the heights above were lying nearly all of his comrades of the Polish Brigade—men who somehow picked their way across Rumania and Bulgaria to Greece and thence to the Allied armies in the West, only to die together here in a futile assault on an impregnable position. We glanced with awe at their resting place. Then the man we had befriended said simply and without pathos, "Now that it is all over and we have won the war, there is no place for me to go. Poland is in enemy hands." He did not need more words to describe the tragedy and the irony which have marked his country's history, if not the human past as a whole.

And so we did what we could at Hunter for the saving and healing of the Polish spirit. Doubtless it was far from what it desirably should have been. But the afternoons and evenings on which we came together to hear versions of Polish poets, to listen while men of substance and imaginative gifts spoke, and sometimes for an hour of music, seem to me to keep their small places snugly in the story of a City the destiny of which now and forever is to harbor the flags of all nations affectionately even while bravely unfurling its own. But always the heartache was in the old men and women. Their children and grandchildren, many of them, were at the College hacking their way through the underbrush of learning to a new life in a country they soon proudly called theirs, with only now and then a wistful glance back at the past.

I shall close the roster of the peoples whom the great hall took into its embrace with the bravest and most sorely tried of all, who during twenty-four hours had their share of freedom and renown and then so many, many days and nights of agony. It was not always a homogeneous group of Hungarians who assembled to commemorate the past and to let their hopes rise like a

chorus in an oratorio stranger and more poignant than any
Bartók could have written, for these men and women held many
allegiances in clenched fists and hearts. They were of differing
religions, political persuasions, social backgrounds. The only
song they sang together was one written to freedom, loved with
a passion we Americans have generally forgotten because we
have not needed to let it surge up in us, loved not wisely or too
well but as an untamed man might love the woman of his
dreams. Because Hunter stands just across the Avenue from the
house occupied by the Russian delegation to the United Nations,
the crowd would merge in one long picket line that swept around
the hated house like the curved tongue of a flame in the wind,
powerless to consume anything except its own rage. Night after
night the police formed their blue rows on foot and on horse-
back behind a portable fence set up and taken down again with
the routine patience which is that of the law. It was impossible
not to be moved and awed by the spectacle, by the infinite pity
of it. But what those who joined the picket line, in fair weather
and foul, could hope to accomplish was meager, indeed, granted
the state the world was in.

I was drawn into this cauldron of emotions primarily because
Sheila Cudahy, the publisher, showed up in my office one day
escorting a handsome though reticent Hungarian, Tibor Horanyi,
once a leader of peasant youth in his country. Both of them were
on fire with an idea which had originated in the imaginative mind
of Roger Straus, that a book ought to be written about Cardinal Mindzsenty, primarily just to remind people that he was
still alive and in prison. Would I undertake the task? I thought
of the endless chores which were mine, of the month by the sea
I needed and wanted, and groaned. But Horanyi was advertised
as a veritable geyser of information, and Miss Cudahy vowed
others would supply whatever he could not produce. Never
before had I undertaken to write a book about any experience
not directly my own. But they were both so very pleasant and
the cause was so good that my consent oozed out quite as would
a promise to marry a comely prince from an indifferently fea-
tured damsel. Then the drama of this book which became more
and more a labor of love began. Whenever I wished to know

something about what was happening inside Hungary, this person or that was whisked in and out of the tortured land. Not all of the information they brought was accurate, but it was the best they could supply. The book when it was finished was everything I could make it, but justice was not done the many who had given to it every whit of insight and knowledge they possessed. It appeared just before the uprising, and some one was able to take a copy to the Cardinal prior to his seeking refuge in the Ministry of the United States.

Incidentally one subsequent experience with it left me filled with awe. The book was very widely translated, so that there accumulated versions in strange tongues like Burmese, Vietnamese and Arabic as well as in more familiar ones. Then I began to hear from convents and monasteries in this country and abroad, where it was read aloud at mealtime. The thought that my words were being dinned into the ears of religious almost the free world round for the first time in my sinful life left me quite limply humble. I could not avoid feeling that, if this or that page had been better, the test to which the whole was subjected could have been met more successfully. And yet I must add that much of the comment which came to me as a result was singularly perceptive.

Could the fate of Hungary have been different? All one can say is that its suppression marked sharply the fading out of a conception of policy concerning Eastern Europe to which the United States had up until that time been committed. This had been based on vivid awareness that the "satellite" countries had been jammed into the Soviet vise much against their will and as a result of the violation of post-War agreements to which the Kremlin had solemnly affixed its signature. We assumed that if we could remind them continuously, through Radio Free Europe and other means, that we were aware of their plight, so strong a thirst for liberty would be kept alive that in the long run tyranny would have to grant its hostile permanence. We also banked heavily on the fact that Stalin was mortal. But if we meant all this in terms of a practical program, surely we would try to handle matters so that in the event of his passing uprisings would take place at the same strategic time in all parts of the satellite world. But in the end the peoples rose one by one, isolated and relatively impotent, and the United States looked on powerless and in fear while the hope for liberty was quenched. And so, after twelve years of brave talk about the liberation of satellite Europe, we reached a point when Soviet might was absolute there, and in another part of the world was buying up the sugar crop in a sensitive land on our own doorstep. We continue to be a great people, no doubt, but if matters proceed as they have been no one may know it save ourselves.

Therewith we shall turn to a period of rejoicing in the history of the College, marked by the inauguration of its Concert Series and its brilliant sequel. One night I had been somewhat sleepily applauding a gala affair in honor of Austrian freedom. During the intermission Lotte Lehmann came to see me, escorting as odd a little man as I had ever met, dressed in formal evening clothes with a spate of decorations across his chest. He all but fitted under her arm, and talked incessantly in German about Mascagni, Richard Strauss and the Emperor Franz Joseph. He was, said Madame Lehmann, with a smile, incomparably great, celestial, was indeed beyond all doubt the most distinguished impresario of Europe. At this moment she accomplished what I was later on to discover was the easiest of her innumerable feats. She referred to his great services to Austrian music. She recounted his misfortunes as a victim of Naziism and an inmate of concentration camps. Meanwhile she found a handkerchief somewhere, crushed it in the palms of her hand, and then deposited into it a few tears as genuine as any I have seen shed. During the preceding months, I had been waited upon by no end of exiled impresarios. Every one of them had fascinated the capitals of Europe, had catered to royalty or at least to princes, and were in a position to lead the American people to new heights of insight and understanding. Concerning all their claims I entertained not the slightest doubt, but in behalf of none of them had the incomparable Lehmann shed a tear. I decided to throw in my lot with Benno Lee and to release the good ship Hunter College Concert Series from its keel.

The times were hard and neither the College nor anybody else had a great deal of money. Not a soul in New York had ever thought of coming to Hunter for a concert for which the price of admission would be exacted. Some of my colleagues thought the little man too bizarre and vowed he would come to no good end. At first I all but agreed with them about the end. The initial houses were pitifully small. But there were two artists who loved and believed in Benno Lee. Lehmann herself, of course. Even if the audience scarce filled a third of the hall, she went through her usual routine, which involved being nervous to the point of absolute exhaustion, repeating the *Ave Maria* until even it was worn to a frazzle, and then going on stage to sing as if she had not a care in the world. Subsequently she drank in the applause and the compliments as if they were brandy and she the most uninhibited guzzler in the history of mankind. The second artist was Emmanuel Feuermann, cellist of incomparable depth and skill, for whom I came to have the deepest admiration and affection even as I did for her who was so soon, alas, to be his widow. Feuermann foresaw the day when the great hall would be packed to the rafters, and was no doubt the first of our artists to sense to the full its beauty and scope. We used to sit together in the wings talking of Vienna and of great music, while we scarce dared to conjure up the shadow of things to come. What a loss it was to the arts and to the great courtesy which is in them when he died, so much before his time!

At any rate, by dint of Benno Lee's groaning and travailing, as well as by reason of the innate rightness of the great hall, matters began to improve. No doubt appearances by two artists whom New York would then move heaven and earth to hear ushered in good fortune. Vladimir Horowitz, frail, reticent and tempestuous, played amidst such downpours of acclaim that when he had finished it was necessary to rescue him from the hundreds who tried to storm the stage and the tiny dressing room. We spirited him out through a hidden exit and into my office where he relaxed with quite cherubic glee. The man who a little while before had thrown every ounce of energy into music was now amiable, utterly tranquil, as genial as a boy with time on his hands. Ezio Pinza, then at the height of powers which would soon be expended prodigally on musical comedy, led a vast crowd to the Hunter door. Many all but adored him; and after his matchless voice had risen to song and encore until very late, it was quite clear that all one needed do was give the public music it craved. But there was no use trying to induce it to come hear somebody of lesser fame. On those evenings when we tried they stayed at home, leaving us to survey ruefully rows of empty seats.

Benno Lee of course knew and loved every artist who had starred in Vienna during the days of yore. My task, until the success of the venture was assured, remained that of presumably genial and persuasive host, explaining to the musicians whose collaboration we desperately needed and to whom we could then pay only a portion of the fee which was their due, that Hunter College had of course been founded so that they could some time enter and give the multitude divine music. Often the personal rewards were very great. Thus I have long since come to believe that Bruno Walter is the beloved of the Lord. It is not merely a question of his utter lack of guile or enmity, or even of his unfathomable gift to fathom the innermost secrets of composers by the use of no more complex a device than loving what they wrote. A special kind of suffering, it seemed to me, had taught him nobility of so rare a quality that one could only bow to it without asking the semblance of a question. We were specially privileged to listen on some evenings while he read from his autobiography. At the time passions were high as the war was raging. But this great maestro was always somewhere where war cannot be, where the human spirit is luminous and tender, and where nevertheless men and women are very much alive.

Then there was Artur Schnabel. He played gloriously, though outwardly with what almost seemed Prussian precision. But when you knew him it became evident that each concert was an act of re-creation, entered into almost ritually. As time went on, he all but made Hunter College a second home. We would often meet at lunch, for he had dreamed of noble deeds to be performed in the great hall, among them a series of concerts in which the whole corpus of the Beethoven concertos would be offered to the public. At the time Schnabel was riding firmly in the saddle of a political *idée fixe*, from which he had to dismount before anything else could be discussed. This was that Stalin was at heart a Social Democrat, with whom the United States could easily arrange the peace of the world if its spokesmen would abandon certain irrational prejudices. Naturally I did not believe a word of this, and at first used to interpose mild objections. But Schnabel would retort grandiously that after all he had played to great audiences in Moscow and Leningrad, that the Russians had a genuine appreciation of music, and that accordingly he could speak with an authority which none of the rest of us could claim. Thereafter I waited patiently until the familiar thesis had been safely put into the stable, and then shared with gusto in the dreams about great music which would then unfold. Alas, just when some of them were about to be realized he suffered the heart attack which all but ended his career. I am sure that had it not been for this the college would have been identified with his later days in a singularly fruitful manner. He was a remarkably generous man who doted on his pupils as if they were his children, and who was just as eager to commend whatever the College was doing for young people as any of the rest of us could be.

There were so many others who came to us not merely as to a concert hall, where everything is impersonal except the dressing room, but to a respected seat of learning in the fortunes of which they were henceforth to have a share. It would be impossible to mention them all, though they make up the roster of the greatest musical talent of more than a decade. The famous singers came, differing so greatly in temperament and in their ability to make of the concert stage the scene of their noblest service to art— Pons, delicate, exquisite and magical; Schwartzkopf, tranquil and reflective, unforgettably beautiful; Tebaldi, who sang like a queen and had the graciousness of one; Seefried, genial, earthy and ready to enjoy a gust of laughter; Gueden, tempestuous and sometimes malicious; and so many, many more. But I shall content myself with just one other reminiscent note, dealing this time with a man to whom we were particularly in debt. Artur Rubenstein surely merits whatever kind of halo Hunter College could place above his head. During the earlier period he played for us at a considerable financial sacrifice—also to the sometimes irate disappointment of Carnegie Hall—and of course the fact that he did so meant that our great hall would be crammed to the last seat. By way of reward (though it cannot really have been that), we entertained him at receptions afterward. Thus there were revealed for our delight his remarkably good nature, his seemingly inexhaustible fund of insight into music, and his amiability as a reconteur. Whereas Schnabel treated a concert almost as if it were a church service, detested encores and thought that appending words at the close was an act akin to sacrilege, Rubenstein seemed to live in a constant act of music making. Playing host to him meant not only hours of the greatest music interpreted with genius, but sometimes additional ones during which the heart and mind were opened to fresh ways of seeing life and art.

A great concert, I think I have learned, is by no means merely a singer or a pianist coming out on the stage and fighting a way through a designated number of pages of music. Music there must be; and it was sometimes astonishing to find that talented artists did not seem to realize that this was an elementary requirement. Their programs were little more than random collections of oddities, picked up here and there with the expectation that the audience would applaud. One tenor I recall especially who spent a whole evening singing ditties which would have gotten a nod from tinpan alley had they not been hopelessly out of date. The heart of the matter is to be found elsewhere, however. It is the thrill of anticipation which ripples through artist and audience alike, welding them into one through the rapture of beautiful sound. I have often thought that musicians and listeners resembled handsome young men going to dances where they expected to meet beautiful girls who would smile on them during an unforgettable evening. Something akin to this, for example, was the experience which the regal Tebaldi made of her concerts. She was not an artist to be flirted with casually. The world she kept at some distance with the magic wand of her personality, but it was always an alluring distance because one wished to cross it. Or in another mode there was Wilhelm Backhaus, a pianist who carried the weight of years graciously, who loved his music as he did people—loved it with a remarkable, deep and memorable kindness. It seemed to me that all he needed to do was to sit down and put his fingers on the keys in order to make one sense both what sort of man he was and what part music played in his life.

And so I have come to believe that on the concert stage the individual artist will always surpass the group—the chorus or the chamber orchestra. The great orchestras are of course another matter, though even here I would argue that the personality of the conductor is the reason one prefers going to see and hear the Philharmonic to listening to the music at home with the help of records. Of course we all have probably likewise had the experience of discerning a favorite among the musicians and through our secret rapport with him making each concert a memorable encounter. At all events, during the years when the Hunter Concert series was in the making, I had ample opportunity to see how great artists prepared for their hours on the stage and how audiences responded. I thought the coolest and most professional was Jascha Heifetz, who seemed to think that the only thing which mattered was his violin; and the most amiable was unquestionably Irmgard Seefried, who always appeared to feel that singing was a kind deed she was performing for herself and the rest of mankind. But the feel of tragedy was also never missing. The time allotted to any artist is fearfully brief. Singers in particular are dogged by their mortality. But I think especially of Solomon, who was our discovery in the sense that we persuaded a manager to book him for an American tour. His first concert here was given at Hunter and proved an extraordinary success. It was, alas, only shortly thereafter that illness ended his career. We sensed the passing of time in other ways as well. One evening we thought that Rubenstein had played with special fervor and depth. He also believed that this was true. His wife lay desperately ill and he remembered her with a prayer in his heart as he played. Often I thought, when the shouting had died down and the great hall was empty, that the spirits of Bach and Schubert, Beethoven, Brahms and the rest, were evoking the men and women who alone could give their music immortality. But there would always have to be other voices, other fingers.

No doubt the thousands who came seldom indulged in such

mournful reflections. They coveted the life which breathes in the patterns of sound the great have woven. Our audiences were of the kind only New York can provide—the young, sophisticated and likely to set exacting standards for program and achievement, and the old for whom music in part evoked memories of concert halls in the Old World. But I recall especially a genial lady of more than ninety for whom these journeys to the great hall were memorable events. She suffered from a form of rheumatism, but when one night a snowstorm blanketed the city and taxis were not to be had, she insisted on going on foot and by subway. It was inspiring to know that, if Hunter had not managed, such persons would have been deprived of much beauty in their lives.

All this meant that Benno Lee was a prince in the realm of impressarios. Since I should have been a complete failure if cast in that role, I have often tried to divine what the secret of success is. Perhaps one cannot really be a master of this trade without a European background. Of course at bottom it no doubt is primarily a hard job of winning artists for one's program, while carefully seeing to it that this is not out of balance. This means catering to and cajoling, while keeping the good will of the fraternity of managers. But no amount of this will succeed unless one can festoon the whole proceeding with wreaths of gilt and glamor. Benno Lee believed in the depths of his soul that Hunter College was the most distinguished educational institution of which the world had so far taken cognizance; and somehow he transferred enough of this extravagant faith to others to make them almost ready to agree with him. But finally an impressario must carry with him at all times, as a reporter does his ballpoint pen, a meticulous, disciplined attentiveness to detail. Every ticket must be what the customer desires, every appointment must be in its proper place, every usher must be a model of efficiency and decorum. This little man lived by a code of carefulness which would make the average drill sergeant seem an advocate of the art of doing what one pleases. At any rate, summoning a concert series into being appears to involve all these things; it is not to be recommended to anyone who is by nature and instinct a beachcomber. Since we were fortunate enough to have on the premises a man who practiced the art to perfection, the enterprise prospered.*

But my conscience was goaded into realizing that we were not doing very much for young musicians, and so another musical venture was embarked upon. This was the Opera Workshop, aided by a group of citizens who banded together to form the Hunter College Opera Association. Two initially unrelated events brought it into being. First, the orchestra which Fritz Stiedry had been conducting since his exile from Germany fell on evil financial days. It had held rehearsals at Hunter, and I had come to be very fond of the earnest, exacting, bespectacled artist for whom the music of Bach was the pinnacle of all things human. We talked of various manifestoes to which the name of Stiedry might be appended—a course in conducting, which actually came into being; a wonderful plan for presenting to the public all of Bach's cantatas, which needed only a generous non-existing angel to get under way; and finally, an opera workshop in which young singers were to be trained after the fashion of Europe. At about the same time Mrs. August Belmont suggested that possibly Hunter College might some time prove to be the place in which youthful Metropolitan Opera singers could be trained. Nothing came of this eventually, but with the help of a modest grant which she very generously secured we decided to see what could be done about creating a workshop.

Stiedry, summoned shortly thereafter to the podium of the Metropolitan, was with us only briefly. But under the leadership of such veterans as Josef Turnau, Rose Landver and William Tarrasch we gradually brought into being, despite formidable difficulties, a kind of ante-room to opera which sometimes had us wondering whether there would be time left to deal with anything else but which prodded us into doing everything possible to make a success of it. Great artists were at our beck and call— Pinza, Thebom, Brownlee, Chapman, Resnik among them. Regina Resnik was of course our very own, for she had been a student at Hunter long before anyone dreamed that opera would

* Benno Lee died shortly after these words were written. May God rest him.

ever be taught under college auspices. My first talk to Freshmen was given in a church to some twelve hundred fidgeting girls, most of whom had their eyes riveted on a clock which ticked solemnly away on a wall. An upper class student sang beautifully. When the chore had been done, I turned to her and said, "You have a beautiful voice. You should see to it that it is well trained!" "I am," she said pertly enough. That was Regina Resnik.

Years later, when the Opera Workshop was getting along as well as could be expected, a roly-poly girl then a student in our High School reported for the auditions. Everyone said she had a beautiful voice, quite untrained but promising. We tided her over, season after season. In due time she had entered the college and there was no doubt in the mind of anyone who followed the fortunes of our Workshop that she was rapidly becoming an adroit and sensitive singer. Then auditions for the Metropolitan were held; and to our infinite delight Martina Arroyo was acclaimed successful. Thus there began for a Negro girl reared in very modest surroundings a career as a singer of opera and oratorio. If all the effort which the successors to Fritz Stiedry put forth had led to no other result, the reward would have even so been great beyond compare.

We never managed to accord a welcome to the theater like the one given to music, though to be sure we offered hospitality to ANTA during a long, hot summer, made room for some community theatrical groups, and once even played host to Harvard's Hasty Pudding Club. But anything resembling repertory was ruled out; it would have meant setting the theater aside permanently for the performing group. This mournful truth I had to convey to quite a number of enterprising persons who yearned for a Park Avenue address. But at least one memorable experience resulted. This was my friendly relationship with Max Rheinhardt during his last years. The great impressario I had come to know in Salzburg, during the summer of 1937, primarily because a European writer friend of mine had fallen in love with a young American actress who was playing a minor role in *Faust*, for which Rheinhardt had devised a truly spectacular setting. She treated this honorable but importunate wooer courteously but cooly; and since he seldom wanted to go anywhere except to the theater for at least a glimpse of his ideal, I became a sort of friendly witness to the quest and in this way saw a good deal of what was going on behind the scenes and therefore also of Rheinhardt himself.

Having to leave Europe and particularly Salzburg because of his non-Aryan blood was a cruel blow to this man who for decades had been in the center of the artistic and cultural life of both Germany and Austria. As a matter of fact, I think that perhaps only Stefan Zweig felt the severance more keenly. The Rheinhardt who came to New York had grown deeply interested in religious reflection. I think he was persuaded that the Church would soon be all that was left of the culture of the Old World. In this mood he discovered Chesterton's play *Magic* and dreamed of giving it a setting which would reveal clearly what he felt was its inner radiance and significance. But there was no "angel" with a flair for this kind of theatrical art. *Magic* he did manage to present, but in a meager and I thought unconvincing setting. It failed, of course. How often I have wished that in spite of everything we had managed to present it in the Hunter theater! But shortly afterward he died, and therewith brought to an end a brilliant page in the history of the drama. I have always felt that he had never been deeper or more brilliant than he was in those New York days.

Student theater was not better or worse with us than it is on other campuses. Young people normally desire to do something rather daring; and so when ours tried they left a great deal to be desired in terms of thespian skill. But there was one annual event which glowed with so much joy and fire that it seemed to me to outshine Broadway. This was the production of Gilbert and Sullivan. The singers were not always superior, and the exclusively feminine cast imposed an added burden on one's credibility. By way of orchestra there was a hodge podge of faculty members and students, who blew and scraped away with abandon. Yet everybody was having such a marvelous time that their happiness was uncannily contagious, and I thought that probably Gilbert and Sullivan pieces cannot really come to life when those on the stage are not in this mood. Anyhow, whatever else there was to do—and I shall add that there was always more than enough—I tossed it aside and went to the revels.

Many another chapter in the story of the great hall might be told. But I shall close with a few references to things which did not leave so pleasant a taste in the mouth. There were evenings when those who had arranged to use our premises proved themselves rank amateurs. On one of these occasions three times as many people came as could be admitted; and the milling crowd of the disappointed had to be dispersed by the police, the fire department and a variety of other agencies. There was another occasion on which an optimistic group assembled an amateur orchestra to play to twelve persons. But I recall with special vividness the day on which the editor of the *Daily News* called to inform me that a mock trial was about to be staged on our premises at which he would be found guilty of diverse crimes and probably hanged in effigy. Inquiry revealed that the sponsoring group of war veterans, later to be unmasked as pro-Communist, had been promised the use of the hall for a concert. I told the leaders bluntly that there was to be no mock trial. During more than a week, the group sang all the more tearful dirges to be found in the hymn book designed by Stalin for consumption in heathen parts. Its members appealed to the Civil Liberties Union, to the supreme officials of the State, and to whomever else could be induced to lend a more or less credulous ear. They buttonholed friends, appealed to patriotic sentiments, distributed broadsides, wrote letters to editors. For a week my office did little except answer calls and fend off the enemy. In the end, of course, there was no mock trial. To have permitted it would have meant turning the great hall into a political forum, which we were determined to prevent.

Of course this caveat against "partisan political activities" did not affect groups which, within the framework of the democratic society, espoused a point of view, however special or eccentric it might seem to us, about matters of civic concern. Some teetered more than a degree or so to the Left, and others were so far to the Right that they all but lay prone. Upon occasion they did not at all like what their opposite numbers had to say; and once I was obliged to take a protesting guest outside to show him what Emerson had written. By and large, however, the ground rules of our game were learned. One episode in particular reveals how tempestuous life in New York can be on the surface, while its inner disposition is hardly affected. The city has in all probability spawned so many groups more or less professionally concerned with its welfare that the average citizen turns problems over to them and proceeds to imbibe the outside world through the innumerable television antennae which dot the roofs. The groups in question are well-intentioned, almost always scrupulously honorable, and led by intelligent men and women. But perhaps their most notable total contribution is to lull the average citizen into thinking that somebody else is taking care of him. When people say that New York is poorly governed, this is what they ought to mean and seldom do. The worst thing that can be said about bureaucracy is that it is bureaucratic. The truth about the average citizen is far more deplorable: he is not a citizen.

At all events, there came an evening when one of our groups boiled Senator Joseph McCarthy in figurative oil. On the next day the pro-McCarthy forces, weaker perhaps in Manhattan than anywhere else in the nation, were on the march. Today it is of course already difficult to believe that this somewhat crude and calculating man should have been able to create so much awe and consternation. But he assuredly did. Our situation was hardly made easier by the fact that a short while earlier I had spoken in Washington about civil liberties and suggested that it was far more important that the American university investigate the Senator than that he probe into it. I added, somewhat provocatively perhaps, that it would help to discover "on what meat this Caesar has fed." The Senator was hardly in favor of the suggestion. Indeed, he reacted with a good deal of vigor. He borrowed the phrase about Caesar and applied it to his foes on a number of subsequent occasions. The mail which thereupon arrived at the College filled several baskets and I have preserved it as a footnote to history. The number of violent adjectives directed to my person was astronomical, though the roster of correspondents who endorsed what I had said was impressively larger than was that of the critics.

It is of interest to me in retrospect to visualize again the manner in which this incredible swashbuckler played his cards. He had assembled a strange crew of helpers, some of them ex-Communists with sharp axes to sharpen further, others young men with an inbuilt urge to paste their egos on billboards, and finally a half dozen or so persons sincerely convinced that the Senator would shove the menace of Communism from American shores. In our case, it was a convert from the Party who tried to be the deadly weapon. He had brought to my office an informer who professed to have proof that a member of our Faculty served as a functionary at meetings of the Party. There was no corroboration. But it was made to appear, in the Senator's counter attack, that only I had stood between a Communist and just retribution. And all the crew, motley though it was, said Amen.

The lesson to be derived from the whole experience is that it is never easy in the United States to maintain, during times of stress, a free forum of discussion. Admittedly ours at Hunter was not without curbs. But on the whole our educational program could be rather nonchalantly continued. No doubt the principal reason why is New York. This tribute I am herewith nailing to its door.

VII.

THE CAMPUS AND THE
WIDE WORLD

The public service which American college presidents squeezed out of themselves and their nerve-racking jobs, particularly during and after the wars against Japan and Hitler, in many instances meant that the leadership which was badly needed on campuses was expertly and rather nonchalantly siphoned off. Something important was gained in exchange, however, though it may not have been visible immediately. The nation, seeing the service and leadership given by educational spokesmen, began to realize that institutions of higher learning are not luxuries but in a very vital sense indispensable reserves of strength. The roster of the victims is a long and distinguished one—Conant of Harvard, Kirk of Columbia, Baxter of Williams, Perkins of Delaware, Eisenhower of Johns Hopkins, Hesburgh of Notre Dame, Wells of Indiana, and many others. These names suggest a spectrum of activities then or now of the greatest urgency: international relations, the release of atomic energy, the manufacture of synthetic rubber, the establishment of an educational policy for the Federal government, the intelligence service, and the conduct of diplomacy.

Few in the fraternity will doubt that a special medal of honor must be pinned on the lapel of Henry Wriston, the indefatigable, gloriously irreverent, many-sided, but always persistently successful president of Brown. What he has written, though there is much of it of uniformly high quality, does not at all give ample indication of the wit, originality, realism and upon occasion iconoclasm of the man who "Wristonized" the Foreign Service, for better or for worse, and in many other ways left a mark on the conduct of affairs in an ineradicable ink whose secret will perish with him. Above all, many of us cherish the memory of his stubborn unwillingness to endorse any shibboleth without having looked skeptically at its reverse side. This caution seemed for a while in our history to be an isolated virtue indeed.

My own service, far more modest in character, has manifestly left a less glorious scar on the tissue of American life, and certainly did not exact more than a pound of flesh from the college I served. From its point of view the most onerous of the burdens I assumed was that of going to Germany in 1950 at the request of John J. McCloy, then United States High Commissioner for Germany, to be his deputy for the beautiful but presumably cantankerous state of Bavaria. He came to the college of a morning on which I happened to be doing a chore I loved, namely teaching in my office a small class in the poetry of the English Renaissance. Suddenly he was propelled into the room and I rather distractedly asked the girls to be patient until this uninvited but importunate guest had ended his visit. To his suggestion that I proceed forthwith to Germany I replied that the Board of Higher Education would never permit me to go on leave for the length of time he indicated, even if Mr. Dean Acheson, wearing all his robes as Secretary of State, were to make the request in person. But, as I have previously indicated, the epistle which that astute diplomat sent to the Chairman of the Board had an extraordinary effect. His colleagues were of the opinion that henceforth Hunter would wear a crown of glory. They sacrificed me on the country's altar stone with an abandon of which I should never have thought them capable. I was off, more than a little against my will, for a tour of duty which lasted eighteen months.

The adventure proved to be very much more interesting and rewarding than I could have foreseen. Not a few have written about Germany's transition from the conquered, despised and dreadfully battered land it was in 1945 to the nation it had become a decade later. I shall set down just a few reflections on the American effort in the hope that the experience they reflect may be of some interest. Certainly the task-force which McCloy led was in several important ways unique. Since there was no pattern to follow, it enjoyed a quite remarkable freedom of action. On the one hand the Department of State had not tied it down with routine directives, though to be sure there was no mistaking the broad outlines of our foreign policy as President Harry Truman had shaped it. But on the other hand, the burden of responsibility for the initiatives taken was often very heavy.

Beyond any question, therefore, the mission would have failed had it not been for the extraordinary qualities of leadership which McCloy consistently manifested. He did not profess to know everything there was to be known either about Germany or about the likelihood that a certain action would prove to be the one which consorted best with the interests and ideals of the United States. He listened a great deal and intently. His major advisers knew always that points of view which seemed to them important would be respected. In the end he not only made up his mind resolutely, but managed to leave it quite clear why he had done so. His secret possibly was an instinctive realization that although a certain distance must lie between the authority of the chief and the views of his aides, there should be no reason for feeling that this distance was impersonal in character. That an operation so vast, many-sided and hazardous (for no one could foresee the future) had to be imperfect in part was a fact Mc-Cloy accepted quite as if he were the mistress of the strange company in *Twelfth Night*; and I suppose it was this tolerance, coupled with constant recognition of true worth, which often seemed to me the most astonishing thing about him. It was not merely a privilege to work with him, but it was also an educational experience to be admired and cherished.

My own mission to Bavaria was to serve as a kind of regent *ex partibus infidelium* in that very particularistic land. Since it constituted by far the largest part of the American Zone, all the problems incident to military occupation had come to roost in serried ranks on its roof and doorstep. Here large numbers of troops were housed in barracks; and it took a long while for the Army's initial "hate the Germans" policy to be transformed into a more constructive outlook. Millions of refugees from the East had meanwhile poured into Bavarian towns and countrysides alike, as a result of the expulsion of the Sudeten Germans, the annexation of Silesia by Poland, and the cruel Russian devastation of East Prussia. Housing, feeding and in some measure taking care of them was an almost superhuman task which had to be carried out even while cities were being cleared of rubble and to some extent rebuilt. Finally Bavaria had come by a reputation which it certainly did not deserve but which for a long while added seriously to its troubles. Hitler had first organized his Party in Munich. The notorious Julius Streicher published a sordid anti-Semitic sheet in Nuremberg, which city was also identified in the public mind with race laws. Furthermore the villa area around Starhemberg Lake, south of Munich, had, during the period of the Weimar Republic, housed a bevy of rabid Prussian reactionaries, among them General Erich Ludendorff. Forgotten were such facts as that many Bavarian districts voted overwhelmingly against Naziism to the bitter end and that the number of Hitler's Bavarian victims was long. The fruits of all these trees were still dangling from countless branches when I arrived in the Land and looked about me to see what might be done. Assets in my bank were that I had earlier come to know the country quite well, and that I could speak German. But there were entries on the other side of the ledger too, among which were that I was a Catholic going to a predominatingly Catholic country, that there existed a strong Socialist and Liberal opposition, and that as an educator I would have to reckon with the heritage of our efforts to reform the schools.

But in Bavaria nothing ever proceeds according to rule. My first welcome to the new post was extended by a newspaper in a small town which applauded the fact that the new Land Commissioner was the president of a "famous college for hunters"— in German *Jaegerakademie*. The point was, to be sure, that perhaps with that sort of professional background I would move to lift the ban on hunting rifles for Germans. The second was that by chance I had known formerly the head of the Socialist Party as well as the standard bearer of ardent Catholicism. The one was William Hoegner, whom we had seen often in Zurich, during his years of exile, where he had written prior to the War a memoir about the rise of Hitler which I vainly tried to have published in the United States. Our country was then regrettably faced with a surfeit of books about Naziism, which no one in particular greatly wished to read. Hoegner's was a colorful personality—he was anti-clerical but with a special nuance, socialist but also in his way a lover of the royal House of Wittelsbach, and very much a city dweller who also knew every mountain and rill in the country. Perhaps my greatest good fortune from the Socialist point of view was that during 1937 I had gone to visit the Prague headquarters of German Social Democracy in exile in order to pay my respects to old Hermann Wels, who alone had opposed in the Reichstag approving the Enabling Act of 1933 which gave Hitler extraordinary powers. This, happily, not a few remembered as a friendly gesture.

The other man was bearded Alois Hundhammer, then Bavarian Minister of Culture and staunch foe of almost everything proposed by American spokesmen to reform education. He was fervently, almost ferociously Catholic. He was also a stern defender of the morals of youth who believed that naughty boys should be rapped on the knuckles, that coeducation was highly unedifying when applied to adolescents, and that above all the study of the classical languages was eminently desirable. Therefore he had stood as a formidable barrier between the reformers from overseas and Bavarian tradition. Unfortunately from their point of view his record as an anti-Nazi had been of the most sterling quality. It so happened that I had met this vigorous crusader in 1948 at an event which still seems to me of great interest.

During that year we had gone to Germany as the guests of General Lucius Clay, so that I could deliver an address in honor of Carl Schurz, who a hundred years earlier had come to the United States as an exiled revolutionary. Then an invitation came to participate in the great conference of German Catholics, the *Katholikentag*. Since I could recall that of 1933—the last permitted by the Nazis, during the course of which Brown Shirts had brutally attacked a throng of marchers, despite the fact that Franz von Papen was in the vanguard—I obtained a permit to travel to Mainz, then in the French Zone, and joined the crowd of more than 200,000 people who for the most part had traveled on foot, in wagons, or on bicycles. Unforgettable was the outdoor assembly on a huge drill ground. We listened for hours to long addresses which only Germans can consume without impairing their intellectual digestions. Round about me were quite a few mothers with children. These sat with a patience unknown in our land. Finally a recording of an address by Pope Pius XII was broadcast, at the end of which the Sovereign Pontiff was recorded as saying, "If you will now kneel down, I shall give you my blessing." And to my everlasting amazement all the little children knelt without prodding. They had listened to every word! It seemed extraordinary that, despite so many years of Naziism, these women had managed to bring up their youngsters as they obviously had done. That night, in the magnificent cathedral of the heavily bombed city, amidst the tombs of the Emperors of the Holy Roman Empire, three representatives of foreign countries spoke briefly—Dr. Veronese of Italy who has since become Director-General of UNESCO, a Belgian lady, and I. What I particularly recall is that from somewhere there had come a marvelous choir of boys, who sang intricate polyphony beautifully, quite as if their young lives had witnessed nothing less enchanting than a vision of Paradise.

At any rate, there I met Dr. Hundhammer, so that when the Department of State invited him to come to this country just prior to my leaving for Germany I did not have to reckon with a perfect stranger. He was to spend a few days in our home, and so I inquired as to what beverage the guest was likely to imbibe. The Department's official reply was "beer"; and accordingly we laid in a store of all available varieties from lager to bock. But when the Doctor arrived, he announced with a flourish that he would like a martini. And so I knew that not everything was hopeless. While it was quite impossible to reconcile Teachers College and Hundhammerism, it became apparent soon that much of the difficulty had grown out of failures of communication and out of vestiges of the Nazi label once so carelessly attached to Bavaria.

In the years immediately following the War it had been light-heartedly assumed that the enemy was hidden in everyone who claimed to be a "conservative." Therewith the monarchists, the Catholic clergy and a good many staunch citizens had been shunted aside in favor of whatever folk the term Leftist could espouse. This had been quite bitterly resented. Much of the trouble grew out of the fact that many of the leading Americans never bothered to make the acquaintance of Germans, except in the most perfunctory way. Both sides therefore talked to each other across a sort of wall, and the resulting misunderstandings were as natural as anything could well be. Hardly had I been seated in my office than, in accordance with the custom of the country, Cardinal Faulhaber called to pay an official visit. I had not seen him since 1933 and found him greatly aged, though there were days when his old remarkable vigor and alertness returned. Meeting him anew was not an unmitigated pleasure, for he professed to be sorely troubled about certain attitudes expressed by the High Commission. I looked up an especially offending document, which had to do with education, and found that what had happened was that the initial term "suggest" had been erroneously translated to read "demand."

It was not easy to counteract the trend while at the same time standing firmly by the policies of my own government. Nor was it, unfortunately, over night that one could change the "enemy" point of view which had been instilled into troops and civilians alike. Sometimes the incidents were harrowing, and it is well that for our own humbling we Americans should occasionally remember our weaknesses. One day shortly after my arrival there took place in Dachau, site of the notorious concentration camp, a meeting of priests and ministers who had once been incarcerated there. Many hundreds came. I have seldom witnessed anything more moving. Numbers of these men still bore on their bodies the scars of prison wounds; but out of the soul of the once captive priest who talked to them there came a message of love and forgiveness, a pledge of hope and of effort in the cause of understanding between men, which, spoken in that place of dread, seemed to have been borne out of another, more human world than ours is. The American friend who had accompanied me and I went away deeply affected, thinking that a small page of history had been turned to the light. But on the next morning there was a different story to tell. I had observed a priest who had come from Westphalia, region round about the city of Muenster from which many clergymen had been sent to Dachau because their Bishop, Count von Galen, had so often vigorously denounced the Nazi movement. This priest had driven down in a battered little car, expecting to proceed on the next day to Rome, where the Holy Year of 1950 was then being observed. As he was leaving the convent where he had stayed over night, he was set upon by one of our Military Policemen, who yanked him out of his car, struck him so hard that the teeth on one side of his face were knocked out, and left him stranded in Munich by draining off his gasoline. None of our police was then authorized to concern himself with a German. The man, who had been drinking, had reverted to the psychology of days gone by. How could one make compensation for an ignominy which in a very real way associated us with Dachau? We apologized, made good the loss of gasoline, and tried in other ways to compensate for what had happened. But it was impossible not to be ashamed. This was not the only time I had reason to squirm for my country. There were far too many such episodes. The United States was often represented by good men, but alas also by lechers, traffickers in women, manipulators of the black market, petty protagonists of illiteracy, and fools. Some of these could gradually be ferreted out. But by no means all.

Not that the Bavarians, for their part, were uniformly noted for sanctity. The calamitous past half-century had witnessed a notable erosion of public and private morals. Though Catholicism was written across the country's brow, the script was often done in a surfacy pigment indeed. A random demonstration must suffice. During our sojourn in Munich, we had as a house guest the eminent Jesuit theologian, Father John Courtney Murray. Priests staying with us were then accorded the privilege of saying Mass in our house. One evening before a feast day, of which the number in Bavaria is legion, Father Murray let it be known that if any of the servants wished to go to confession the next morning he would be at their disposal. We had a fairly large retinue, all of them presumably loyal sons and daughters of Mother Church. Evidently our butler, who ruled his colleagues with iron and velvet combined, transformed the invitation into an order. At any rate, when the new day dawned, I waited two hours for Father Murray to complete his exercises in spiritual sanitation and left for the office. The only comment he made later on was, "I now know what overtime means!" Admittedly the fact that women so greatly outnumbered men when the disastrous conflict had ended gravely affected the moral climate. But no doubt the sources of trouble lay deeper and were in part the frustrations and the sense of life's meaninglessness which had developed during the two wars.

But it would be quite unrealistic not to insist that there is another Bavaria—a *Bavaria sancta*, a holy Bavaria, as well. In the crypt which one enters to the rear of the Buergersaal in Munich one can kneel with many others beside the simple tomb of Father Rupert Mayer, Jesuit who from Goebbels' point of view was a prophet perennially bobbing up like a rubber ball. He preached against the Nazi disorder, was often imprisoned and beaten, but could not be disposed of once and for all because of his extraordinary popularity. A recent German work of reference says of him laconically, "likely to be beatified," which means that if all goes well he will some day be declared a saint. There are many people in Munich who cherish his memory more than they do anything else on earth. We had not known Father Mayer. But it was impossible not to esteem and cherish noble women who had been his staunch allies in a dark time—Princess Pilar, unmarried daughter of the Wittelsbachs, who gave away almost all of her meager fortune for the alleviation of distress; her mother, of the royal lineage of the Spanish Bourbons, whom refugees from Franco, Syndicalists though they were, insisted after her death on carrying to her grave because she had symbolized for them everything that was noble and holy in Spain; and Elizabeth von Schmidt-Pauli, whose Hungarian blood was never tamed and whose books were episodes in her own crusade against evil forces.

When I think of this aspect of Bavarian life as we knew it there comes to mind especially memories of young people—of art students at the Conservatory who spent their evening hours discussing questions of spiritual moment; of the many who gathered at the Ludwigskirche on Sunday mornings to hear Monsignor Guardini preach so simply and well; and of the sons and daughters of workers who cherished ideals of spiritual dedication. If there were such a science as the geology of religion, doubtless its practitioners in our time would distinguish between many layers of insight. In Bavaria these layers would have been numerous. All I wish to say is that I should be quite unfair if I did not insist that while many of them were near the surface and subject to erosion, others could not be seen unless one probed deeply. Especially memorable was a gift not a few had of distinguishing between human frailty and inhuman malice. The great Bavarian portrait painter Leo Samberger was constrained to do a likeness of Hitler, whom he had once or twice seen passing by. The face which looked out from the canvas was so diabolical that when the Fuehrer saw it he flew into a rage and ordered the portrait's destruction. But fortunately a few of the preparatory sketches survived. One of these, by reason of a friend's generosity, is in our possession. I do not display it save when there is question of good and evil.

McCloy's major tasks were these: to strengthen the central government so that it would be in a position to assume democratic responsibility with a reasonable chance of success; to establish an effective German economy, so that the burden of financial support could be lifted from the shoulders of the American taxpayer; to liquidate war guilt cases which had not yet been resolved; and meanwhile to do what could be done to bring to the Germans understanding of what freedom and civic responsibility are. But in addition the year 1950, when the defense of Korea had grown into a full-fledged military action, ushered in two other problems. It was decided to re-arm the Germans and at the same time greatly to strengthen our own military garrison. Memorable was the day, shortly after my arrival in Germany, when I was asked what I thought of German rearmament. The proposal, I shall confess, quite astonished me. Everything conceivable had been done to impress upon the vanquished Germans that they were never again to bear arms. In Oberammergau, for example, all the hunting rifles, many of them heirlooms, were collected, laid side by side on the main street, and then demolished by a tank. No citizen of Bavaria, exception having been made for the police who carried rather innocuous looking pistols, was permitted to own any weapon. Even farmers whose property was invaded by wild boars had no recourse except to petition Americans to hunt the marauders down. And now suddenly we wanted German divisions! Meanwhile of course we had persuaded a great part of the citizenry that militarism was a wholly evil thing.

The Germans were often bewildered by the conflicting pressures to which they then were exposed. Veterans groups, as I amply found out by speaking at the universities, were likely to be anti-militaristic because of resentments, both of the blind and bloody alley down which Hitler had led them and of the contempt and hostility long shown them by us and our allies. Women often very sincerely wanted no new militaristic enterprise. Dozens of them came to my office to plead that if there was need of German youth the tasks assigned to them should be those normally entrusted to non-combattants. Then of course there was pressure from the Russian side. This assumed as usual divers forms. On the one hand, threats of the taking over of Western Germany by the Communists, presumably on the basis of an invasion, were widely circulated, especially in smaller cities along the border. Thus in one town near that border every business man received during the fall of 1950 a post-card from the East bearing a picture of a telephone pole and a caption, "You will hang from this!" The message was all the more ominous because the individual designation of each pole was indicated. On the other hand, there was the more legitimate fear that if Western Germany were to throw in its military lot with the United States, the reunification of the country would be rendered more difficult. For at the time it was still possible to entertain the view that through diplomatic action a peace treaty restoring independence to Germany at least from the Oder to the Rhine was possible. The Russians played skilfully on both trumpet and harp.

There really was very little military strength at hand with which an invasion could have been resisted. The American division and the air power on which it could rely might have carried out at best a withdrawal operation, in the hope that Communist armies would halt at the Rhine. Once I wrote a speech which I was to deliver on McCloy's behalf at an assembly in Bavaria, containing Benjamin Franklin's famous line, "If we do not hang together, we shall hang separately." My chief struck this out with the notation, "Too uncomfortable!" And indeed there had been drawn up a plan of evacuation which to me meant only that if an invasion actually took place, I would get as far as Memmingen, there to be captured and put on a train for Siberia. Additional units of Americans were therefore welcomed, despite all the difficulties attendant upon housing and living close to them. It was the argument that Germans could not expect American boys to defend them unless they in turn did something about defending themselves which eventually brought about acceptance of rearmament. Yet the decision was a momentous one; and when the original plan for a European Defense Community had to be modified, by reason of French unwillingness to endorse it, the implications seemed even more grave.

The restoration of the German economy led to what is often referred to as a miracle but it was perhaps only the natural consequence of having put together ingredients from which success was almost bound to come. In the first place, the influx of millions of expellees added greatly both to the number of excellently trained graduates of scientific and technical schools and to the size of the skilled labor force. Hand in hand with this there came a strong augmentation of salesmanship ability. For example, nobody entitled to reparations through the "dismantling" process wanted the then rather bedraggled Volkswagen plant. The British and the French thought that their own automotive industries were wholly prepared to meet any demand which might arise. But in a short while the combination of a brilliant designer (Porsche) and a very competent industrial manager (Nordhoff), counting on the good will of working men and women who had nothing, to do everything they could to get something, resulted in an enterprise which today symbolizes the amazing economic recovery of West Germany. And of course it is only one symbol among many. Nor can one overlook the stable currency, which held fast primarily because at the outset the support of the Marshall Plan was effectively used. The total achievement is very remarkable and indicates that American action and planning, when they are of high quality, can reap successes far beyond any which Communism can obtain.

On the other hand, I shall say parenthetically, we seem not as yet to have found ways of dealing effectively with countries whose economic development has not advanced beyond the primitive level. Thus while the reorganization of the Formosan economy would seem to merit the praise lavished on it, life in Liberia remains, after more than a century of ties with the United States, about as devoid of signs of progress as are a bandit's morals. Possibly one reason why this is so is our inability, psychologically, to live ourselves into the core of societies lacking what we have come to take for granted. A major explanation is that we cannot resort to ways of creating incentives which Communism never fails to employ. If for the sake of bringing about industrial expansion one organizes slave-labor camps and virtual chain-gangs, it is easy to achieve results very cheaply, while not greatly lowering the standard of living which the unfortunate serfs have previously known. No great value attaches to the life of the common man in China, for example. Beyond that, incentive is created by holding out the chance that if an individual acquires some rudimentary industrial skill he can escape from slavery. The Communist economy in later stages must face serious problems, but the initial impulse is powerful. The conclusion suggests itself that perhaps we would do better if at least at the outset we concentrated our efforts on fifteen or twenty countries where our own special skills can be put to effective use rather than scattered largesse everywhere.

At any rate, it was a notable experience to observe what was happening from the special vantage point of Bavaria. All the phenomena of industrial change and post-war recovery manifested themselves. Munich was fast growing out of the clothes it had worn as a governmental and cultural center. Agriculture outside the city which was steadily encroaching on the land, was rescued from a desperate shortage of man power by exiled peasants from the East. The once quiet valley of the Inn, as pleasant and romantic an area as one could hope to hike in, was changing almost spectacularly as one hydro-electric plant after another was built to make more industrial power available. Refugees were starting new enterprises in abandoned ammunition dumps. But here again the impulse which came from the American desire to help create a viable economy encountered almost as much traditional resistance as did the suggested educational reforms. There was a sort of alliance between the landed aristocracy, the peasants and the clergy in support of the doctrine that industry breeds crime and radicalism. The Bavarians stoutly resisted the effort to break up the large estates, and in the end these remained pretty much what they had always been, save when later on the equalization of burdens tax forced some of the proprietors to unload a few acres. In so far as small business was concerned, all but the few who profited looked askance at our efforts to create a free economy by disavowing the principle that a pharmacy, for example, could be opened only by some one licensed to operate it.

Upon occasion the friction was rather amusing, but sometimes it revealed differences of aim and outlook which were quite baffling. One of Munich's grievances was that although the city's supply of water came from a huge mountain reservoir where the precious fluid was practically distilled through a bed of limerock, the Army insisted on a dose of chlorine as prescribed by the rule book. This meant that before the elixir of life, Munich's far-famed beer, could be brewed properly the chlorine had to be extracted again. But I suppose that this additional effort was well compensated for by citizens who professed to be unable to stomach the germ-proof, Americanized water which ran from the taps. I found similarly beguiling a conversation with a bishop. We were riding through a pleasant rural country when we came upon a brand-new little factory. My companion crossed himself just as if he had suddenly met Satan. The factory, he explained, would not merely drain off the girls from the farms and expose them to grave temptations but, since it was to manufacture stockings made of perlon, the whole region would soon suffer cultural erosion. I gathered that the vision of farm girls putting on that sort of hose brought more of a promise of moral deterioration than he could face with equanimity. And indeed there were prelates who stoutly and triumphantly resisted the invasion of their dioceses by factories and similar establishments of the devil.

But as I have suggested there were ways in which the scene conjured up moods that were grave and even sombre. Thus there was a form of Bavarian anti-Semitism which had nothing whatever to do with Naziism but was nevertheless very real. Its root was a kind of peasant repudiation of the Jew as a component part of urban society; and it reached so far down into the soil of things that one could not easily believe that what we were doing officially about anti-Semitism was going to wither it away. Few of these people would have applauded anything Hitler did. Some of them as a matter of fact were heroic under the onslaught of his doctrines and his henchmen. Yet their myth was very much alive inside them. I had often to think of it while we faced some of the multiform aspects of the enterprise known as "building German democracy." We had created a new press more or less in the image and likeness of our own. To some extent we had "reformed" the radio and even the schools. In dozens of towns we had stationed earnest young men who tried hard to form women's organizations, PTAs, civil liberties groups, youth forums and similar instrumentalities of democratic living. Undoubtedly they did introduce a leaven. But one could not help feeling that in the end the Bavarians would remain what they had always been, just as Virginians will perennially be Virginians. The Bavarian dearly loves freedom, but it is not our kind. He is tolerant of others because fundamentally he is tolerant of his own foibles. Yet unless the changes which are coming over a Europe increasingly shaped by technology affect his country, he will go right on being a person who on the one hand piously makes a pilgrimage to some shrine like Andechs and on the other has a love affair at Fasching time.

When one thought of freedom in Germany, it was of course to Berlin that one's heart and mind turned. For here was a beleaguered island which by reason of its people's resolve and of the decision of the United States would not be swallowed up in the Russian sea. We had caught glimpses during 1948 of the air lift which made Free Berlin's survival possible—a magnificent, courageous mission on wings, which has always since seemed to me like a giant eagle constantly in motion to carry not prey but succour for the spirit of Europe as well as for millions of human bodies. But I had not seen the city since the war.

The opportunity to do so came when it was agreed upon to make an official ceremony of the presentation of a Freedom Bell to Berlin in November, 1950, thus symbolizing the unity between Germans and ourselves which had saved the western part of the city at least from slavery. General Lucius Clay was to come from the United States to deliver the presentation address, and McCloy and some of his aides would attend, each bringing with him a German designated by some branch of his government. The Bavarians chose Dr. Hundhammer and we were off. Berlin when we arrived that night was assuredly drab enough, for rain was falling on Tempelhof airfield and winter was in the air. I am sure my wife, who was wretched with a severe cold, felt that the city of which we had so many memories was doing its worst by her.

But when morning came we had as we drove to Schoenberg, from the Rathaus tower of which the bell was to ring out, a view of the magnitude of the devastation caused by the war. No one who did not at some time look out on the sahara of rubble the once proud metropolis had become in the days of its torment can imagine what it was like to realize that for mile after mile old landmarks had been swallowed up in a nothingness so vast, silent and terrible that it seemed impossible mankind would not learn from this alone the dread meaninglessness of war.

It was still drizzling as we entered the Rathaus. Then, as we came out on the balcony facing the square to take our seats, amazement of another kind was ours. For instead of the few hundreds we had thought might be standing there, there were scores and scores of thousands—so many in fact that the last of them were little more than dots on the horizon. Men, women and children were standing there in such dense array that it was all but impossible to believe there could be so many people in the world.

Tears came to General Clay's eyes as he began to speak. Then when he had finished and was about to press the button which would make the bell ring, the sun broke through the clouds. The faces of the crowd made up of people wearing spare, worn clothes, turned upward toward the tower and the sun. Never again in all probability would anyone who was there see so luminous and moving an expression of hope. It was as if more human beings than one could see had come up out of a spiritual dungeon, the counterpart of that in *Fidelio*, to have joy in the belief that American good will and leadership would insure both peace and liberty. It left me abashed and curiously afraid. What would the world be like if we did not manage? There was in Berlin that day no doubt we would manage. As we were leaving, women came one after another out of the crowd to press my wife's hand because she was an American who had been there on this day with them.

Afterward having savored the courtesy and hospitality of General Maxwell Taylor, then the commandant and in every sense a noble and resolute solider, we accepted Dr. Hundhammer as our guide and went to visit some laboratories belonging to the research institute called the Max Planck Gesellschaft in honor of the great German physicist who had likewise been one of the bravest among Hitler's German foes. Our bearded Bavarian friend had often been pointed to with smiles of recognition in which there was also a bit of malice, for Berlin was primarily a Socialist and Protestant city where some of his pedagogical theories would have fitted not at all. But on that day he was certainly the only German who escorted his American hosts on this kind of tour.

One thing we saw was quite unexpected. There was in Berlin, we knew, a great microscope, then possibly the largest in the world, counterparts of which had been carted off to the United States and Russia. But in our honor a young scientist revealed something much more marvellous—a new electronic microscope, looking for all the world like a large-sized flashlight, with the help of which one could actually see the movement of electrons across the surface of a molecule. It was the first time I had seen what has since been called the "dance of the atom," the rhythmic motion which delvers say proceeds to the accompaniment of music, which if we could hear it would surround us constantly.

I said to the scientist that it now seemed to me quite impossible
to credit older theories which had sundered mind and matter.
He answered almost reverently that this appeared to be so.

I returned to Bavaria musing on the fact that I was after all
fortunate to be in a state the Cultural Ministry of which could
worry on the one hand about whether growing youngsters were
spanked sufficiently, and yet on the other take time out to consider the mysteries which Science was for the first time enabling
men to know were there. Maybe I had to undertake a little re-
education of myself, too. For this vigorous traditionalist, who
rather than do business with Hitler had given up all academic
pursuits in order to open a shop where boots were cobbled, and
who as a result had lived through a dreary time without ever
having said "Siegheil" or lifted his hand in a phony salute, was
also one who would not agree to sponsor any American idea in
which he did not believe. This was service to freedom, too; and
though I continued to feel that some of the things with which he
was concerned were strange and old-fashioned, yet the longer I
reflected the odder it seemed that arguments about such matters
were vital to American foreign policy. We did not debate very
strenuously about them any more, and instead tried to see if we
could improve the teaching of the Social Sciences and dry up the
sources of Naziism.

This last concern, oddly enough, flung me into an adventure
which blended cynicism with awareness of poignant tragedy.
The old Jewish community of Munich had been virtually ex-
terminated. One of the few members of it who returned from
the slave labor camps was an excellent physician, whose skill in
medicine had somehow proved his salvation. But now the osten-
sible chief was a man who hailed from another part of Germany,
who arrived with a brand-new wife, and who bore the title Dr.
Auerbach because he had extracted a university degree in some
quite unorthodox way. We had inaugurated the practice of inviting to dinner representatives of the various political parties,
of the three major religions, and of other civic groups. Questions
of some moment were discussed. It was at that time the only
opportunity which men of diverse groups had to meet and see
that possibly the matters which divided them were not of as

much moment as those which they entertained in common. Out of these meetings there was born the first Christian Social— Social Democratic coalition in post-War Germany. Of this I was quite proud. But another result was a series of random discourses by Dr. Auerbach.

Then came the day when a United States court indicted him for various alleged defalcations, and it became my duty to notify the Bavarian government of the fact. A special Cabinet meeting was called; and infinitely to their regret the Bavarians inaugurated the trial for sundry misdemeanors of a man they had hitherto walked round gingerly and often on tiptoe. This trial dragged on long after I had left Bavaria; and during the course of it peccadillos were revealed which did not add up to a crime of any kind but on the other hand were not a bouquet of roses exuding the aroma of sanctity. One day after I returned to Hunter, a student asked to see me. She was Dr. Auerbach's daughter, by his first marriage, who had come to the United States after her mother had been divorced. We talked and it was decided that out of her meager savings she wished to send flowers to her father so that his prison cell would be a little brighter. I arranged to have them delivered. Whether they reached him prior to his despondent suicide, I shall never know. But I have always hoped that this man, who certainly was not a hero and yet no great villain either, had seen his child's gift for a little while before he died.

Some forms of organization did meet with a cordial response in Bavaria. My wife came back from visiting camps of refugees— including people who had been evacuated from their homes or had been expelled from their homelands—filled with a resolve to do something. Accordingly she brought together a number of German and American men and women for the purpose of launching a Good Neighbor movement. Perhaps the initial incentive was provided by the hope of spending a pleasant afternoon at the house of the Land Commissioner. But the idea caught fire, and ten years after we left Munich the Good Neighbors were still flourishing. This taught me some kind of lesson. Maybe talking to people about attitudes we wished them to adopt was not likely to accomplish much, unless we stayed for a long time and kept up the sources of contagion. Maybe what really mattered was to join in a common effort to be doing something which was just plain human and so required no sales talk.

Another development which deeply impressed me, though we had nothing to do with it, was inter-religious dialogue. Having realized, as a result of common suffering under Hitler, that however grave the cleavages between Lutheranism and Catholicism might be, the religious situation in the present-day world demands mutual affection and respect, a surprisingly large number of things were happening to break down old barriers and to create a measure of unity which, while it might never become complete, would nevertheless substitute cooperation for ancient hostility and recrimmination. In this respect I knew to my chagrin that the Bavarians had greatly outdistanced ourselves. Sometimes the new climate manifested itself vividly. One day I was asked by a Lutheran bishop whether I would speak at a conference of the Gustavus Adolphus Society. This had been for generations, he explained, a rather fire-eating kind of organization at the meetings of which the Pope had been duly roasted to an oratorical cinder. It was now undergoing a change: since the Catholic Minister President of Bavaria likewise addressed the throng, it was doubtless the first time in history that two officials holding allegiance to the Church of Rome were headlined as speakers to the Society. I am sure that Gustavus Adolphus, if his spirit was in a position to concern itself with such matters, must have been greatly astonished. As it turned out, the major address was given succinctly and unexpectedly by a little merchant who had come all the way from Weimar to explain what religion meant to a man living under Russian domination. He did not shed tears or adopt a false pose. But he said very feelingly that when he went back home and told his friends that an American and a Bavarian Catholic, representing two states, had spoken at the meeting they would be immensely comforted by the thought that not all governments were godless.

I shall say little more about our adventures in Bavaria except to indicate that they came to be steeped in a form of friendship which lingers in the memory as one of the great experiences of our lives. It was a time concerned with humble folk as well as important ones. We often had as our guests the Cardinal and the magnificently vital old Crown Prince, Rupprecht of Bavaria. Many of the great writers and artists gave us a cordial welcome, among them Hans Carossa and Gertrud von le Fort, the latter one of our time's geniuses whom we least appreciate. But very probably it was just going about and meeting folk which served our country best. When I arrived in Munich I found that my chauffeur had attached to the official car a blue light and a siren with which he was wont to roar through the streets with or without the Land Commissioner. Very sadly he removed them, and we drove thenceforth without disturbing the peace. But people even so came to know who we were. One day we stopped at a roadside tavern for lunch. The waitress asked me if I were Professor Shuster, for the academic title was the greatest accolade of respect a Bavarian could manage. Having admitted the fact, I remarked that a group of people seated in a corner seemed to be enjoying themselves immensely. "Why shouldn't they?" she countered. "After all, they have just come from a funeral." And apparently from one end of the country to the other people were, despite all their problems, difficulties, worries and quandaries, always just coming from funerals.

Perhaps it was the proudest day in my life when, shortly before I left, I heard McCloy say to the group of German Minister Presidents assembled in his house, as it was the custom to arrange at regular intervals, "Why cannot we have in the other states the excellent cooperation given to us in Bavaria?" When I came to Munich the reason for my presence was that relations between ourselves and the Bavarians had reached a kind of sub-zero latitude. Could I not say to myself, the mission had been accomplished? Unfortunately it was immediately necessary to add that I had really done very little except talk to people in their own language, talk to them whenever they wanted me to do so, in the spirit that the new world upon which we were entering would require of us on both sides the largest measure of friendly cooperation for freedom and justice that we could manage. Anybody else could have done equally well, had he been able to break down the barrier of cultural understanding and with it, perhaps, the wall of prejudice which had needlessly been erected by American and Bavarian alike.

The major phenomenon doubtless was recovery from the devastation visited on town and city. The ravages of a war as brutal as the one Hitler began cannot be veiled from those who loved the city Munich once was, and who knew its gables and towers, its blend of Romanesque, Renaissance and Rococo—a Munich which was of one mood when the snow fell and the Christmas carolling began, and of quite another as the crowd moved to the Theresienwiese for the circuses of October time, when beer seemingly never ceased to gurgle on its way down throats and roasted chickens tumbled endlessly from spits. But I fancy that a youngster strolling from the Stachus to the Ludwigstrasse today might well have difficulty realizing that much of what greeted his eye has risen anew out of the rubble. For the urge to rebuild has been a mighty one. Perhaps I had never realized how strong it was until I stood for a little while, during the Eucharistic Congress of 1960, beside the plaque which marks the place where Cardinal Faulhaber is buried in the cathedral now so white and clean that it almost seems to have been erected yesterday.

Nearly ten years earlier, my wife and my son and I had come here for Mass at midnight time on Christmas Eve. We sat, as it was the custom for representatives of the State to do, in one of the choir stalls, huddled under a blanket which we had somewhat sheepishly brought with us. The old Cardinal, wearing the heavy vestments which were appropriate for the occasion, leaned forward on his throne. The roof of the cathedral, which had buckled under a bomb explosion, had been patched in a rather desultory manner, and the tall windows from which the glass was gone had been boarded shut. Through the frosty air the singing of the choir was borne from an organ loft at the far end of the cathedral. Meanwhile the wind knifed its way through tiny places not quite blanketed. It made no noise whatever, being as persistent as a cat slinking along the top of a garden wall, and coaxing a constant flutter out of the altar candles.

Never have I been so cold. As the hour and a half of the Mass neared its final moments and we rose, I fancied myself an icicle absurdly tilted upward from the floor. Such was the Frauenkirche of 1950, and naturally this was a great improvement over the ruin which had gaped out at the passerby five years earlier. In the vast unlighted reaches of the cathedral, round the tall pillars erected during the gothic time, stood a great crowd, remaining patient and reverent during the long Mass. After it was over the Cardinal, flanked by young men carrying candlesticks in which fat tapers gleamed, went out through the people, blessing all and sundry with a gloved hand. He had, one realized, seen Munich in the days of its ancient regal splendor, and had himself at the time been quite doughtily monarchist and patriotic.

There followed the triumph of Hitler, after which the Cardinal had gone to another church, named for his patron saint Michael, to preach the sermons against anti-Semitism which made him a marked man. He had to live through nights when Nazi terrorists tried to break into his household, ransack it and take his life. On one of them he was saved when by chance a passing woman, tall and blond as Brunhilde, flattened herself against the door and somehow overawed the mob. Then, finally, peace came bringing with it the first pathetic Corpus Christi procession. Altars were set up on heaps of rubble, and from one to the other the Cardinal went, carrying the Sacred Host, while bands of the faithful followed as best they could. Oddly enough, there was a film of that procession, made by a Communist who when I met him was no longer one.

These experiences had greatly changed the Cardinal. Calling on him, in the interests of peace between Church and State, I invariably walked past the huge police dog who lay in the entry way and eyed me with an air of reluctant tolerance and up the stairs to a seat under the impressive portrait which Leo Samberger had painted when the Cardinal was in his prime. Now he was old and, I learned, likely to offer unexpected morsels of advice. There was a morning on which he spent virtually all the time counseling me against kissing his ring. We were living, he thought, in a time when that kind of ceremonial was bound to be misunderstood. On another occasion he surmised that the

Church in Germany would be curbed and silent. But when he died, Bavaria gave him a funeral the like of which has seldom been seen. It was quite as if the immense throngs of Bavarians who lined the streets knew that a great era in the history of their country had ended. Yet a new one was emerging, too, in the modernity of which remnants of the past would be embedded, quite as the restorers of the cathedral have salvaged and built into the walls whatever of art the roaring fire kindled by the bombing had not destroyed.

I cannot get Bavaria out of my memory without being quite personal about our sojourn there. Gloom descended on our days in Munich by reason of the death of a friend who though he could not lay the slightest claim to being human was as amiable if sometimes as exacting, even exasperating, as one of our own breed could well be. Kleiner, a long lean dachshund came to me originally, by courtesy of my wife, because at the age of two he had proved to be the most resourceful and determined of chicken thieves. His citizenship in the country estate on which he had been born was therefore summarily revoked. He came from as noble a lineage as his folk could boast, but this only meant that he was funnier looking than usual. We had never previously enjoyed the company of so individualistic a guest, though we had sheltered collies, a police dog, a wire-haired terrier, and a pup of greatly garbled ancestry. For his part Kleiner for a time looked upon us, I think, as stray menials whom he had fallen upon during transitory, tedious days; and it was not until after a series of mishaps had befallen him that he began to accept us with a measure of nonchalance and affection.

There is an essay by a forgotten German writer of the eighteenth century which describes his own dachshund in vivid detail; and as time passed I concluded that this stubborn but beguiling villain had certainly been Kleiner's ancestor. Both delighted, for example, in walking, but during the course of a stroll viewed every other canine and every human being with infinite disdain, while bestowing on trees, flowers and mysterious patches of grass an attention worthy of a botanist, indeed of the great Linnaeus himself. They were also alike in regarding with hostility everybody in uniform, be he postman, soldier or member of the clergy. And when he could terrify a housemaid or a guest, Kleiner took infinite delight in pressing home the point. But of firecrackers he lived in mortal dread and was wont to spend the whole of the Fourth of July evening upstairs under a bed. Among his possessions were faculties of spatial diagnosis which continue to baffle me completely. During the war, with its attendant shortages of gasoline, I often came home by a bus which halted an eighth of a mile away from our house at a point constituting the corner of a rectangle opposite from where that stood. The intervening space was filled with houses, people and dogs. When the bus stopped and I got off, Kleiner was instantly apprized of the fact by some mysterious Ariel of his acquaintance. He immediately proceeded to the house door and sat with one ear impishly and efficiently exposed to the sound of my footsteps. This was only one of several comparable feats. How he did them I shall never know.

More remarkable still was his addiction to the arts. When the piano was played softly, he was moved to melancholy and upon occasion to tears; but a *polonaise* or something of the sort would evoke a dismal howling suggesting desert spaces and huge moons. I was beguiled into devising a theory according to which his remote forebear had been an Egyptian jackal, given to weird incantations native to the land of Cleopatra. But it was as a devotee of the motion picture that Kleiner really came into his own. We owned a projector, and during the time when our house was humming with young people we often sat looking at movies. Kleiner would rush in gleefully and take his station in a front row of his own devising. Watching with rapt attention, he would growl appropriately if a dog or a rabbit (he had a special hunter's interest in rabbits) appeared on the screen; and sometimes he would tiptoe behind it to see if the visitor had left tracks. He did not manage to induce the stray kitten who one evening walked through a door to fall in love with the movies, but he did treat it in the spirit of a jovial equality, accepting buffs on the nose with resignation and permitting pilfering from his dish. Otherwise to and fro across the living room rug they went, engaged in a combat of wits. Any other cat encountered in the garden was a mortal enemy, but until the day when our tramp kitten vanished as inexplicably as it had come, he treated it hospitably and also cautiously, even as so unpredictable a creature demanded.

But there came a day a little before our leaving for Germany when, with advancing age, Kleiner developed a "heart condition" which upon occasion called for digitalis. My wife decided that he must go to Europe with us; and so he occupied his own small cabin on the *Coronia*, wherein I fear he uttered more than sighs. In due time we arrived in Paris and at a hotel, where an emissary of the Department of State had arranged for us to spend a few hours. He entered the hostel with more than a bit of reluctance, but since he was on a leash he had willynilly to ride up with us on the elevator to our room. Once inside my wife relaxed her grip before I had a chance to close the door. Down five flights of stairs went Kleiner, lover of nature as he was, out into the courtyard. When we had recaptured him, it took almost all of the drug we had with us to calm his heart. All night on the train to Frankfurt he was snuggled up on my berth; and then, after some days of sniffing about in the flowers of the garden just outside the house in which we were guests for a few days, he came to his Munich home. By this time he must have fancied himself a world traveler. There were many people to learn to know, and plenty of chance to walk. I sadly fear that our German servants also catered to his natural addiction to gluttony.

But, alas, there came a morning when he was simply tired out. He submitted graciously to all the petting and cajoling we heaped on him. The digitalis he took with an air which indicated that although he knew we meant well, the medicine strengthened our hopes rather than his body. I put him on a blanket in the sun before going off to a conference in Frankfurt. That we were very fond of each other I am sure he knew as well as he did that Munich was far from home. I shall not forget that when I turned round at the gate, his eyes were on me with a kind of summary of the dedication of long years. When I came back the next day, he was gone. Whenever I come to that corner in Stamford he had always identified with me, I think of him. And sometimes when I pass through the door of the house, it is all I can do not to stoop and make believe that he is there . . .

I shall end these remarks with a tribute to my chief. McCloy had many a difficult problem to solve, many a decision to make which would affect the climate of history for years, and many a chance also to take the easy way rather than the hard one. But no doubt the one task which weighed most heavily on him was that of liquidating as far as he could the cases of war criminals which were either pending or in need of review. The men imprisoned in Spandau under joint Allied auspices were beyond the pale, because their fate depended in part upon what the Russians were prepared to do; and at the time the sole word in the vocabulary of the Kremlin was "Nyet." But there were many prisoners in Landau. Death sentences had been meted out to some of them. Other cases clamored for review. German public opinion stirred uneasily every time it was pointed out that there was still no end to a situation which in its view was identified with a policy of vengeance.

McCloy arranged to have a review of all the cases made by competent American jurists. The panel was a distinguished one. The conclusions arrived at were varied, but among them was one to carry out some of the death sentences, involving men who undoubtedly had been guilty of heinous crimes, and to pardon Alfred Krupp, heir to the great Essen fortune. The second decision was oddly enough to bring down on McCloy's head the denunciations of various Britishers, though paradoxically it was British juridical opinion which had weighted the scale in favor of a pardon. For obviously the young Krupp had had nothing whatever to do with the iniquities attributed to his firm, except that his father had died before the Nuremberg Court was able to pass judgment on him. But the first, involving a decision to take human life five years after the war was over, called for almost superhuman fortitude. German opposition was strong, perhaps above all because the new Government did not wish to be saddled with a reputation for the same hardness of heart which had characterized the Nazis.

Day after day, night after night, McCloy paced the floor. I had ample opportunity to see how troubled in spirit he was, not merely because it was his duty to determine whether men would live or not but primarily for the reason that the image of the

United States which would inevitably be created would mean so very much for the future. In the end there were confirmations of death sentences, not as many as some people had wished for but still a fateful number. Now there occurred a kind of marvel which I am sure merits a place in the nation's annals because it indicated what we can do as Americans when we act with wisdom, intelligence and foresight. Shepard Stone, in charge of McCloy's public relations, gave to the German press information and explanation in advance, so carefully prepared and adapted to German opinion that when the news came out it was accepted almost as if no other solution of the problem had been possible. It was, on the part of a veteran of the New York *Times*, as admirable an action in behalf of our country as one can well imagine. It is a merited tribute when I say that this carefully planned solution of a major problem was characteristic of a task force admirably led, without which in my judgment the present history of West Germany might well have taken a different course.

I shall offer sundry additional leaves from a notebook concerned with a variety of persons and enterprises which only the time in question could have assembled. When the Second World War broke out, I was wearing two national service hats neither of which fitted unusually well. The first was a stern cockade worn as a member of one of New York's Enemy Alien Boards, which organizations have not as yet been given their due. The Boards were appointed to "screen" Germans, Italians and Japanese who for one reason or other had been corralled by the FBI. Each convened in the Department of Justice Building in Foley Square at six o'clock sharp. Evening after evening ours remained in session until close to midnight. I kept a small but comfortable room at the Players' Club, with a tiny window and an even smaller adornment in the shape of a handbill dated 1741 which advertised the fact that the role of the King in *Richard the Third* would be played by "a Gentleman who has never hitherto appeared on any Stage." Who he was I do not to this day know. And, appropriately enough, few of the ladies and gentlemen we interviewed had thitherto been in any sense renowned. When the hour of nightly release had arrived, and I

was back at the Club, I ran smack into exuberant actors just
released from Broadway and confronted the psychically rubber-
cushioned FPA, who at that hour was sure to be playing billiards
with abandon. I munched a sandwich, drank a bottle of ale, and
tumbled into bed to dream of spies whom the morrow might well
uncover.

My distinguished colleague on the Board was Henry Pitney Van
Dusen, later on to be President of Union Theological Seminary.
He was a citizen of the utmost probity whose patriotism was
never an excuse for blindness or hardness of the heart. And
good this temperateness was, for the men and women mustered
into our presence by the Attorney General's representative were
for the most part a forlorn and motley crew. They included small
business men, servants, artists down at the heels and persons
dedicated above all to the pursuit of leisure. We interrogated a
Japanese cook who in response to a query as to what he thought
of the situation then obtaining said: "Me always work like horse,
now me got vacation!" We listened to the sad tale of a Jewish
emigré couple who had subscribed to a pro-Nazi sheet of some
kind in a desperate effort to persuade Long Island neighbors that
they, too, were Aryans. And then, of course, there was the Japanese merchant, vouched for by practically everyone of consequence in the community in which he lived, whom we released
but who later on proved to be a spy of some distinction.

But no doubt the Board on which we served would have passed
mutely out of history had it not been for the case of Ezio Pinza,
illustrious basso, whom the Attorney would dearly have loved to
intern for the duration. The debit side of the ledger contained
two items alleged to be of moment. The first was some scroll or
other which Pinza had exhibited with a measure of gusto because it had come straight from Mussolini. Viewed in the light
of the scramble there had once been in the very best circles for
nods from the Duce, this seemed a rather trifling matter. The
second item was thought to be of greater significance. On the
evening after the grandiose annexation of a few square feet of
French territory by the Fascists, following the German break-
through, the exuberant basso had opened a French singer's dressing room door and said, "Aha, the Italians can lick the French!"

It was this vile deed that was primarily responsible for his many nightly encounters with us. These the Attorney seemed to have felt would lead to a conviction and therewith to a laurel wreath for his brow. Pinza's amatory prowess, admittedly considerable, was reviewed in detail, presumably for the purpose of demonstrating that some of those he temporarily adored were possible enemy aliens. And on the other hand the singer's wife, flanked by relatives and friends, bared all his more recent domesticities with a quite touching desire to save him from serfdom. In many ways it was a beguiling, if sometimes, heart-searing spectacle. But at long last Dr. Van Dusen's patience was exhausted. He said to the Attorney with a truly Presbyterian lack of inhibition that if he did not cease and desist forthwith, the Enemy Alien Board would speedily be deprived of one member. Not to be outdone, I added another to the list of potential absentees. It is scarcely necessary to report that Pinza was thereupon decently paroled, no doubt to walk past the dressing room he had so grossly invaded, silently and on tiptoe.

When the genuinely onerous duties of the New York Board had ended, the Department of Justice established Appeal Boards at various interment camps; and since I happened to be somewhat of a specialist in German affairs, I of course found myself in Santa Fe, New Mexico, at a camp for Japanese. My acquaintance with them had up to that time been virtually non-existent, but the experience was in every way rewarding. The city itself, with which I had had only a fleeting acquaintance, was naturally suffering mildly from the war but it had lost none of its familiar habits. Every afternoon promptly at four the thunder rumbled high up in the Sangre de Christo mountains, and shortly thereafter the rain came down in torrents for twenty minutes. An hour later not a sign of moisture was discernible anywhere. This and other phenomena beguiled me no end, as also did, if the truth must be told, the Japanese.

These had been assembled hastily from many corners of the Southwest; and in the first flush of Pearl Harbor shock it had perhaps not been too difficult to believe everyone a potential traitor. But time had passed, nerves were less ragged, and the never slumbering conscience of the United States had stirred.

The Attorney's representative was an estimable person who had been given a question to ask that was couched in the reverberating diction which for me will always be associated with the War: "If the Emperor Hirohito summoned you and requested you to undertake some action inimical to the best interests of the United States, what response would you make?" Most of the internees had a difficult time calculating what they were expected to do about so formidable a query. But one afternoon we had before us an elderly gentleman who could make neither head nor tail of the question. The Attorney rephrased it. "The Emperor Hirohito," he said, "calls you. He tells you, do something bad against the United States. What will you say?" A look of comprehension immediately came over the weatherbeaten face and we had the reply: "Me tell him—got wrong number!" Since then I have come to know many Japanese and to have a high regard for them. But I shall always have a special place in my heart for the old man and his telephone reply.

The second hat I wore was that of membership on a Committee formed to advise the Department of State concerning its newly organized cultural relations program. This program had come into being after President Roosevelt's Good Neighbor Policy was inaugurated, for the purpose of improving relations with our Latin American neighbors. Just how it happened that I was appointed to it remains a minor mystery, but it was for me a fairly fateful association because in one form or other it has lasted until the present time (UNESCO, in a very real sense, owes its origin to the Committee). Being summoned for the first time to the Department of State, during the early forties, was something like being invited to dine with a hitherto mysterious King. The old building with its high ceilings and seemingly endless corridors, during the summer months ahum with the whirring of fans, was then still a haven for secrets and striped trousers. There were no security regulations, but nobody entered the premises apparently without being by nature unaddicted to running off with documents.

Being one of the members expected to give sage counsel was for me then, and might indeed still be, a memorable experience. The presiding officer, G. Howland Shaw, then Assistant Secretary, seemed to me a kind of civilian relative of Robert E. Lee. Duty was for him also the sublimest word in the language, but he approached it with the courtesy of a Virginia gentleman, seemingly persuaded that it would be all the more binding on one if it were greeted as a sometimes unwelcome but nevertheless respected friend. Later on, after leaving the Department, he was to devote himself with all his heart to the cause of underprivileged boys and so earn, though he shied away from every advertisement of the fact as if it were the plague, a place in the shrine of those who have nobly served American youth. But at the time we were struck by his vast knowledge of Byzantine and Islamic art, gained during many years as a representative of the United States in Turkey; and it was apparent to each of us that if we were going all out for cultural relations he was as good a model as any we could propose.

A number of distinguished men served on the Committee— Henry Wallace, then Vice President (he came when he could, and invariably astonished me by seeming to be asleep and then suddenly proceeding to comment with great force and originality on the subject under discussion), James T. Shotwell, James Bryant Conant, Archibald MacLeish, and Ben Cherrington among them. But unquestionably our intellectual primate was a man of whom the majority of Americans have probably never heard, but whose name would assuredly be a household word if learning and wisdom were as widely respected amongst us as are batting averages and closeups. Waldo Leland was at the time the guiding spirit of the American Council of Learned Societies. In and through this organization he did more to foster scholarship at home and intellectual commerce abroad than any other American of his time. To me association with this master of acrid though always kindly wit, a devoted servant of the idealism which alone can make wit beneficent, was worth as much as any year at a university. It was he who devised standards for our cultural relations activities which were probably more exacting than the routine of the old diplomatic service could live up to but which, had they been made the norm, would have removed any danger that a cultural relations officer could sometime be termed an "ugly American." But let me add, lest my portrait of

Waldo Leland be misleading, that he was also a good companion. During the years of prohibition his ability to ferret out good Virginia bourbon was unparalleled and as a host at dinner he represented the greatest tradition in that art.

We also had amongst us spokesmen for organizations who were quite without guile but who did feel that if cultural activity was to prosper some of it must assuredly be channeled through their offices. The American Council on Education has had a number of able and far-sighted leaders, but it will certainly never again have at its helm a man like George Zook. No doubt he literally slaved himself to death for it, and so perhaps became what today would be termed an "organization man." Still he built his empire with so much zest and so little of malice toward anyone that it was a pleasure to observe his success. He found a rival of sorts in Stephen Duggan, founder and director of the Institute of International Education, who felt that if cultural relations were to prosper in any sense, student exchanges would have to occupy a front row. Sometimes to the relative amusement of the rest of us, the two manoeuvered spryly for position; and in the end the Department of State showed magnanimous impartiality by dividing a certain amount of largesse between them, though I hasten to say that in both cases it was by no means a lucrative enterprise they coveted but an opportunity to be of service.

I shall add that Stephen Duggan became a cherished friend; and it is still a poignant memory to have been involved in some measure in the tragedy which befell him. When Stephen transferred the leadership of the Institute to his son Lawrence, whose years of service with the Department of State had won acclaim, I assented after some hesitation to become Chairman of the Board. It was shortly thereafter a proud evening for an illustrious old man when he could sit in the great hall of Hunter College and listen to a commencement speech by his son, which was also a statement of what to his mind the nation's cultural position in the world was destined to be. From where I sat on the stage I could see Stephen in the front row of the mezzanine, radiantly happy over what seemed the beginning of a promising career in educational service. Then, alas, only a few days later, the inexplicable tragedy occurred. The body of Lawrence was found on the street, far below the office window from which he had either leaped or been thrown. In all probability, no one will ever know what really happened. Certainly we of the Board did not. The unfortunate man's name had previously been stricken with emphasis from the list of government employees slated for security investigation. All anyone could do was reckon anew with the finality of death. The father did not indicate to anyone that his heart was broken. But all of us who knew him realized it was.

Meanwhile the Committee carried on until the grim tasks of war diverted attention from every other concern. But there was evolved during the course of manifold careful debate and ceaseless experimentation a philosophy of cultural relations which built on what the nation had done in the past (for instance, to its great credit, utilizing the indemnity arising out of the suppression of the Boxer Uprising for the purpose of establishing scholarships for Chinese students), but none the less striking out also in new directions. Many divergent points of view were expressed, and sometimes the clash of opinions sounded quite like the din of battle. Not a few of the country's best, Thornton Wilder and Ralph Turner, Gilbert Chinard and Morton Zabel among them, reported from farflung fields. And as I have indicated the work done lead eventually to new conceptions of cultural relations, one of which was to find its expression in the creation of UNESCO.

Next I accepted what from some points of view was the most difficult and in a macabre way interesting assignment of my career. The War Department and the Department of State both decided to send to Europe Historical Commissions whose task it was to be to secure from captured German generals and Nazi officials information which it was thought might be useful in evaluating wartime developments. I was, let me cordially admit, flattered by Secretary Robert Patterson's invitation to accept the direction of the War Department's Commission, primarily because of my high regard for him. The mission was supposed to remain a secret one, but it was only a short time after our arrival in Europe that we were discovered by the press and duly interrogated. I concluded at that time, and have had ample opportunity to corroborate the opinion since, that the Intelligence branch of the service (to which we were attached) is the least satisfactorily equipped to withstand the assaults of the news-gathering agencies. It does admirably when nobody asks questions. But when somebody does, as in the ominous case of a flyer lost over Russia, it violates all the public relations commandments.

At any rate, we found ourselves in Montdorf, Luxembourg, where many of the then most notorious of the world's citizens were incarcerated under the aegis of as peppery and esoteric an army officer as has ever been corralled for duty by the Armed Forces. Outside there was a fountain from which mineral water flowed for the benefit of what in happier times were citizens suffering from gallstones, dyspepsia and rheumatism. The gentry with whom we were to deal, many of whom would in a short while be transferred to Nuremberg for trial, were afflicted with far more grievous maladies. They were then the most hated people in the world, not infrequently for wholly adequate reasons. It was through the process of making the best of the assignment that I acquired the friendship in particular of two deputies, Oren J. Hale (later on to be my valued deputy in Bavaria), then a Colonel but now as before Professor of History at the University of Virginia, and Frank Graham, at the time no doubt Princeton's most illustrious economist.

We were to be closeted for some days with Hermann Goering. He had surrendered to an American general while wearing his airforce uniform festooned with various decorations. When we met him the uniform was a bit shabby and the decorations were gone. But this extraordinary swashbuckler had lost none of his verve or presence of mind. The time during which he had lorded it over a segment of the world had ended, and the vast collections of jewels, works of art and hunting lodges he had acquired in his role as a "Renaissance man" had vanished. Yet he continued to maintain his aplomb and to exert a curious fascination on other prisoners and indeed on the younger American officers with whom he came into contact. Arnold Wolfers used to say that Goering should have been sent to the Island of St. Helena to serve as a resource for historians. I am not sure. He might have beguiled someone into accepting his point of view.

The information I secured from him was accurate enough, when the question had to do with matters already amply explored, but his comment on other events was colored by his delight in playing a game of wits. Thus one day I asked him to tell me who had set fire to the Reichstag. "Professor," he replied, for he had ferreted out who I was, "we didn't start the blaze. Neither did the Communists. The fire was an accident resulting from carelessness." He then embarked on an elaborate theory of the "accident." The reason why he did this was of course clear. Knowing that if he continued to accuse the Communists he would not be believed, and that on the other hand a confession of Nazi guilt would have scored a point against him, he took refuge in an interpretation which he could make sound extremely plausible. Nevertheless, recent research appears to have proved that his answer was correct. In all such forms of dialectical embroidery he took great pleasure. But there were times when this mask, which he wore almost with frivolity, fell momentarily. His analyses of Hitler were shrewder and more candid than I realized at the time; and sometimes he threw light on his own character which was quite as startling and revealing. One afternoon, after asking why war had been declared on the United States, I outlined a theory of which I was then fond, namely that if after Pearl Harbor and President Roosevelt's response, Hitler had gone to the Reichstag and deplored the Japanese attack with sufficient vigor, it would have been virtually impossible to persuade the Congress to send American troops to Europe. In that case, it would have been equally impossible to inflict the total defeat on Germany. This would of course have altered the course of history more or less deplorably.

This was the only occasion on which I saw Goering at a loss for words. Finally he said, "If I believed that, Professor, I would go upstairs and commit suicide." I replied that in view of the precautions taken (the "guests" ate with spoons only, and the window panes in the resort hotel had been replaced with a plastic compound) that would be difficult. He smiled sardonically. "A man can take his life any time he wants to," he said. His words were destined to come back with a bang when the news was flashed from Nuremberg that he had cheated the hangman with poison. But he returned to the discussion several times. Goering of course knew, as we at that time did not, that the Japanese had failed to inform the German government in advance of their intention to bomb Pearl Harbor. As time went on, we gathered further information about the Fuehrer's extraordinary decision. Admiral Doenitz described in detail the precautions taken by the German Navy to avoid clashes with the United States during the course of submarine warfare. The instructions given were meticulous and were carried out by the commanders despite the very serious restrictions of movement which resulted. In fact the sudden declaration of war did not permit redeployment of the submarines until considerably later. That is why the attack on shipping off the coast of the United States was so long delayed.

General Wilhelm Keitel, who told everything he knew in the obvious hope that by so doing he could escape the hangman's noose, gave a remarkable account of the impact of the news on Hitler. This was confirmed by General Jodl. The Fuehrer drove to Army Headquarters in a mood of great elation, toting a bottle of champagne which he invited the generals to share with him in honor of the Samurai caste. This, he said, had now proved its mettle and was henceforth due to rank historically with the Aryan-German folk. Then, without conferring with anyone about the fatefulness and magnitude of the step he was about to take, Hitler convened the Reichstag and read a declaration of war on the United States. Therewith he removed every vestige of a chance that Germany's mad bid for the control of Europe would succeed. It was, I may add, impossible to discuss this or any other problem with Ribbentrop, once the Minister of Foreign Affairs. He had completely lost his nerve and lived in a state of chronic depression. Gone were his power and influence, and he now seemed unable to remember that they had ever been his.

Noteworthy was a day spent with Franz von Papen, then detained in a house which was under British command. The sun was shining brightly as we neared the dwelling, and I saw a pair of naked legs dangling from a window sill on the second floor. These, it was explained to me, belonged to von Papen, who was

accustomed to taking this kind of abbreviated sun bath whenever conditions permitted. The house had been wired, so that the discussion between us was, I realized somewhat to my discomfiture since I had known the man, being duly put on records somewhere in the cellar. Papen can only be understood, it seems to me, if one conceives of the fag-end of an aristocracy anxious to play a part in the drama of the regeneration of mankind. More than any other German of his time, he pitted his wits against those of Hitler. The trouble was not merely that Hitler's were of very much better quality but also that generals and others relied upon by Papen to redress the balance were even more unintelligent than he. At any rate our conversation was completely honest. Papen said pretty much what he has since published in his memoirs. But at the end of the day, he conjured up in his imagination the almost incredible havoc which had been wreaked on German cities, not merely in the populous ones like Berlin and Frankfurt, but in small and once almost miraculously beautiful places like Hildesheim and Wuerzburg. When the whole vision had passed before his mind, he began to sob at the realization of his own impotence and ignominy. I sat there knowing that the record downstairs would end in a whimper such as history has often known.

The generals were on the whole cast in a different mold. Most of the notable ones who had survived sat with us and answered questions. We respected men like Heusinger and Speidel, good soldiers worthy of any country's armies. Some others we detested. I came to have a special regard for Heinz Guderian, Armenian by birth, who had arrived in Germany to study at Von Seeckt's Reichswehr staff college and had stayed on with that organization. He had about as little political savoir-faire as a boy in a prep school, but of tank warfare he had known, alas, as much as anyone did. When I first met him he was as full of tales of combat as even Othello in his day had been. We talked of the Blitzkrieg in France, and then of Hitler's unrealistic, indeed quite unbelievably cruel ideas about winter campaigning in Russia. It was blood-curdling to hear about inspection trips in the neighborhood of Moscow during the course of which the General had found his men frozen to death in their light uniforms beside

tanks which could not move because the oil had congealed in the
cold. I very much wanted to bring Guderian to the United States
so that he could write his story. But instead he was carted off to
various degrading prisons and finally to Nuremberg; and when
I saw him again later on in Munich the fire in him had died low
and a variety of resentments were the central objects of his concern. It had always seemed to me that it was a blunder to hail
generals who had lost the war before a court for trial. What can
a soldier do but try to win the battles which the civilians make
it necessary for him to fight? It is true that the noblest of German officers, men like Von Beck and Von Hammerstein, would
not engage in Hitler's wars. They merit a special citation. Yet this
does not seem to mean that others less quick to grasp the real
nature of this government were necessarily derelict.

The punishment inflicted on Germany by reason of Hitler's
ambition and crimes was and is so staggering that the imagination cannot drink it in. I shall not comment here on the physical
destruction, at which anyone who walked about the streets of
cities could only stare with horror and amazement in 1945. The
moral damage inflicted was at least equally great. And so perhaps the most poignant recollection I have is of a former SS man
interviewed in the internment camp near Heidelberg. He was at
first only a name on a list. The dossier indicated that he was a
university graduate and that he had written a dissertation on the
Greek sources of the church hymn, *Te Deum laudamus.* How, I
asked myself, did someone like that happen to be detained here
in the detested uniform of Hitler's praetorian guard? I sent for
him.

There came into the room a dejected little man who kept twin-
ing his fingers round a worn piece of headgear. It turned out
that he had been a Catholic priest, a member of a religious order,
with a woebegone record. His family had been intimately acquainted with that of Himmler; and after that most sinister of
Hitler's lieutenants was safely established in power, he had suggested to this priest that he join the SS, not of course as a
potential warrior but as an intellectual. There was an additional
recommendation, to the effect that a good SS man must marry.
The unfortunate monk knew no women other than a spinster at

the postoffice who sometimes smiled at him when he came to post letters. To this fair lady he proposed, and they were joined in some kind of wedlock. His occupation for several years thereafter was to prepare the attack on the Christian Churches which was to follow Hitler's victory. At my request the priest wrote out in detail what the plan Himmler had inspired was to be like. There was first of all to be staged in every town and city of Germany a dramatization of the witchcraft trials of the late Middle Ages; and this was to be followed by an all-out attack on the alleged superstition of the Churches, in the spirit of Rosenberg's *Myth of the Nineteenth Century*. There was then to take place the proclamation of the "German Creed," held to be the religious core of the Nazi Empire destined "to last for a thousand years." The priest had been charged with doing the historical research required.

When on the day before I left the camp he called to deliver the last segment of his report, he was obviously in a state of great agitation. He kept twirling the worn little hat in his hands and was obviously unwilling to leave. I then asked whether he had something on his mind. Finally he blurted out, "What will happen to me? Will they kill me?" I replied that in my judgment, if he had committed no crimes other than work for Himmler as he had reported, I considered it very unlikely that anyone would propose capital punishment for him. He threw himself on his knees, held out his clenched hands, and said, "You must not let them kill me. . . . I am afraid of what will happen to me when I die!" It was a gruesome experience, which opened up a view of the depths of a tortured spirit. I may add that he was eventually released and died, before his time, of natural causes. May God have mercy on his soul!

Yet, viewed in its entirety, this tour of duty had its lighter moments as well. Not a few who were caught in the mesh of imprisonment were estimable persons who might instead have been awarded medals for heroism. Some were a sort of oafish folk, taken up somehow in the swathe. Finally there were those who had unquestionably fought as hard for Germany as was at all possible, and who nevertheless were estimable fighting men. One of these in my opinion was Admiral Doenitz, submarine commander who to the bitter end revered Hitler as the incarnation of German power and ambition. It was impossible to agree with any of his judgments about the war, or about the reasons why it was fought. Nevertheless all the while one could not help feeling that here was a naval officer of genuine quality—one about whom, had he been an American and a lover of freedom, we might have spoken a eulogy. Marshal Kesselring, who had commanded the German forces on the Italian front, was at the time described as a particularly fiendish character. But the fact is that although he was housed in a rather primitive camp which subjected him of necessity to many indignities, he was as unruffled by them as a middle-aged count might be at a ball for debutantes. Our mission had acquired an increase of personnel in the form of a brigadier general who spoke not a word of German and therefore banked heavily on the prowess of his aide, a young lieutenant who had graduated from a Middle Western university. Regrettably the two of them had never discussed the matter. The general had merely studied his subordinate's record and noted therein that two years of collegiate German had been victoriously endured. When the time came to interview Kesselring, the lieutenant, in whose demeanor I observed something akin to advanced seasickness, was invited by his commander to proceed with the investigation. No face has, in my experience, ever revealed more shades of purple and vermillion. What he said made no sense whatever. Then the Field Marshal very courteously inquired if the lieutenant would care to speak English. All was then smoothed over when Kesselring further promised to draw a map of the battle chiefly of interest. When finished this was really a sort of little masterpiece which no doubt the general proudly displays to his guests even to this day.

I derived from this and many other lessons at least one new educational objective. Why could so few Americans speak a foreign language with any sort of proficiency, and what could be done to remedy the situation? Undoubtedly the reasons were twofold. The doctrine of utility which for so long a time colored our national educational outlook led inevitably to the conviction that for an American knowing how to speak and write foreign languages served no good purpose whatsoever. And of course the prevailing pedagogical doctrine was so violently opposed to every concept of intellectual discipline that any utterance to the effect that studying another language could be of value in the training of the mind merely raised goosepimples on pedagogical flesh. But after the second World War we simply had to have people who could converse with their fellow human beings in alien tongues. The other reason for our failure was then revealed. By and large, the art of teaching a foreign language was hardly practiced in the United States. From this point of view Hunter was an oasis. Therefore I cooperated wholeheartedly later on with every effort made to remedy the situation.

Looking back on my experience of 1945, interviewing prominent Germans in varying ways guilty or innocent of implication in Hitler's purposes, I am impressed by the large number of citizens over whom he ruled who understood perfectly what his sinister purposes were. Very many of them—so many that not even the French Resistance has a firmer title to glory—died for their convictions. On a recent trip to Paris I walked down an obscure street not far from the École Militaire, in the heart of which is the tomb of Napoleon, and came upon a convent wall bearing a plaque on which is inscribed very simply that here had lived a priest who as a result of his association with the Resistance had died in Cologne by the guillotine during 1948. How could I avoid thinking of many Germans who had perished in the selfsame way, among them some dear personal friends? And I cherished anew the conviction that when Konrad Adenauer, born to generations of city dwellers, accomplished the historic deed of spending days and nights as a guest of General Charles de Gaulle, symbol of conservative rural France, in a farm-house in Columbey-les-deux-Eglises, which is a rustic town if ever there was one, the strongest bond which united them was the knowledge that those who had died obscurely for the freedom of Europe did not have the Rhine as a boundary between their spirits.

I believe that mankind cannot afford to forget that Naziism, born in an Austria which was infected but not conquered by it, triumphed in the German heart of Europe because it had within it a fury and an evil hardly less than diabolical. As the gifted

German historian Michael Freund has candidly averred, Hitler was a man of great native ability, perhaps even of a certain genius, who was overwhelmed too early in life by the social and intellectual forces which at the time gave Vienna its true form, so that he was psychically unsettled by the corruption of spirit that was about him and came to be that corruption's terrible manifestation. I retain in my mind, as a vivid illustration of the innate horror of what he summoned into being, memories of an experience my wife and I had driving from Freiburg in the Breisgau to Breisach on the Rhine during the summer of 1937. We were coming back from Prague and the sombre funeral of Thomas Masaryk, and had left Freiburg late in the afternoon. Suddenly the landscape was dotted with Brownshirts who were beating every bush. Two of them halted our car, and I ventured to inquire what they were looking for. A vile traitor, one answered, was trying to escape from Germany and they were heading him off. We drove on and eventually put up for the night at a Breisach inn. About ten o'clock, as we were sitting after a late dinner, a most fiendish din arose. "What are they up to now?" our old waiter mumbled in mingled revulsion and despair. We soon knew. The Brownshirts had captured the unfortunate pilgrim to freedom, whoever he may have been. All night long the howling of the successful huntsmen kept everyone in Breisach awake. Theirs was a curious, indescribably barbarian and sadistic clamor.

Whenever I think of Naziism, the experience of that night returns. For though one did not hear then the screams and the sobbing of those who tumbled in the putrid fumes of Auschwitz and Theresienstadt one listened, it seems to me, to something still more appalling—to the bestial laughter of men who in their madness were putting to death thousands of years of the hopes of mankind. I remember Sir Edward Grey saying as the first World War began that the lights were going out everywhere in Europe. On that night, lying in my bed near the cathedral of an old Rhenish town, I heard what human wolves can say in the dark.

The final act in this often bizarre but always interesting drama was a trip to Rome. My principal objective was to interview

Ambassador Ernst von Weizsaecker and other German diplomats who at the time were living in Vatican City under a grant of immunity. But since some historians were then nursing the idea of a history of the Great War written on the basis of international scholarly collaboration, I also had this very much in mind. The idea was destined to come to naught primarily because the various governments concerned were hoarding their documentation and putting "Top Secret" labels on nearly everything of importance. The carting off of German archives to Washington, London and elsewhere was another deterrent, and of course the wall the Russians built around themselves was not to be breached. Yet at the time it seemed a promising way to approach the study of the greatest tragedy in the record of man; and so I was interested in seeing whether the Vatican could be induced to participate by suspending its age-old rule that documents concerning persons still living were not to be made public.

Therefore, having completed my talks with the Germans, which took place well in advance of Weizsaecker's sensational trial in Nuremberg, I went to call on Father Leiber, the physically tiny but extraordinarily astute Jesuit who was then Pope Pius XII's most intimate adviser. We had met and talked at great length after the Austrian Anschluss in 1938, so that seeing him again was in a sense a resumption of ties cut off by the war. I outlined my plan and was greatly pleased by the cordial and favorable reaction. No doubt it would have pleased Father Leiber if data concerning, for example, the often criticized signing of a Concordat with the Nazis in 1933, could have been presented to the world in some appropriate form. Two days later, I had a private audience with the Pope, whom I had not seen since he had visited the United States as Cardinal Pacelli. His Holiness was most affable and immediately said in German that he knew what I had discussed with Father Leiber and that he was ready to lift the ban and permit me to study the documents relating to Naziism and the War! This was a very great deal more than I had expected; and I had, alas, to explain that in all probability the work would have to be done by some one else. "In that case," His Holiness replied, "we shall have to reserve our decision until we have been informed as to who is to receive permission." He was obviously a bit nonplussed. Never in my life have I regretted so deeply not being free and financially able to undertake a task. It need hardly be added that when the news was bruited about the Vatican many a prelate's eyebrows were raised. The experience was, indeed, unusual, and it is hardly to be wondered at that some of my friends still do not quite believe it real.

Rome was at the time a confused city the moods of which alternated between gratitude that the storm clouds of war had been lifted and despair about the political and financial situation. Not far beyond the outskirts of the crowded metropolis the Communist Party had created a powerful arsenal and formed the cadres of a military force ready if circumstances permitted to march on Rome even as Mussolini had once done. At that hour it was still the presence of United States troops which insured the peace. But life at the Vatican was seemingly tranquil. One was escorted to a private audience with the usual pomp; and when I returned the great hall was filled with GIs waiting for the Pope to appear and say a few words. Normally he was greeted in right lusty fashion. But the great Papal offices were not disturbed by such things. They were still busily looking at the world piece by piece, *sub specie aeternitatis*. Meanwhile below St. Peter's a daring feat of archeological excavation had been carried out under the direction of Monsignor Ludwig Kass, Pope Pius' closest German friend, who before his exile had played an unsuccessful part in the struggle through which Hitler had come to power. Perhaps, indeed an inglorious part.

It was absorbing to have, by reason of old associations with the Monsignor, a preview of the early Christian world now lying bare under the mighty edifice erected at a time when the splendor of the Catholic religious Empire was made manifest in broad arches and a soaring dome. By authorization of the Pope, the debris of centuries had been removed without the knowledge even of the canons of the cathedral. Now one could see again the walls of the ancient basilica of Constantine, move about among sarcophagi, many of them beautiful, in which the faithful of the first centuries had been interred, and peer down at the place where, it was believed, the body of Peter had been laid to rest after his martyrdom. In those troubled days, when the future often seemed very dark, one could not avoid feeling that this old world was more contemporary, closer to the spirit of our age, than the Renaissance cathedral which rose spectacularly above the ground. It seemed fitting that by chance a German, exiled from his country so shaken by the fever of the age, became the architect of this reconstruction of a period of suffering and spiritual dedication. It was only because the preparation of a tomb for the lately deceased Pope Pius XI had brought to light what seemed part of an imperial Roman wall that the excavating was begun. But who can be in Rome without feeling anew, each time more deeply, that this city is above all the shrine of what is most vital in the experience of the West, the almost unimaginable tragedy of our race, the struggle of power against insight, the hopeless opposition of the transitory to the timeless? And so I went again and again to see the work of art in which this experience seems to me to have been expressed more clearly and movingly than in any other—Michaelangelo's Moses, in the church of St. Peter in Chains.

The journey to Italy was also to have for me certain more mundane educational implications. The only way to get from Frankfurt to Rome was by car. I discussed the situation with the transportation officer and suggested that since the cultural climate of Italy was most salubrious he might wish to give some erstwhile college student under his command an opportunity to profit intellectually. But it was not his function to cater to eggheads of any age; and so I was accompanied across the Brenner by a young man equipped with a spyglass and a mouth organ. He hailed from the mountains of Tennessee and I soon applied the name of that state to him, at his locally patriotic request. Whenever opportunity afforded, I discoursed on the wonders of Italy and assumed that possibly new vistas were opening to his imagination. But disillusionment soon set in. We arrived in Rome on a warm day, and having safely deposited me at the Hotel Majestic he went off to the appropriate barracks to rest for a strenuous tomorrow, which would probably necessitate driving me to Vatican City in the morning and waiting until noon. In due course we journeyed to St. Peter's, the vastness of which I had eloquently described. He parked the Chevrolet in the shade, climbed into the back seat, and put his feet out the window. "Tennessee," I inquired, "aren't you going into the cathedral?" "Naw, sir," he answered. "I just don't care much for churches." And he never set foot inside. We drove to the Protestant cemetery one noon, while waiting for the Italians to recuperate from siestas, with comparable results. He said that by reason of a lack of interest in dead men he would stay outside and not visit the graves of Keats and Shelley. This despite the fact that I had recited a stanza from the "Ode to a Grecian Urn." Some days later, we drove out to Naples so that I could confer with historians working diligently at Seventh Army Headquarters. He had two or three hours of waiting before him. Outside Caserta there is a great old Roman acqueduct, and I hopefully suggested that he might have a look. "How old is it?" he asked dubiously. I replied with some enthusiasm that it had probably reached the ripe old age of more than two thousand years. "Naw," he said firmly. "I ain't interested. It ain't got no modern improvements." He meant what he said and gave the acqueduct not so much as a glance. Though on the verge of despair, I tried once more. Of all the monuments in Italy, it seemed that the Leaning Tower might awaken in him a mild form of curiosity. And sure enough, we drove through Pisa on a beautiful moonlit night. There, across the Campo Santo it stood, leaning less perhaps than I had said it did but making a genuine attempt none the less. "There it is," I said with as much fervor as I could awaken in my soul. "There is the Leaning Tower!" He dutifully took a look and ventured the comment, "Well, sir, the doggoned thing sure does lean!" That was the end of my effort to teach a measure of art appreciation. I should long since have known how difficult it can be to educate a human being, but Tennessee made it abundantly clear that it may sometimes be impossible. I have often wondered whether my friend the transportation officer had devoted a good deal of time and thought to figuring out which of his charges would profit least from an Italian journey. But no doubt this was assuming he would have expended more energy on a problem than was his custom. He had merely looked at his men and picked a random sample.

By the time the Second War ended, it was plain as day that only through heroic effort could mankind cleanse its hands of blood. Was it not impressively true that the literature born of that struggle talked of no heroism save triumph through brutality? The bright young Americans who have since written about war in the Pacific differ not a whit in this respect from the equally bright young Germans whose books describe the fighting on the Eastern front. And so, though cursed from the outset perhaps by a lack of realism, the wish of the peoples for some kind of international organization able to prevent the outbreak of another, still more devastating conflict could not be gainsaid. The United Nations was born in San Francisco; and its Charter contained a modest clause to the effect that international understanding was to be promoted through education. It was with this effort that I was to be in some measure identified from the beginning and for more than fifteen years. Perhaps nothing in my history has seemed to many people either so futile or so questionable.

Yet the Department of State had, through its advisory Committee, early given much thought to the problems of educational exchange and reconstruction which would emerge when the War was over. For how could anyone doubt that, in view of ideological conflict and technological advancement, schooling would become more vital than ever before? It was of course true that the people of the United States had done relatively little thinking about education in the world at large. This was not surprising, for we had persuaded ourselves that the less the Federal Government "meddled" in the schools the better off we should all be. Nevertheless shortly after war broke out in Europe there was established in association with the Governments in Exile a permanent Conference of Ministers of Education, having its seat in London. With this the Government of the United States cooperated. Meanwhile the hope that the schools would become agencies through which understanding between the nations could be fostered and the rise of movements akin to Naziism prevented also grew more fervent. Mr. James Marshall, then a member of New York City's Board of Education, formed a group to promote the concept of an international educational organization to serve the purposes thus envisaged. With this I was also associated.

In conformity with the UN Charter, a conference was then called into being at the close of 1945 for the purpose of planning the structure of an international organization, drafting its constitution, and preparing for the formal launching. The American delegation, of which I was a member, was headed by Archibald MacLeish. It now became apparent that educational reconstruction, even in the form of aid to the devastated countries, could not be a major objective, since it was believed that the Congress would oppose any appropriations for such a purpose. Against this decision our colleague, the greatly respected Alexander Mieklejohn, protested at length and in vain. How remote from present realities this caveat now seems! We have sponsored any numbers of vast enterprises of the self-same kind in many parts of the world. There was nothing else to do but set to work to create an educational instrument for making War and Naziism things of the past. A preamble to the proposed Constitution was drafted jointly by MacLeish and Etienne Gilson, the noted French philosopher. It combined the conviction that since "wars begin in the minds of men," it is these minds which must be taught to cherish peace, with the belief that there exists a "moral solidarity of mankind," which creed Gilson had earlier expounded with great eloquence at Harvard. These convictions, noble and in some measure correct though they were, now seem to most people so unlikely to cure the miasmas of modern power politics that they are viewed on the one hand with more than a trace of irony and on the other are somehow held to display a dearth of noble patriotic sentiment.

Yet in London that year it did not seem unrealistic to acclaim them. The great city was still breathing heavily under the burden of war. About other decisions to be taken, there was, however, more than a little conflict. The scientists in attendance, persuaded that they alone could keep a genuinely effective international dialogue going (for were they not the custodians of a universally accepted and valid body of truths?), insisted that the word Science must appear on the organization's masthead. Indeed, they proclaimed that if this wish were not endorsed they would take themselves elsewhere—thus presumably proving that the "moral solidarity of mankind" was less complete than was being assumed. This somewhat imperialistic venture into the realm of nomenclature naturally revived the ancient debate between the sciences and the humanities. If the child was to be baptized Education and Science, then by Jove it must have a third name, which after some argument became Culture. For my part, I have never been quite able to see why Science is not a part of Culture, but anyhow this is the story of the entry into history of the United Nations Educational, Scientific and Cultural Organization.

I have alluded to London in 1945; and perhaps an episode may resurrect the character of the time. We had arrived by ship at Plymouth, and my modest luggage included a case of grapefruit to be delivered to a friend's friend. Never have impedimenta been more awkward. The train which was to take us to London was crowded, particularly with women and children who had somehow survived a long ocean voyage in compartments designed for troops. There was neither light nor water in the coaches. Through a seemingly endless night we jogged along, with the sobs of uncomfortable children always in our ears. But stupidly I could think of nothing but the grapefruit, which had perforce been tossed on a heap of luggage. The carton was, however, intact when we alighted; and after it had been taxied to its destination, the apartment of a well-to-do citizen, I discovered that the welcome accorded it was literally unbounded. The reason became apparent a few evenings later when I went to the same home for dinner. My host offered excellent Scotch from a cellar which had survived the war. The meal consisted, however, exclusively of twenty-four oysters which had been garnered in from a private bed. Two daughters had returned quite famished from a Japanese internment camp outside Shanghai and now consumed with relish everything the family's ration cards provided. I suggested that they come to call on me for such a supply of candy bars, et cetera, as I could get from a PX; and never again do I expect to see a small mound of Hershey bars and similar entities disappear in so tiny a fragment of the twinkling of an eye. In that kind of London our preamble did not seem out of place.

During the winter of the next year, the first General Conference of UNESCO convened in Paris. The city had recovered more than a little from the state of desolation in which I had seen it during the summer of 1945. Roast duck was being served again in the Tour d'Argent if one did not mind paying outrageously for it, and the garish and to me always sinister Hotel Majestic, where the Conference was held, hummed with discourse and the clatter of typewriters in the service offices. François Mauriac, one of the French delegates, predicted that an organization reared in such an environment could come to no good end. But as a matter of fact the Conference brought together a brilliant group of diplomats, scholars, writers and artists. The presiding officer was Léon Blum, not yet quite recovered from the rigors of a Nazi prison; and I suppose that no one who was there will forget the words of hope and determination he addressed to the gathering. But what we conjured up seems now to have been compounded largely of Picasso-like doves and Klee rainbows. The trouble was that nobody had been able to think through just how the world was to accomplish what the Constitution of the organization prescribed. Most of us were quite certain that some device in which we had a good deal of confidence, whether it happened to be radio broadcasting or the study of philosophy, would bring mankind the coveted blessings. What took place as a result was that the program drawn up moved out into so many directions at the same time that with all the good will in the world the new agency could not get very far in any. To make matters worse Julian Huxley, who through an odd chain of circumstances was elected Director-General, proclaimed that the brand of Scientific Humanism to which he had given birth was to become the official philosophy of the organization. His statement of it was issued in a green brochure pleasant to behold but to spokesmen for competing varieties of Humanism it seemed diabolically inspired. And so for a time if anyone suggested that UNESCO had a doctrine of any sort, a dozen kinds of lightning flashed on the horizon.

The American delegation was a quite variegated one and therefore difficult to fuse into a unit. But in the end we seemed to rally round Professor Richard McKeon's principle that whether something was to get into the UNESCO program would be determined by its value in serving the cause of peace. Unfortunately no one had drawn up a dependable list of the ingredients of peace, and so the discussion was often badly blurred at the edges. I suppose that no one was genuinely satisfied with the results of the Conference. To begin with, the Russians had not put in an appearance. William Benton, then Assistant Secretary of State, made heroic efforts to obtain from Moscow a reply to the invitations addressed to the USSR. He then tried to confer in person with Stalin. But when he reached Berlin an icy wind, figuratively speaking, had blown in from Siberia and the journey to Moscow was not permitted. It was clear that in the circumstances the defenses of peace could be erected in the minds of men only with extreme difficulty. More generally, it was uncertain whether the suggested program made great sense or whether the organization created to put it into effect was adequate. But there was hope in all our minds and hearts. At all events we had renewed acquaintances across national boundaries after a long period of isolation and that fact alone seemed to promise well for the future.

I shall permit myself to sketch an idyllic interlude because it serves to recall the now almost unbelievable relief which the end of the war ushered in, particularly for those of us who had previously seen what havoc and deprivation could do to human society. Some members of the delegation went to Paris in the more leisurely way, traveling on the *SS. America*, then on her maiden voyage. Before leaving, we were received at the White House by President Harry Truman who instead of rising at his desk and speaking a few perfunctory words ushered us into the garden and made an impromptu address which was marked by uncommon good sense. Then, as on many later occasions, I was impressed by the intellectual temper of a man whose political education had doubtless not been wholly orthodox but who had learned to cherish the welfare of the nation with temperateness, without chauvinism, but with great fortitude.

Let me refer parenthetically to another experience with Mr.

Truman which perhaps revealed an additional segment of his character. The Rosenwald Foundation had underwritten a study of segregation in the Nation's Capital, and a committee was formed to supervise the endeavor. Of this I was the chairman. As usual the findings of the research workers, headed by Joseph Lohmann, who was later on to abandon sociology in order to embark on a busy career as Sheriff of Chicago, presented its findings in several stout volumes. But there was issued also a succinct and carefully written General Report, of which we were perhaps inordinately proud. On the appointed morning, Channing Tobias, James Carey and I met at the White House to present a copy to the President in the hope that he might say something favorable and quotable about it. But the time was evidently not right for that. Mr. Truman regaled us with stories about his last campaign. He described the foibles of reporters. He narrated the histories of the various and indeed often curious gifts which were grouped about him in his study. But not a syllable could we extract from him about our literary masterpiece. It was a consummate illustration of political artful dodging. Later on, during President Eisenhower's first campaign, I resorted to television one evening for the good of my civic soul. There the General was, with a copy of our Report in his hand! Even when deferred, recognition is good for the soul.

At any rate, here we were, relaxing on the *America* though conferring earnestly every day about the Conference which lay ahead. It seemed almost too good to be true that we were once more in a world where nothing was rationed, and where the sea manifestly existed in order to swish against the sides of a luxury liner. Best of all there was an opportunity to exchange experiences. Thus I came to know William Benton's extraordinary dynamism and imaginativeness. Having demonstrated that he was one of the world's most successful salesmen, he now made it the purpose of his life to sponsor and render effective ideas which he thought consonant with the vision and the welfare of the United States. Education had become, as it would remain, a major concern. He could toss off ideas in almost bewildering sequence, not all of them tenable, perhaps, but some remarkably stimulating and significant. With all this went a verve, a tirelessness and a good humor which all but left one breathless. Chester Bowles was also with us, being likewise a delegate to the UNESCO Conference; and it was fascinating to see how the personalities of the two men, so long closely associated, diverged and converged again. Later on when Bowles became Governor of Connecticut he had an opportunity to name some one to the Senate for a year. He dangled the prize before me, but I realized with a trickle of transitory sadness that it was not for me. He held it out to Benton, too, who at first shied away from it as from temptation but then later on rather reluctantly accepted. Then he discovered that for him the Senate opened up vistas of unimagined interest. A very good and responsible Senator he was, and I still regret deeply that the wheel of political fortune eventually turned against him.

This idyl of a voyage, so much like a trip through fairyland despite the work there had to be done, conjures up its amiability anew when I recall a frivolous experience. Two men of moment, Senator Thomas Murray and Mr. Philip Barry, were among the passengers assembled in the bar at cocktail time when our ship came to rest in the harbor of Cobh. A delegation representing Ireland came aboard to hold out the hand of welcome. One member of it was a tall and handsome representative of the Catholic clergy attired in a frock coat. The Senator and Mr. Barry were by this time in a mellow mood. Seeing the clergyman, they were moved to surmise that he might perchance be a dignitary of high rank. The Senator, deeming me an authority in such matters, came to ask my opinion. Spurred on by some demon, I said, "Senator, he undoubtedly is the Bishop of Cobh." He returned to confer with Barry, and thereupon the two went over to address the "prelate." I could see and hear the Senator bowing low and murmuring respectfully, "Your Excellency, I am Senator Murray and this is Mr. Philip Barry, the playwright." "I'm pleased to meet you," responded a booming voice. "I'm Father Hogan of Youngstown, Ohio." I considered it expedient to disappear; and indeed for some days thereafter the Senator eyed me with some suspicion.

One other experience containing a fragment of frivolity comes to mind, though its import is serious and calls to mind some things already said. Secretary Benton was troubled by the fact that very few members of the American Delegation could understand or speak French. For it was already becoming apparent that our country's great linguistic weakness, which would plague us for many years, was a barrier to understanding. Accordingly he set a kind of example by pausing whenever he could to ask the French equivalent of an American phrase. One such inquiry led to the discovery that when you offered a tip it was polite to say, *Pour vous*. All went well until the day of our departure. The Secretary came down the main stairway of the Crillon, with a bundle of francs in his hand, greeting the various personages who waited expectantly with an appropriate reward preferred with the remark, *Vour pous*. But after all people have been known to do worse for no equally good cause.

The fortunes of UNESCO during the years that followed were varied, upon occasion stormy, and never specially wreathed in the smiles of good fortune. Unfortunately some groups in the United States acted as if the organization had been taken over by the Devil or the Kremlin. Their attacks are among the strangest in my experience. The American Legion was for a time in the vanguard; and Ray Murphy, a distinguished attorney who had been for a time its president, was enjoined to make a careful investigation of all UNESCO's misdemeanors. This he did with the remarkable probity which has always characterized him. The report he eventually made was a quite eloquent expression of faith in the use of education for the promotion of human betterment and international understanding. It did no good whatever. The Legion, flanked by the DAR, continued to condemn UNESCO in ringing terms as a subversive organization, though with the passing of time public opinion generally paid less and less heed to them.

The new agency gradually streamlined its program. It did a number of useful, sometimes even remarkable things. To its iniative is due the writing of an International Copyright Convention, which has had a highly beneficent effect even though, with the exception of Poland, no country in the Russian bloc has signed it. From the scientific point of view, it has wrestled with the problem of arid lands and taken part in the planning of an

International Atomic Energy Agency. Educational research has been fostered, notably in three institutes established in Germany and two centers of experimentation in community education, the one in Mexico and the other in Egypt. Effective leadership has been exercised in the promotion of East-West cultural understanding, and in the exploration of educational needs in Latin America. In addition UNESCO has acted most skillfully as a clearing house of educational information at a number of levels.

Today UNESCO is rapidly becoming what the old Committee of the Department of State had envisaged, namely an international educational agency of genuine stature concerned primarily with two tasks—the creation of a center for the pooling of information and advice for all major institutions of learning; and the making of an instrument for surveying, and in some measure carrying out, the advancement of education in the world's newer countries. To both these efforts the Government of the United States has subscribed with constantly increasing readiness and confidence. Undoubtedly UNESCO still has fewer virtues than may seem desirable. But it has found that it has a most important part to play in the drama of mankind and has tried to prepare itself adequately for the part. The basic weakness with which it has to contend, as do all other international organizations, grows out of its inter-governmental structure. Unavoidably, to some extent inexplicably, the sessions become tugs of war between alien points of view and between nations which lack the means to attain the educational goals they desire to reach and other nations which are more affluent. Sitting on the Executive Board of UNESCO and representing the United States, I have felt more than once that great problems which ought to arouse international concern are side-tracked while the discussion has to do either with aspects of the East-West conflict or with the special desires of the more handicapped states. Indeed the discussion is often very trying.

Debate with the Russians plunges to unfathomable depths. Sometimes—I cannot document this for fear of doing a disservice to a colleague who for all his allegiance to the Communist cause would like to be a human being with a claim on freedom—I have had the feeling that if a promenade on some terrain outside the realm of commitment were possible, one would meet a man with a warm desire for friendship and a quite unmistakable longing for freedom. But that promenade is always, always made impossible because of watchful eyes. Often I am persuaded that we ourselves are too inexperienced in the ways of the Communist world to take advantage of the situation. All that I shall say is that I have seen warmth come into the eyes of a Russian by reason of a deserved compliment one has paid to him. Yet almost immediately thereafter it has been necessary to conclude that this warmth must pass unrecognized, because some agent of Khrushchev was probably walking about with a thermometer.

Still I have greatly appreciated having a seat in the front row while something probably unparalleled in the history of man is taking place. This is the developing strong thirst for education in even the humblest parts of the world. During times when transportation was difficult and travellers were few, men and women dwelling in relatively primitive areas may have been content to live ignorant lives close to the soil. But today the average simple native can compare his lot with that of the foreigner who comes again and again into his ken. Why cannot he prosper likewise, he asks? The rumor also reaches his ear that the Russian Communists have an infallible recipe for improving his lot. Little news reaches him about the fate which Communist engineering has meted out to the little man in all the countries to which it has been applied. Through some grapevine of local gossip he may hear now and then that there are refugees in Hong Kong. But that there is desperate hunger in China, or that there are chain gangs of slaves reaching from one end of the horizon to the other, remains in so far as he is concerned a secret. The United States is in his view a fabulously rich capitalist country. If everybody living in it were to travel on one less gallon of gasoline per month, schools could be built in India. Nobody really knows about how much this country is doing for the underprivileged abroad. Nobody realizes how heavy the pressure of taxation is on the aged, or indeed upon the young with families. By talking so much about the automobiles and refrigerators we have and the Russians do not, we may have dug a ditch under our feet. The average visitor who goes to Russia is kept a thousand miles away from Vorkuta and similar camps. But everybody who comes to the United States sees the East Bronx, the Negro slums in Newburgh, the worst part of Brooklyn. Very few know about anti-Semitism in Russia. But who has not heard of segregation in our South?

It seems to me that I have, by reason of my service with UNESCO, acquired an insight into these matters which is valuable to me personally and which I take every opportunity to transmit to my countrymen. But for some reason or other they do not know how mighty the upsurge is, or how well one can gauge the strength of it by sitting in on the counsels of UNESCO. Most people continue to believe that this organization has some kind of grandiose plans for ushering in peace through text-books. I most assuredly wish it had a plan. Anything on earth which could effectively prevent bombs from dropping on New York or Moscow has my wholehearted support in advance. One can merely report that this is not what is being attempted. UNESCO is working hard to help make schools rise in the jungles. It is attempting to help young people living in good comfortable neighborhoods realize that the rising generation everywhere is like them. I cannot imagine that any agency could plot for itself a larger task or one more likely to prove worthwhile if it were accomplished.

These, then, are some of the experiences of an American college president whom the fortunes of the time upon occasion diverted from the ordinary business of academic life. I fancied they brought with them a measure of awareness of human society as formed by calamity and hope alike which could not have been acquired within the academic community as such. Perhaps through a special kind of osmosis a little of awareness and quandary, of blended seeing of wide horizons and baffling human detail, rubbed off on my colleagues. Certainly they listened most courteously to what I had to report and at least upon occasion made me feel a bit like Marco Polo. But in retrospect I am not sure. It must be said that a college president can never permit himself to become a humdrum figure. If he cannot be seen beyond the rim of the campus he will not be visible inside it either. But after all there are other areas in which exploration is possible and which may well be more directly in keeping with academic life. If a president were to devote as much time to scholarly inquiry as I did to public service he might eventually open some little door of his own on the hidden world of the mind with which colleges and universities are primarily concerned. As I have indicated, I am not sure. Any man's chronicle can concern itself only, for better or for worse, with the part he has chosen, or has been persuaded, to create for himself.

VIII.

AFTER HOURS

One aspect of our educational enterprise which, though manifestly important, has been referred to so far only in passing is concerned with the almost unbelievable numbers of adults who come after work to take courses in a bewildering variety of subjects. For every one who did so a quarter of a century ago, there are now three. Indeed, if space and instructors had been available, the growth would have been more marked. We at Hunter insisted on courses which were at least reasonably like those offered by a self-respecting college. That is, we did not teach people how to play bridge, or try to siphon business from the places where one learns to dance the rumba. Nevertheless the crowds knocked more and more insistently on our doors. No doubt they were to some extent egged on by employers who attached value to education, but I honestly think the majority merely wanted to "improve their minds," as the phrase has it.

Well, certainly one must reckon primarily with the average decent person's desire somehow to participate in what is going on. Everybody who has in one manner or other got on some kind of stage and spoken to the public knows that the response is easier to evoke than to deal with after it has been evoked. Upon occasion a little piece in a popular magazine or a few remarks made over a network will bring so many messages, pro and contra, that the task of responding to them is almost overwhelming. And so, perhaps, what the "college for adults" really is can be defined only in terms of eagerness to participate in the discussion of things which matter. No doubt there is some naïveté about it all. But I have met with a suffcient number of classes or groups formed of such people not to feel entirely sure that what happens to them and their compeers will be of the greatest importance to the future of America.

When Hunter College was founded in 1870, the demand for education was relatively elementary. The work-day was long and the household chores exacting. Young ladies in number came to the new institution to be prepared for school teaching; but the course of study provided did not offer quite as much as our High School does today. So far as one can now determine, graduates then knew a little about the classical literatures and the ethical philosophy underlying them, though most of the information was absorbed from translations. They had some awareness of the famous buildings and art works of Europe, though the dearth of illustrated manuals, now become quite commonplace, was a serious handicap. Of classical music, exception having duly been made for a Chopin nocturne or a passage from the Moonlight Sonata played on the home piano, most people had little inkling. The repertory which the radio stations now offer a half-willing listener was beyond the dreams of any save the very few who spent long periods of time in Europe. With this there were, to be sure, many and varied ancestral ties. Germany was in the foreground then, bequeathing to the New World a wide range of interests, from Goethe to Heine, from Schiller to Socialism (the bugaboo of the time), or in more mundane terms from pictures of steamers on the Rhine to cuckoo clocks. America was therefore not at all isolationist in outlook, except possibly in so far as Great Britain was concerned, but was likely to be sentimental and dubious of the value of its own culture.

Yet as a matter of fact that culture, though it may hardly have affected the urban masses, was genuine. There was a sense of community which for all its patriotic emotional roots—the Civil War had left a deep imprint—grew out of a common concern for basic values. It was true that great social problems had not only not been solved but were in what might be termed a state of troubling gestation. The battle against the sweatshop was still to be fought, and political corruption would have to tighten its grip on the cities before reform could begin. Citizens with some education spoke and wrote graceful and effective English. Most of them were specially concerned with the religious beliefs in which they had been reared, though few could be cajoled into considering a change. In short, the early generations of Hunter graduates seem to have acquired a measure of graciousness we now miss, but not much awareness of beckoning horizons. The literature they read was not the product of a mind in a state of upheaval. Emerson's or Longfellow's imagery was homely because there was no other kind anybody knew. It was compounded of wagons and stars, of ploughing the earth and sowing the grain, of animals and smithies.

Now, I think, the people who come in quest of further education feel a longing for a comparable kind of simplicity. They live in the midst of things and of forces which are immeasurably bigger than they are. The daily route leads from an apartment house to a large and complex office. They must consider social and political problems in the light of statistics which dwarf the individual to insignificance. Social scientists tell us, for example, that by 1965 two million youngsters will be hailed each year to the courts for some kind of delinquency or other. Traffic in the congested cities will transform the streets into torrents of humanity. Reading the annual report of the Pennsylvania Railroad, for instance, conjures up so bewildering an array of problems facing just this one small part of the transportation complex that the imagination can hardly take it in. And in still another dimension, the drama played on the world stage is so overwhelming in scope that the individual must feel utterly helpless under the impact of it. What shall one make, for example, of the presence in Asia of a Chinese Republic which in the not too far distant future may have a billion citizens? Or what, indeed, of an economy which, under the weight of automation, may reduce the work-week in factories, offices and shops to three days?

I believe that in the midst of all this a great many people urgently feel the need for self-identification. They are not content to be numbers only. What then could be more natural than attaching oneself to a personality or an institution, in the hope of finding a comradeship which is to some extent also a partnership? Undoubtedly this quest is swelling the rolls of churches and synagogues. It seems to me that this trend is by no means as much the expression of a desire for conformity as it is a half-instinctive yearning for shelter. And so it also is with the college.

To have a place to go to in which one counts, at least in some small way! To feel that through learning something one also finds out a little about being oneself! One cannot forever live in the midst of things too big to understand. Somehow, somewhere, the world of experience must take on a human dimension.

Naturally there are ways in which the modern city dweller is far more fortunate than his human ancestors were. All the social and medical services function much better. He is insulated against want to an extent which would once upon a time have seemed impossible. Drudgery to the verge of physical exhaustion has practically disappeared. But there are also ways in which life is harder and more lonely than it has been. For instance, it is often said that technology, by creating leisure, has given the average man the status an aristocrat enjoyed in earlier times. But the differences are very great. The aristocrat had money with which to purchase an estate, ride to hounds, take trips, and if he was so minded books and works of art. But even for our working urban population we must assume an allocation of one room for every adult, though this will mean an improvement over present conditions. What will a man do in that room? "Leisure is that from which one escapes by going to work," Georges Bernanos said resignedly.

If what I have said is in some small measure correct, the challenge to the educator is very great indeed. In order to make my view of that challenge explicit I shall describe two experiences which seem as pertinent as they were unusual. During the summer of 1938, Adolph Hitler came to Rome to visit Benito Mussolini, his newly found ally. During the preceding months the street leading to Vatican City and to St. Peter's, which stands majestically in the foreground of that realm, had been widened to create an approach both stately and regal. It was broad enough to permit the passing of large automobiles flanked by guards, as well as for sidewalk throngs which might applaud or at least observe whatever cavalcade came along. It was announced that Hitler would be escorted to the basilica. But on the appointed day the staunch old Pope, Pius XI, ordered the great doors to be closed and locked. This was for all who witnessed it a quite breathtaking deed. For it opposed a moral action to the mighty configuration of power which all but held Europe in its maw. The Pope's gesture said more plainly than words could have done that Naziism was ethically reprehensible. With it, the little man everywhere could identify himself, if only in thought. It restored the dimension of freedom even for those who in many a dire way were not free.

The second experience was the receipt of a personal letter from President Franklin Delano Roosevelt on the morning after the invasion of North Africa by American troops. The letter stated that a lady he had known since his Hyde Park boyhood was seeking a job and that he would appreciate it if I would see her and if possible help her to find employment. My acquaintance with the President was slight, resulting as it did from the purchase of his town house for Hunter. It has continued to amaze me that a man in his position could concern himself at that time with a mission of mercy entirely without political implications, but even more that he had turned the matter around in his mind until he had come up with my name. The explanation is, of course, that he was accustomed to doing kind things for people. Perhaps he had any measure of weaknesses and faults, but kindness was a habit with him, and that one does not form on the basis of a special arrangement of one's white corpuscles.

I have related these experiences because they point to things people desperately want and have to find. How shall one continue to be a warm, interested, intelligent person in a world of crowds and machines? Is there anything education can do to help? Here we are at the opposite end of the street from the place where the aim is primarily to train scholars. Not a few exponents of higher education think we have no business being there at all. For obviously what all these people, who in coming out of crowds form another crowd, seek is not so much learning, or intellectual excellence, as the Good in the sense in which Plato conceived of it. What they really want is to sit and talk with somebody worth talking to. We shall have to find teachers who can be that sort of person. Most of the education they will offer will be primarily group experience. The students will belong to orchestras and choruses, will look at art and speak their minds about it, will be busy with others trying to gather through a measure of experimentation some insight into the wonders of natural science. There will be discussion groups, ranging all the way from some concerned with problems of the social and political order to the ideas packaged in great books. Gradually the citizen will learn to create his own education because he will build his own community.

I shall say no more about the matter here except that when I think of what this pattern of education may well some time be, the future somehow seems bright. Ours is an era when for better or worse the fences created by space and time are disappearing. One can now visit the Pygmies or the Sikhs, the Eskimos or the Tennessee mountaineers. The traditional isolation which gave them seclusion has ended. In a comparable way, time is no longer a barrier. Primitive oral cultures now everywhere come squarely up against the literate culture of industrial society. Why then should it not also be possible to attack the ultimate fences of urban society? Why should not education be the weapon? When I ask these questions, I recall with gratitude that of all this Hunter's community center was a tiny lantern in the window.

I should like to close quite sentimentally by talking about the light in my own house. More years ago than it is consoling to remember, I was teaching during a summer at Notre Dame. A girl stood under what they call the "Golden Dome," with a little gold ornament on her throat and a light in her eyes. Some time later we were married. We took many things more or less in stride. A few of them were very hard to take. There is no reason why I should talk about them here other than that we stood our ground together. Perhaps a little of our buoyancy rubbed off in the process. But I believe we managed somehow to keep our chins up and whistle in the dark. A good many things never came our way which it would have been pleasant to see come. Then there were twenty-one years at Hunter. That many years is a long time, but no doubt ever arose that we accepted them together, made them together, loyally and with affection. It is often said a wife is the shadow of her husband, or that a husband is the shadow of his wife. That is not true of us. We made one shadow, and for it I am in this place saying thanks.

INDEX